INDICATORS OF EDUCATION SYSTEMS

INDICATEURS DES SYSTÈMES
D'ENSEIGNEMENT

MEASURING WHAT STUDENTS LEARN

MESURER LES RÉSULTATS SCOLAIRES

ORGANISATION FOR ECONOMIC CO-OPERATION AND DEVELOPMENT
ORGANISATION DE COOPÉRATION ET DE DÉVELOPPEMENT ÉCONOMIQUES

ORGANISATION FOR ECONOMIC CO-OPERATION AND DEVELOPMENT

Pursuant to Article 1 of the Convention signed in Paris on 14th December 1960, and which came into force on 30th September 1961, the Organisation for Economic Co-operation and Development (OECD) shall promote policies designed:

— to achieve the highest sustainable economic growth and employment and a rising standard of living in Member countries, while maintaining financial stability, and thus to contribute to the development of the world economy;

— to contribute to sound economic expansion in Member as well as non-member countries in the process of economic development; and

— to contribute to the expansion of world trade on a multilateral, non-discriminatory basis in accordance with international obligations.

The original Member countries of the OECD are Austria, Belgium, Canada, Denmark, France, Germany, Greece, Iceland, Ireland, Italy, Luxembourg, the Netherlands, Norway, Portugal, Spain, Sweden, Switzerland, Turkey, the United Kingdom and the United States. The following countries became Members subsequently through accession at the dates indicated hereafter: Japan (28th April 1964), Finland (28th January 1969), Australia (7th June 1971), New Zealand (29th May 1973) and Mexico (18th May 1994). The Commission of the European Communities takes part in the work of the OECD (Article 13 of the OECD Convention).

The Centre for Educational Research and Innovation was created in June 1968 by the Council of the Organisation for Economic Co-operation and Development and all Member countries of the OECD are participants.

The main objectives of the Centre are as follows:

— *to promote and support the development of research activities in education and undertake such research activities where appropriate;*

— *to promote and support pilot experiments with a view to introducing and testing innovations in the educational system;*

— *to promote the development of co-operation between Member countries in the field of educational research and innovation.*

The Centre functions within the Organisation for Economic Co-operation and Development in accordance with the decisions of the Council of the Organisation, under the authority of the Secretary-General. It is supervised by a Governing Board composed of one national expert in its field of competence from each of the countries participating in its programme of work.

ORGANISATION DE COOPÉRATION
ET DE DÉVELOPPEMENT ÉCONOMIQUES

En vertu de l'article 1ᵉʳ de la Convention signée le 14 décembre 1960, à Paris, et entrée en vigueur le 30 septembre 1961, l'Organisation de Coopération et de Développement Économiques (OCDE) a pour objectif de promouvoir des politiques visant :

- à réaliser la plus forte expansion de l'économie et de l'emploi et une progression du niveau de vie dans les pays Membres, tout en maintenant la stabilité financière, et à contribuer ainsi au développement de l'économie mondiale ;
- à contribuer à une saine expansion économique dans les pays Membres, ainsi que les pays non membres, en voie de développement économique ;
- à contribuer à l'expansion du commerce mondial sur une base multilatérale et non discriminatoire conformément aux obligations internationales.

Les pays Membres originaires de l'OCDE sont : l'Allemagne, l'Autriche, la Belgique, le Canada, le Danemark, l'Espagne, les États-Unis, la France, la Grèce, l'Irlande, l'Islande, l'Italie, le Luxembourg, la Norvège, les Pays-Bas, le Portugal, le Royaume-Uni, la Suède, la Suisse et la Turquie. Les pays suivants sont ultérieurement devenus Membres par adhésion aux dates indiquées ci-après : le Japon (28 avril 1964), la Finlande (28 janvier 1969), l'Australie (7 juin 1971), la Nouvelle-Zélande (29 mai 1973) et le Mexique (18 mai 1994). La Commission des Communautés européennes participe aux travaux de l'OCDE (article 13 de la Convention de l'OCDE).

Le Centre pour la Recherche et l'Innovation dans l'Enseignement a été créé par le Conseil de l'Organisation de Coopération et de Développement Économiques en juin 1968 et tous les pays Membres de l'OCDE y participent.

Les principaux objectifs du Centre sont les suivants :

- *encourager et soutenir le développement des activités de recherche se rapportant à l'éducation et entreprendre, le cas échéant, des activités de cette nature ;*
- *encourager et soutenir des expériences pilotes en vue d'introduire des innovations dans l'enseignement et d'en faire l'essai ;*
- *encourager le développement de la coopération entre les pays Membres dans le domaine de la recherche et de l'innovation dans l'enseignement.*

Le Centre exerce son activité au sein de l'Organisation de Coopération et de Développement Économiques conformément aux décisions du Conseil de l'Organisation, sous l'autorité du Secrétaire général et le contrôle direct d'un Comité directeur composé d'experts nationaux dans le domaine de compétence du Centre, chaque pays participant étant représenté par un expert.

Foreword

The General Assembly of the OECD project on International Indicators of Education Systems (INES) met in Lugano, Switzerland, in September 1991. That assembly reviewed the first set of OECD education indicators, and recommended that they be published in *Education at a Glance: OECD Indicators*. After the decision by the CERI Governing Board and the Education Committee in early 1992 to continue to develop education indicators, four networks with voluntary country participation were invited to pursue the conceptual and methodological work needed for the measurement of new indicators in different domains:

- Network A, led by the United States, took up the challenge of developing and measuring indicators of student learning outcomes;
- Network B, with strong support from Sweden, was requested to develop measures of education and labour market destinations;
- Network C, under the leadership of the Netherlands, was given the task of measuring indicators of schools and school processes;
- Network D, supported by the United Kingdom, was invited to chart the expectations and attitudes to education of the various stakeholder groups in OECD societies.

The General Assembly will convene again in June 1995 when Member countries and the people involved in the INES project will take stock of what has been achieved, examine the organisational framework of the sets of indicators produced so far, and explore the possibilities for further developments. To facilitate this review, each network has prepared a report describing the conceptual, methodological, and political problems encountered in constructing its respective clusters of indicators. The four reports are presented to the INES General Assembly as background and reference documents. Collectively, they offer a rich account of innovations, successes and failures in indicator development at the OECD, information that is essential for a review of perspectives and options for possible future work.

The content of each report has been discussed and endorsed during plenary sessions of the networks. The contributors are mostly members and national delegates to the networks, although in some cases distinguished independent experts have also contributed. For each network, members reviewed all the papers and suggested modifications where needed.

The preparation of this report was made possible thanks to the support received from the United States, the lead country of Network A, and particularly the National Center for Education Statistics, United States Department of Education, which contributed generously and co-ordinated the production of this report. This volume was prepared by the former Chair, Gary Phillips of the US National Center for Education Statistics, with the assistance of Jay Moskowitz of Pelavin Research Institute, Washington DC, in co-operation with Norberto Bottani and Albert Tuijnman of the OECD Secretariat.

This report is published on the responsibility of the Secretary-General of the OECD. It represents the views of the authors and does not necessarily reflect those of the OECD or of its Members countries.

Avant-propos

L'Assemblée générale du projet de l'OCDE sur les indicateurs internationaux des systèmes d'enseignement (INES) s'est réunie à Lugano, en Suisse, en septembre 1991. Elle a passé en revue la première série d'indicateurs de l'enseignement de l'OCDE et recommandé qu'ils soient publiés dans *Regards sur l'éducation : les indicateurs de l'OCDE*. Après que le Comité directeur du CERI et le Comité de l'éducation eurent décidé au début de 1992 de poursuivre l'élaboration d'indicateurs de l'enseignement, quatre réseaux, auxquels les pays participent volontairement, ont été invités à effectuer les travaux conceptuels et méthodologiques nécessaires pour mesurer de nouveaux indicateurs dans différents domaines :

- le Réseau A, mené par les États-Unis, s'est donné pour mission d'élaborer et de mesurer des indicateurs des acquis des élèves et étudiants ;
- le Réseau B, qui bénéficie d'une importante aide de la Suède, a été invité à mettre au point des mesures relatives à l'enseignement et aux débouchés professionnels ;
- le Réseau C, dirigé par les Pays-Bas, s'est vu confier la tâche de mesurer les indicateurs des établissements et des processus scolaires ;
- le Réseau D, soutenu par le Royaume-Uni, a été invité à décrire les attentes et les attitudes à l'égard de l'enseignement des diverses parties prenantes dans les pays de l'OCDE.

L'Assemblée générale se réunira de nouveau en juin 1995, ce qui permettra aux pays Membres et aux personnes participant au projet INES de faire le bilan de ce qui a été accompli, d'examiner l'organisation des séries d'indicateurs élaborés jusqu'à présent, et d'étudier les prolongements possibles. Pour faciliter cet examen, chaque réseau décrit dans un rapport les problèmes conceptuels, méthodologiques et politiques auxquels il s'est heurté dans la construction de sa propre série d'indicateurs. Les quatre rapports sont présentés à l'Assemblée générale du projet INES à titre de documents de référence. Ensemble, ils rendent compte en détail des innovations introduites avec ou sans succès dans la construction d'indicateurs à l'OCDE, autant d'informations qui sont essentielles pour étudier les perspectives et les options qui s'offrent en vue de la poursuite des travaux.

Le contenu de chaque rapport a été examiné et approuvé au cours des sessions plénières des réseaux. Les auteurs sont dans leur majorité des membres des réseaux et des personnes déléguées près d'eux par les pays, encore que dans certains cas des experts indépendants de haut niveau aient aussi apporté leur concours. Pour chacun des réseaux, les membres ont passé en revue tous les rapports et, le cas échéant, suggéré des modifications.

Ce rapport a été élaboré grâce à l'aide reçue des États-Unis, qui assurent la direction du Réseau A, et en particulier du National Center for Education Statistics du Département américain de l'Éducation, qui a généreusement contribué à sa publication et en a assuré la coordination. Cet ouvrage a été établi par l'ancien président du National Center for Education Statistics, Gary Phillips, avec l'aide de Jay Moskowitz du Pelavin Research Institute à Washington, en coopération avec Norberto Bottani et Albert Tuijnman du Secrétariat de l'OCDE.

Ce rapport est publié sous la responsabilité du Secrétaire général de l'OCDE. Il reflète les opinions des auteurs et ne représente pas nécessairement le point de vue de l'OCDE ni celui de ses pays Membres.

Table of Contents/Table des matières

Part/Partie 1

Developing Student Achievement Indicators
Mise au point des indicateurs de réussite scolaire

Chapter/Chapitre 1

National Experiences Using International Student Outcome Indicators
L'utilisation des indicateurs internationaux de la réussite scolaire :
l'expérience des différents pays

Jay Moskowitz

Chapter/Chapitre 2

International Comparisons of Student Achievement: Problems and Prospects
Comparaisons internationales de la réussite scolaire : problèmes et perspectives

Thomas Kellaghan and Aletta Grisay

Chapitre/Chapter 3
Réflexions sur quelques indicateurs inaboutis
Reflections on Some Unsuccessful Indicators

Aletta Grisay

Chapter/Chapitre 4

Calculation and Interpretation of Between-School and Within-School Variation in Achievement (*rho*)
Calcul et interprétation des variations de la réussite entre écoles et à l'intérieur d'un même établissement (rho)

T. Neville Postlethwaite

Part/Partie 2

Developing an Indicator of Cross-Curricular Competencies
Mise au point d'un indicateur de compétences transdisciplinaires

Chapter/Chapitre 5

Cross-Curricular Competencies: Rationale and Strategy for Developing a New Indicator
Les compétences transdisciplinaires : raison d'être et stratégie de mise au point d'un nouvel indicateur
Uri Peter Trier and Jules L. Peschar

Chapter/Chapitre 6

Measuring and Comparing Democratic Values
Mesurer et comparer les valeurs démocratiques
Loek Halman

Chapter/Chapitre 7

**Personality Theories and Developmental Processes: Their Implications for Indicators
of the Quality of Schooling**
*Les théories de la personnalité et les processus dynamiques :
incidences pour les indicateurs qualitatifs de l'enseignement*

Helmut Fend

Chapter/Chapitre 8

Problem-Solving and Communication Skills as Part of Preparation for Real Life
*Les techniques de résolution des problèmes de communication dans la préparation
à la vie réelle*

G. Douglas Hodgkinson and Michelle Crawford

Part/Partie 3

Developing an Indicator of National Education Goals
Mise au point d'un indicateur d'objectifs nationaux de l'enseignement

Chapter/Chapitre 9

Goals Orientation and Attainment in Learning Systems
Le choix des objectifs et leur réalisation dans les systèmes d'enseignement

Marit Granheim and Sten Pettersson

Chapter/Chapitre 10

The GOALS Study: Analysis and Implications
L'étude GOALS : analyse et incidences

Astrid Eggen Knutsen

Preface

by

Gary Phillips
National Center for Education Statistics,
US Department of Education, Washington DC, United States

In recent years several events coalesced to increase attention on international comparisons of student achievement. Politicians focused attention on how much is spent to educate children and the quality of the product that is being produced. Also, analysts in many countries expressed the opinion that children in school today will not be capable of participating in tomorrow's global economy. As a result of this attention, educational reforms aimed at improving student outcomes are being launched in all OECD countries.

Network A of the project on International Indicators of Education Systems (INES) is responsible for developing and preparing student outcome indicators. The network is made up of representatives from 19 OECD countries, including academics, researchers, school inspectors, and government officials. Over the past three years, these network members have prepared achievement indicators in mathematics, science, and reading literacy. In addition, considerable efforts have been directed towards the development of a "survival kit" indicator, which would take into account both schooling and societal influences, and of an indicator of national goals, designed to provide contextual information on which to base international comparisons of student outcomes.

The chapters collected in this volume were prepared to assist the network in developing student outcome indicators. Some chapters were prepared by consultants in response to methodological problems. Other chapters provided the network with background information needed for understanding conceptual issues. Finally, some chapters provide reports on specific network activities.

The volume is organised in three parts. Part 1, edited by Aletta Grisay of the University of Liège (Belgium), discusses both the difficulty of developing international comparisons, and national interest in these comparisons. In a series of mini-case studies, Chapter 1 illustrates how INES has encouraged nations to develop their own publications on indicators. Chapter 2 lays out some of the conceptual and data issues that the network confronts in preparing the indicators. Chapter 3 explores some of the network's empirical investigations of potential indicators. Chapter 4 presents an example of the methodological rigour that the network attempts to bring to its work.

Part 2, edited by Jules Peschar of the University of Groningen (the Netherlands), presents information prepared as part of the development of a Cross-Curricular Competencies (CCC) indicator. In 1991, it was proposed that the network should explore the development of an indicator of skills which young men and women need to live in a modern, democratic society. These skills include a knowledge of democratic values, an ability to solve problems and to communicate, and a sense of self-concept. The chapters in this part present the rationales for developing a CCC indicator and some of the conceptual thinking which supports its eventual realisation.

Another long-term interest of network members lies in linking measures of student outcomes to national goals and policies. Part 3, edited by Marit Granheim of the Norwegian Ministry of Education, Research and Church Affairs, describes a network activity labelled "Goals Orientation and Attainment in Learning Systems" (GOALS). Chapters 9 and 10 discuss the theories underlying GOALS and the results of a pilot study aimed at developing a basis for data collection. Chapter 11 provides a sense of the conceptual work prepared for GOALS.

While the focus of Network A since 1992 of the INES project has been on developing student outcome indicators for *Education at a Glance* (OECD, 1992, 1993 and 1995), the network has also begun to develop a longer-term perspective. Chapter 12 concludes with an attempt by network members to outline some of the issues and components of a strategic plan for producing student outcome indicators.

Préface

par

Gary Phillips
National Center for Education Statistics,
Département américain de l'Éducation, Washington DC, États-Unis

Ces dernières années, sous l'effet de plusieurs événements connexes, les comparaisons internationales touchant la réussite scolaire ont suscité un intérêt croissant. Les politiciens ont appelé l'attention sur les montants consacrés à l'éducation des enfants et sur la qualité du produit obtenu, et les analystes de nombreux pays ont fait valoir que les enfants qui fréquentent l'école aujourd'hui ne seront pas capables de participer à l'économie mondiale de demain. En raison de cet intérêt, des réformes de l'enseignement destinées à améliorer les résultats obtenus par les élèves ont été entamées dans tous les pays de l'OCDE.

Établi dans le cadre du projet sur les indicateurs internationaux des systèmes d'enseignement (INES), le Réseau A est chargé de concevoir et de mettre au point les indicateurs ayant trait aux résultats des élèves. Le groupe, qui se compose de représentants de 19 pays de l'OCDE, réunit des universitaires, des chercheurs, des inspecteurs scolaires et des agents de gouvernement. Au cours des trois dernières années, ses membres ont préparé des indicateurs de compétences en mathématiques, en sciences et en lecture. En outre, le réseau a déployé beaucoup d'efforts en vue de l'élaboration d'un indicateur de « survie », qui tiendrait compte des influences exercées à la fois par l'école et par la société, ainsi que d'un indicateur d'objectifs nationaux visant à fournir des informations contextuelles sur lesquelles il serait possible de fonder les comparaisons internationales de résultats scolaires.

Les chapitres réunis dans le présent ouvrage ont pour objet d'aider le réseau à mettre au point les indicateurs de résultats des élèves. Certains ont été rédigés par des consultants en réponse à des difficultés méthodologiques. D'autres ont fourni au groupe les renseignements de base nécessaires à la compréhension de problèmes conceptuels. Quelques-uns enfin donnent le compte rendu d'activités spécifiques du réseau.

Le volume comprend trois parties. Revue par Aletta Grisay, de l'Université de Liège (Belgique), la première partie traite à la fois des difficultés inhérentes à la production de comparaisons internationales et de l'intérêt des pays pour ces comparaisons. A l'aide

17

d'une série de mini-études de cas, le chapitre 1 illustre la façon dont le projet INES a incité diverses nations à produire leurs propres recueils d'indicateurs. Au chapitre 2 sont exposés certains des problèmes conceptuels et des problèmes de données qu'affronte le réseau dans l'élaboration des indicateurs. Le chapitre 3 examine quelques travaux de recherche empirique effectués par le réseau sur d'éventuels indicateurs. Quant au chapitre 4, il fournit un exemple de la rigueur que le réseau entend apporter à ses travaux sur le plan de la méthodologie.

La deuxième partie, revue par Jules Peschar, de l'Université de Groningue (Pays-Bas), présente les informations rassemblées dans le cadre de l'élaboration d'un indicateur de compétences transdisciplinaires (CCC). En 1991, il a été proposé au réseau d'envisager la mise au point d'un indicateur sur les compétences dont les jeunes ont besoin pour vivre dans une société démocratique moderne. Ces compétences englobent la connaissance des valeurs démocratiques, la capacité de résoudre des problèmes et de communiquer, et le sens d'une image de soi. Les chapitres réunis dans cette partie exposent les raisons pour lesquelles on développe un indicateur de compétences transdisciplinaires et certains aspects de la réflexion conceptuelle qui étayent son éventuelle réalisation.

Les membres du réseau s'intéressent aussi à long terme à l'établissement de liens entre les mesures de résultats scolaires et les politiques et objectifs nationaux. Revue par Marit Granheim, du ministère norvégien de l'Éducation, de la Recherche et des Cultes, la troisième partie décrit l'activité du réseau sur le choix des objectifs et leur réalisation dans les systèmes d'enseignement (GOALS : Goals Orientation and Attainment in Learning Systems). Aux chapitres 9 et 10 sont analysées les théories qui sous-tendent cette activité et les conclusions d'une enquête pilote destinée à créer une base pour le recueil des données. Le chapitre 11 donne pour sa part une idée du travail conceptuel effectué pour GOALS.

Si, depuis 1992, le Réseau A s'est surtout attaché à mettre au point des indicateurs sur les résultats des élèves pour la publication *Regards sur l'éducation* (OCDE, 1992, 1993 et 1995), il a également commencé à élaborer une perspective à plus long terme. En conclusion, dans le chapitre 12, les membres du réseau tentent d'esquisser certains aspects et composantes d'un plan stratégique visant la production d'indicateurs de résultats des élèves.

Developing Student Achievement Indicators
Mise au point des indicateurs de réussite scolaire

Introduction

by

Aletta Grisay
University of Liège, Belgium

This first part of the volume provides insight into several levels of the preparation of *Education at a Glance* (OECD, 1995). It begins with a summary of some of the work that countries have produced, provides some understanding of the problems faced by the network in selecting its indicators, and ends with an examination of the statistical criteria and techniques used in analysing some of the indicators themselves.

Chapters 1 to 4 present several aspects of the network's efforts towards the publication of the third edition of *Education at a Glance* (OECD, 1995). Chapter 1, by Jay Moskowitz, examines the impact the first and second editions of *Education at a Glance* (1992 and 1993) have had on educational policy-makers in the countries covered. In Belgium (Flemish Community), Finland, Switzerland and the United States, the publication was used as a model on which to base reports of the student outcomes of national or sub-national groups. The publication of these books, which gauge national educational achievement, arose out of national policy-makers' interest in the OECD indicators.

In Chapter 2, Thomas Kellaghan and Aletta Grisay explore some of the difficulties encountered in making international comparisons, using student achievement data taken from national and international sources. While dependence on these sources of data has made the OECD indicators set vulnerable to certain pitfalls, the network is currently exploring ways to reduce this dependence. For example, an assessment of cross-curricular competencies, one of the alternative approaches noted by Kellaghan and Grisay, is currently being designed by the network. (A detailed description of this effort is provided in Part 2.) The chapter concludes with a description of several alternative approaches to measuring student achievement in a range of countries.

The effects that the drawbacks of using varied sources of data have had on the OECD education indicators are discussed by Aletta Grisay in Chapter 3. Specifically, she presents those indicators that did not meet the network's criteria for publication. The ratio of material learned and material taught, and the evolution of reading competency indicators, failed on account of the age of their data, and the complexities faced by any effort to update them. Another indicator, which measured the variation of mathematics scores between classes within schools and between schools within countries, also failed to meet the network's quality standards. Both the home/school language difference and computer literacy indicators could not overcome several statistical obstacles and were consequently rejected by the network.

As statistical methods and techniques play a significant role in the measurement of student outcome indicators, Chapter 4 is designed to present the reader with an in-depth treatment of one of these techniques. This technique, *rho,* is useful in measuring the difference in variation between two groups, relative to the variation within them. Chapter 4 provides an overview of the different types of group to which *rho* may be applied, and then uses this technique to explain the variation in results among the OECD countries.

Introduction

par

Aletta Grisay
Université de Liège, Belgique

La première partie de cet ouvrage donne une idée des diverses étapes de la préparation de *Regards sur l'éducation* (OCDE, 1995). Elle commence par un résumé de quelques-unes des publications produites par les pays, aide ensuite à mieux comprendre les problèmes qu'affronte le réseau dans le choix de ses indicateurs et se termine par un examen des critères et techniques statistiques utilisés pour analyser certains des indicateurs eux-mêmes.

Les chapitres 1 à 4 décrivent, sous plusieurs de leurs aspects, les efforts déployés par le réseau en vue de la publication de la troisième édition de *Regards sur l'éducation* (OCDE, 1995). Dans le chapitre 1, Jay Moskowitz examine l'incidence qu'ont eue les première et deuxième éditions de *Regards sur l'éducation* (1992 et 1993) sur les décideurs du secteur de l'enseignement de divers pays. En Belgique (Communauté flamande), en Finlande, en Suisse et aux États-Unis, l'ouvrage a servi de modèle à des recueils d'indicateurs de résultats scolaires établis à l'échelon national et infranational. La publication de ces rapports, qui permettent de jauger les niveaux nationaux d'instruction, découle de l'intérêt témoigné par les décideurs des pays cités pour les indicateurs de l'OCDE.

Au chapitre 2, Thomas Kellaghan et Aletta Grisay examinent quelques-unes des difficultés rencontrées en procédant à des comparaisons internationales à l'aide de données sur la réussite scolaire issues de sources nationales et internationales. La dépendance à l'égard de ces sources de données expose certes l'ensemble des indicateurs de l'OCDE à certains écueils, mais le réseau explore en ce moment des moyens de réduire cette dépendance. Il est, par exemple, occupé à mettre au point une évaluation des compétences transdisciplinaires – qui représente l'une des méthodes proposées par Kellaghan et Grisay pour mesurer la réussite scolaire. (On trouvera dans la deuxième partie une description détaillée de cette initiative.) Le chapitre se termine par la description de plusieurs autres approches permettant de mesurer la réussite des élèves dans divers pays.

L'incidence des inconvénients qu'entraîne l'utilisation de sources de données de qualité variable sur les indicateurs de l'éducation de l'OCDE est examinée par Aletta Grisay, dans le chapitre 3. Elle présente en particulier les indicateurs qui n'ont pas répondu aux critères du réseau et, à ce titre, n'ont pas été publiés. Ainsi, les indicateurs relatifs au rapport entre les matières enseignées et les matières apprises et à l'évolution des compétences en lecture ont été refusés en raison de l'ancienneté des données utilisées et des difficultés pour les mettre à jour. Un autre indicateur permettant de comparer les résultats obtenus en mathématiques entre les classes d'une même école et entre les écoles d'un même pays n'a pas non plus réussi à répondre aux normes de qualité du réseau. Les indicateurs concernant la différence entre la langue parlée à la maison et la langue de l'enseignement et les compétences en informatique n'ont pu surmonter divers obstacles d'ordre statistique.

Comme les techniques et les méthodes statistiques jouent un rôle significatif dans la mesure des indicateurs des résultats scolaires, le chapitre 4 offre au lecteur une analyse approfondie de l'une de ces techniques, le *rho*. Celle-ci est utile pour mesurer les variations entre deux groupes par rapport aux variations à l'intérieur de chacun d'eux. Le chapitre présente un aperçu des divers types de groupe auquel le *rho* peut s'appliquer, puis utilise cette technique pour expliquer les variations des résultats obtenus parmi les pays de l'OCDE.

National Experiences Using International Student Outcome Indicators

L'utilisation des indicateurs internationaux de la réussite scolaire : l'expérience des différents pays

by

Jay Moskowitz
Pelavin Research Institute, Washington DC, United States

The publication of the first international report on education indicators (*Education at a Glance,* OECD, 1992) aroused considerable interest around the world. As the countries compared were all OECD Members, the publication led to political debate and increased public interest in many Member countries concerning the state of their education systems relative to other industrialised nations.

This chapter presents the experiences of four countries that have produced publications similar in type to *Education at a Glance.* The reports prepared in Belgium (Flemish Community), Switzerland and the United States are similar, one (Finland) is quite different from the rest. The information on each country was provided by an official involved in the production of the country volumes, in response to a set of questions. These mini-case studies are presented in Sections 3 to 6. The similarities and differences are summarised in the concluding section. This chapter will begin, however, with a summary of international reactions to the results published in *Education at a Glance* (OECD, 1992).

*

*   *

Note de synthèse

La publication du premier rapport international sur les indicateurs de l'enseignement (Regards sur l'éducation, *OCDE, 1992), qui offrait aux pouvoirs publics la possibilité de comparer utilement les indicateurs de l'enseignement au niveau international, a suscité dans de nombreux pays un vif intérêt de la part des administrations et des instances dirigeantes. Des recueils d'indicateurs inspirés de* Regards sur l'éducation *ont été par la suite mis au point en Belgique (Communauté flamande), en Suisse, aux États-Unis et en Finlande. Les descriptions suivantes des expériences vécues dans ces pays ont été rédigées en réponse à un questionnaire concernant le mode de présentation et la production de ces recueils.*

En Belgique où les Communautés allemande, flamande, et française contrôlent la quasi-totalité des aspects de l'enseignement, la Communauté flamande a décidé de ventiler les données utilisées par l'OCDE. On s'est donc servi dans le rapport flamand (De School op Rapport) *de données provenant de diverses sources internationales et flamandes afin de comparer la Communauté flamande avec d'autres pays de l'OCDE. Cet ouvrage a été, et continue d'être, fréquemment évoqué par la presse.*

En Suisse, on a établi un ensemble d'indicateurs destiné à comparer le système éducatif des différents cantons. Le premier document national publié par les Suisses, qui s'inspirait de Regards sur l'éducation (OCDE, 1992), *offrait une description du pays tout entier dans une optique internationale, situait chaque canton à l'intérieur du pays, et donnait un aperçu des cantons eux-mêmes. Ce document a été bien reçu et ses résultats sont actuellement utilisés à titre de référence dans des publications spécialisées.*

Aux États-Unis, tous les secteurs de l'administration s'intéressent à la contribution qu'apporte la réussite scolaire à la prospérité. C'est pourquoi, le ministère de l'Éducation a publié The Condition of Education, *un inventaire annuel des statistiques de l'enseignement américain. En y insérant des données provenant de* Regards sur l'éducation, *on a pu, dans la publication intitulée* Education in States and Nations, *faire des comparaisons entre États et pays. Cette publication fait actuellement partie d'une action menée pour permettre de mieux comprendre et comparer plus facilement les données internationales sur l'enseignement.*

En Finlande, où Regards sur l'éducation *(OCDE, 1993) a bénéficié d'une large publicité, une version en finnois du document a été établie; elle comprend la traduction partielle des tableaux et des textes, ainsi que des articles écrits au titre du projet INES sur les indicateurs internationaux des systèmes d'enseignement. Les travaux d'INES ont également permis l'élaboration d'indicateurs provisoires qui reflètent le niveau d'instruction de la population des communes.*

Tous les livres publiés dans les pays cités répondent au besoin de pouvoir comparer les indicateurs afin que les décideurs de l'enseignement soient en mesure de jauger l'évolution du niveau d'instruction de leurs pays. C'est parce que ces pays avaient en commun le désir d'adapter plus étroitement à leur situation les travaux de l'OCDE tout en se servant des données et de la présentation de Regards sur l'éducation *qu'ils ont publié des ouvrages issus de* Regards sur l'éducation, *qui sont à la fois des versions plus fines et correspondant de plus près à leurs propres besoins.*

*

* *

1. International Reaction

Governments and political bodies of many nations took notice of the results of *Education at a Glance* (OCDE, 1992). For some, the published information was a rude awakening. For others, the results were both pleasing and surprising; and major newspapers in OECD countries covered the release in various ways.

Newspaper stories usually gave brief coverage to the release of results and provided a run-down on how the country in question was faring on certain indicators, with the "Per Pupil Expenditure" indicator mentioned most often. More extensive stories analysed the country's ratings and often linked *Education at a Glance* (OCDE, 1992)'s findings to national and international educational reform movements. Some of the longer stories were supportive of the national education system; others used *Education at a Glance*'s evidence of poor national performance. One British story used *Education at a Glance*'s findings to dispute ministerial statements on educational spending (*Daily Telegraph*, 25 September 1992).

In short, *Education at a Glance* (OCDE, 1992) was an international success in that the report allowed comparisons of education indicators that were of certain policy relevance; and education experts used *Education at a Glance* as a ready and accessible frame of reference for factual debate about their country's own education system.

2. National Utilisation

In most countries, an examination of national-level comparisons provides local officials with only limited information on which to base policy decisions. Similarly, in federal countries sub-national information is required. In fact, several countries subsequently and independently developed indicator reports, based on the format of *Education at a Glance,* which provided additional data on the national education system, so that the OECD indicators could be interpreted against improved contextual information.

Belgium (Flemish Community), Finland, Switzerland and the United States provided information on how their national indicator reports were designed, and how they were received. These reports are referred to as *mini-case studies.* A questionnaire on various aspects related to the preparation and impact of these national reports was sent to national delegates, who were invited to:

1. Describe the rationale for preparing the document and discuss the major issues that were addressed.

2. Describe whether *Education at a Glance* data were used and how. What national data were available to augment *Education at a Glance* data?
3. Provide an example of new ways (compared to *Education at a Glance*) in which the indicators were presented in the national reports.
4. Provide suggestions, based on national experience, of how *Education at a Glance* might be modified and improved.
5. Discuss the reception given in your country to the national indicator report. For example, who used it? And what discussion did it generate?

The questions were designed as a uniform guide to the presentation of the mini-case studies. These follow, in the form of individual responses from the four nations that produced books similar in type to *Education at a Glance*.

3. The School on Report: Flemish Education in an International Context
by **Luc Van de Poele,** University of Ghent, Belgium

Belgium has relatively recently (1970) become a federated state with a central government, cultural communities, regions, provinces, and local authorities. The communities, of which there are three – Flemish, French and German – have gradually taken over most of the responsibilities for education policy from the former central government. The current federal government only makes decisions regarding the beginning and end of compulsory education, the minimum conditions for graduation, and the general structure of education. Except for such restrictions, education policy in the communities has become autonomous.

The OECD has traditionally included aggregated data for Belgium in its reports, which were not of direct use to the communities precisely because of the aggregation. The Flemish Community thought that indicators and data analyses should be performed on disaggregated Belgian data, and took it upon itself to put together a book similar in style to *Education at a Glance,* comparing the Flemish Community to other OECD nations. Unlike previous analyses, this analysis is of direct use to the Flemish Community; and the publication of the book represents one of the many steps that the communities of Belgium have taken in order to gain autonomy in education policy.

Data Sources

While the Flemish report, *De School op Rapport,* was based on *Education at a Glance* (1992), only about 40 per cent of the data came from the OECD; and those data were used to make international comparisons between the Flemish education system and those of other countries. One example is the Network B database, which was used to calculate three indicators upon which the OECD did not focus. One of those indicators (Index of Gender Differences) was subsequently included in *Education at a Glance* (1995).

Another 40 per cent of the data came from Flemish sources. These data described the evolution of the Flemish education system, with much attention given to the differences between the ideological "networks" (e.g. the Catholic, official, and provincial education systems) and issues of special interest in Flemish education (e.g. percentage of repeaters). There were no international comparisons made in this section.

The remaining data were used for international comparisons, but they did not derive from the OECD. Among the data sources used were information gathered by the European Community, the International Association for the Evaluation of Educational Achievement, and the Flemish Education Ministry's analyses of statistical yearbooks from different countries.

Presentation

Most of the Flemish indicators report is composed of bar-charts for the indicators and related information. Each indicator is accompanied by an interpretation and brief analysis. However, distinct differences exist between the Flemish book and *Education at a Glance*. For example, the indicators for educational attainment of the population and computer use in education are presented in country profiles, not bar-charts.

Profile presentations give a better picture of several aspects of a country at once, making comparisons between the general educational conditions in the countries easier. In the case of the computer education indicator, for example, the presentation gives a good picture of how computers are used in schools in different countries (see Figure 1.1).

Reception

The Flemish government used a professional publisher to distribute the book, of which over 2 000 copies were sold. For a government report, it was a great success. The book was launched at a national press conference, and all the major newspapers carried at least one article covering the book's release and reviewers' first impressions of it.

The book turned out to be more than a momentary flash. Months after its release, BELGA (the national news agency) distributed a story based on the book. The authors of the book also received some personal press coverage. The principal authors were interviewed on radio and television, and a few interviews took place on prime-time television news programmes.

Most of the press coverage focused on results from the use of the *European Values Study* data, for the indicators generated with those data illustrated educational issues over which there was public concern. Although the data had been previously published, the Flemish book highlighted their close relation to education and gave them greater public exposure.

Figure/*Graphique* 1.1. **The use of computers in particular subjects**
Utilisation de l'informatique dans certaines disciplines

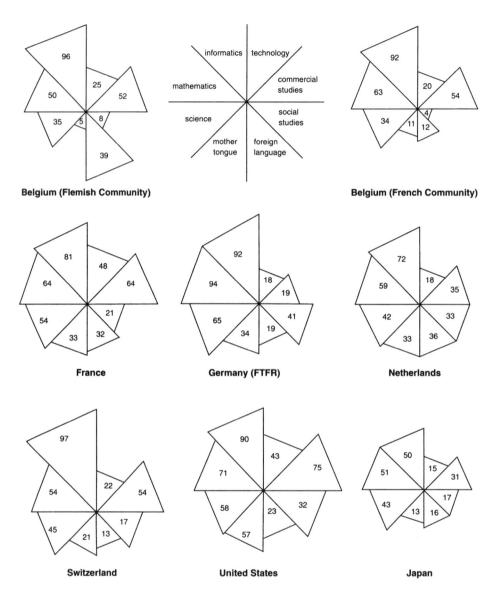

Belgium (Flemish Community)

Belgium (French Community)

France

Germany (FTFR)

Netherlands

Switzerland

United States

Japan

Note: The percentages of computer co-ordinators indicating computer use in particular subjects correspond to the areas covered by the triangles.
Source: De School op Rapport, Ministry of Education, Flemish Community.

4. National Education Indicators for Switzerland
by **Anna Borkowsky,** Federal Statistical Office, Switzerland

Profiting from the experience of developing a set of Swiss national education indicators has been one of the major goals of the active participation of Switzerland in the OECD's INES project. To talk of Swiss national education indicators is inaccurate, however, because the purpose is to develop a set of indicators for comparing cantonal education systems.

A complete set of indicators will give a picture of the Swiss education system as a whole. That picture is important to a country where educational policy and responsibility are traditionally fragmented, not only between the cantons, but also between different sectors of public administration. Each indicator provides an international perspective of the country as a whole, places each canton within the context of the whole country and, at the same time, allows a glimpse into the fascinating and often not very well known realm of the neighbouring canton.

Switzerland could obviously benefit from the high level of expertise which had gone into the construction of the set of international indicators, as well as from the aura of legitimacy surrounding an international project managed by the OECD. The first of the Swiss national documents, published in 1993, is thus an "offshoot" of *Education at a Glance,* but it is also intended as the starting point of a national series, with a second document to be published in 1995.

The whole process of participation in INES is an example of the increased readiness of the Swiss to compare and evaluate recent innovations in their education systems. Other examples are the first OECD examination of the country's educational policy, conducted in 1990, and a national research programme on the efficiency of the Swiss education system(s), running from 1993 to 1998.

Data Sources

Education at a Glance data provide the core of the Swiss indicators report. Only indicators for which Swiss data at the cantonal (or at least regional level) could be constructed were included. For practical reasons eight OECD countries were selected for the international comparisons: Austria, France, Germany, Italy, Japan, the Netherlands, the United Kingdom and the United States.

The international list was supplemented with some country-specific indicators, such as "Home and School Language", that had not been used in *Education at a Glance.* Other indicators highlight features of the Swiss education systems, including the selection into streams within lower secondary education and the differentiation of general and vocational education at the upper secondary level. A third group of indicators enlarges the results section by showing the effects of education in areas other than the labour market.

For the first publication in 1993, data on political, social, and cultural participation were used. For the second publication in 1995, we plan to include some indicators on the

Figure/*Graphique* 1.2. **University diplomas**
Diplômes universitaires

Percentage of age groups obtaining a university diploma (1988)

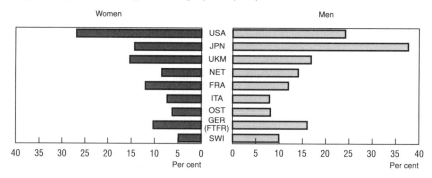

**University diplomas in Switzerland according to gender and linguistic region (1990)
(not including non-resident foreigners)**[1]

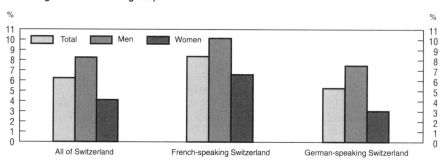

**Intercantonal comparison of age groups obtaining a university diploma (1990)
(not including non-resident foreigners)**[1]

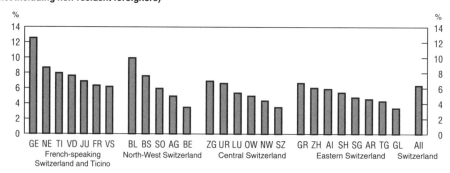

1.   Number of licences and diplomas by per cent of population in the same age group.
Source: Swiss Federal Statistical Office.

relationship between education and health. This group of indicators depends on data from studies that, in general, are not internationally comparable and are not repeated annually. Nevertheless, we think they are a valuable addition to the more traditional labour market indicators published in *Education at a Glance* (1995).

Presentation

The presentation of the indicators followed the model of *Education at a Glance* rather closely, although inter-cantonal comparisons were included and a strict adherence to a two-page format for each indicator was followed. The texts are generally longer and more "theoretical" than those in *Education at a Glance*. An example below illustrates the format used throughout the publication (Figure 1.2).

The innovation at the national level consisted in presenting the whole set of indicators, and in assembling data usually found in different places, in a systematic, comparative perspective. However, it is easy to become lost among the plethora of interesting information. We would wish for more synthetic or concentrated indicators and for more help in placing indicators within conceptual frameworks. In this respect, the 1993 version of *Education at a Glance* already represents an improvement over the 1992 version. Our rigid framework forced us to present only one (or at most two) aspect(s) among the many different aspects of an indicator, at the cost, of course, of neglecting much interesting information. There might, nonetheless, be merit in curbing the number of indicators developed at the international level.

Reception

The reception given to the publication by the Swiss public was quite positive among both users and readers, thanks primarily to the amount of information provided and the comparisons between cantons which this allowed. The results shown in the document have been used to provide background information in special publications for educators; and both its reception and its use point towards its continued value for future study.

5. Education in States and Nations: A US "Offshoot" of *Education at a Glance* by **Tom Smith,** National Center for Education Statistics, United States

In 1983, when a widely read publication entitled *A Nation at Risk* highlighted both the condition of American education and its essential role in securing the nation's prosperity, international comparisons of mathematics and science achievement were among the cited evidence. It appeared, then, that US students were being increasingly outperformed by students from other countries, including some that educated their students at a much lower cost. That publication by the National Commission on Excellence in Education, which was appointed by the Secretary of Education suggested that, at a time when a nation's prosperity was more than ever before determined by the collective capacity of its citizenry, the US education system seemed not to be performing as well as it could.[1]

A few years later, in 1986, the US National Governors' Association issued *A Time for Results,* a report similar to *A Nation at Risk* in its tone, in the nature of its evidence, and in its recommendations. *A Time for Results* stated even more strongly than *A Nation at Risk* that global economic competition meant that the most appropriate benchmarks for education system performance were now global. This report by a *national* association of *state* governors was at once an assertion that education was a national concern, and that it was still primarily a state and local responsibility.[2]

Since publication of *A Time for Results,* Americans have seen much activity on education policy at the interstices of authority and between the separate branches and levels of government. The Federal government and the nation's governors combined their efforts formally at the Charlottesville, Virginia, "Education Summit" in 1989; and the subsequently formed National Education Goals Panel and National Council on Education Standards and Testing both included members from the Congress, the White House, the US Department of Education, and the ranks of governors and state legislators; and agreement on six (later eight) national education goals followed the Charlottesville summit.

A commitment to reach world-class education performance levels is explicitly expressed in National Education Goals 4 and 5. Goal 4 declares that US students will be first in the world in science and mathematics achievement by the year 2000. Goal 5 asserts that every adult American will possess the knowledge and skills necessary to compete in a global economy.

By joining efforts with the Federal government, the governors did not intend to share the management of the public schools. However, they did agree that the Federal government had an important role to play in the collection and dissemination of comparative data needed to manage the quality of American education.[3] The US Department of Education's National Center for Education Statistics (NCES) has for many years carried out such duties. One of its efforts, *The Condition of Education,* is an annual compendium of statistical information on American education, including trends over time, international country comparisons, and some comparisons among various groups (by sex, ethnicity, socioeconomic status, and so on). This publication contains very few state-by-state comparisons, however.

Education in States and Nations is a logical next step, and a valuable US companion to *Education at a Glance.* It not only allows state-to-state and country-to-country comparisons, but also state-to-country comparisons. For perhaps the first time, states can compare their support for education, the participation of their youth in the education system, or their educational outcomes with those of a number of industrialised countries, including some that may be quite similar in size and wealth. In other words, on a variety of measures, education in US states can now be compared internationally.

Data Sources

Education in States and Nations includes 16 indicators chosen to take the maximum advantage of the data available in *Education at a Glance*. Indicators from *Education at a Glance* (OECD, 1992) were selected for use in *Education in States and Nations,* if they were relevant to states and if comparative state-level data on the indicators already existed. The indicators are grouped into four categories: 1) background, 2) participation, 3) outcomes, and 4) finance. The data come from a variety of sources.

Most of the data on countries come from the OECD. The data on individual states come primarily from the NCES, the Department of Labor's Bureau of Labor Statistics, and the Department of Commerce's Bureau of the Census. In addition, results from the 1992 NAEP (National Assessment of Educational Progress) study of mathematics achievement of American eighth-graders have been statistically linked to results from a similar study of the mathematics achievement of 13-year-old students in various countries, conducted in 1991. This linkage allows comparisons of academic achievement between states and countries.

Presentation

The presentation of each indicator includes an explanation of what it measures, why it is important, and key results from a comparison of countries and states. Throughout the book, comparisons are most often made between "like-sized entities": between the United States and the other large and relatively wealthy countries that compose the so-called Group of Seven, or "G-7" countries: Canada, France, Germany, Italy, Japan and the United Kingdom; but the book also compares US states to all the OECD countries, including the smaller and relatively less wealthy ones. Comparisons with like countries can be more meaningful than some others, essentially because certain common and influential factors, such as state size and wealth, are relatively constant.

In addition to the explanations and key results, the presentation of each indicator includes separate tables for states and countries and a graph that displays states and countries together. The graphs are, in most cases, simple bar-charts, with the states and countries listed in order, from highest value to lowest. This type of graph highlights the distributional aspects of the data (*i.e.* where countries and states stand in relation to one another and the magnitude of the differences between them). Where appropriate, notes on interpretation describe special circumstances affecting indicators that warrant particular consideration in making comparisons. Data sources are listed at the bottom of each table and graph. Because some of the terms used in this report may not be familiar to all readers, a glossary is included. Finally, appendices include supplementary data and technical information on how the indicators were developed.

To illustrate with one example, Figure 1.3 shows the bar-chart for Indicator 14, from *Education in States and Nations.* Note that current public education expenditure as a percentage of GDP/GSP attempts to show what *public* investment states and nations make in education in terms of the economic resources available to them.

Figure/*Graphique* 1.3. **Current public expenditure on education as a percentage of GDP/GSP,
by country and state, 1988**
*Dépenses publiques courantes d'éducation en pourcentage du PIB/PSB,
par pays et par État, 1988*

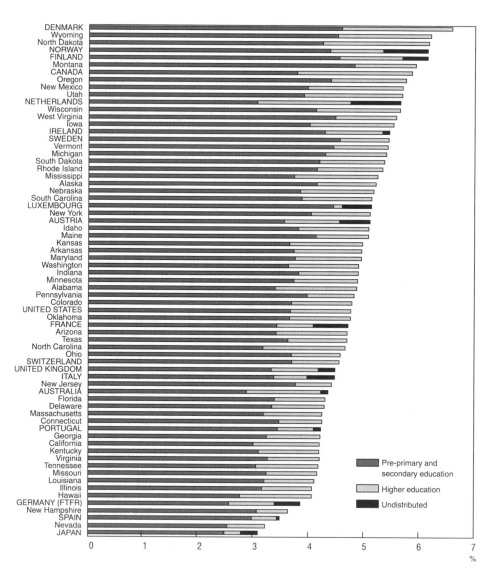

Sources: US Department of Education, National Center for Education Statistics, Common Core of Data Survey, 1988/89; Financial Statistics of Higher Education Survey, 1988/89; and Integrated Postsecondary Education Data System Finance Survey, 1988/89. *Statistical Abstract of the United States 1992*, Table 684; OECD.

As one can surmise from the chart, NCES chooses to use current public expenditure, rather than total expenditure. Our position is that public expenditure better represents the public investment and commitment to education than does total expenditure; and that current expenditure is less influenced by exogenous demographic factors than is capital expenditure, and so is a less volatile measure. It takes NCES a not insignificant effort to tease current and public expenditures out of the total expenditure figures that some countries turn in to INES. The modification to *Education at a Glance* that would help NCES most is a commitment from participating countries to send in complete financial data, with accurate breakdowns for current and public expenditures.

Reception

Education in States and Nations has received considerable press attention, although, because it came out just a few weeks prior to the release of *Education at a Glance* (OECD, 1992), some journalists confused the two publications. (One journalist, for example, credited the OECD with producing our report comparing the US states to the OECD countries.) The press coverage also focused overwhelmingly on the mathematics examination indicator developed by the US National Assessment of Educational Progress (IAEP/NAEP), the only achievement indicator that was available to us.

The first edition of *Education in States and Nations* is just one part of an overall NCES effort to improve the accuracy of comparing the education systems of different states and countries. NCES, which is acting as the representative of the United States in the OECD's INES project, has commissioned a study in connection with that project to improve the comparability of financial data on education between countries. It is hoped that this study will help to improve the quality of the financial data gathered for future editions of *Education at a Glance* and *Education in States and Nations*.

6. Education Indicators: Development in Finland
by **Reijo Laukkanen,** National Board of Education, Finland

In the 1990s, decentralisation and deregulation are the main themes in Finnish education policy. At the beginning of 1993, the system of state subsidies was renewed, allowing municipalities to receive a lump sum of money for education; and the municipalities can now decide how to use this resource. The curricular guidelines were revised at the beginning of 1994, and, through this change, the municipalities, schools, and parents will have greater choices of subjects and more latitude in defining the overall content of education. Deregulation has largely meant that, in most cases, the national guidelines for local decisions are broad. This new policy has also meant changes in the national strategies guiding the education system. The most prominent new emphases in the national strategies are on definitions and the development of evaluation strategies, causing great interest in the development of national indicators for education.

Preparation

The OECD *Education at a Glance* publications, especially the 1993 version, have received wide publicity in Finland. One reason for this is the possibility of comparing the Finnish education system with that of other countries. Another reason is that these publications provide a model for defining and using education indicators.

To give all interested groups an opportunity to become acquainted with *Education at a Glance,* the Ministry of Education decided to prepare a Finnish version of the 1993 version, which consists of two parts: 1) a partial translation of texts and tables of *Education at a Glance* (approximately 100 pages), and 2) articles on the work done in International Indicators of Education Systems project (INES) (approximately 80 pages).

The preparation of the first part has demonstrated the difficulties that arise in translating OECD definitions. For example, it was not easy to find an accurate Finnish counterpart for the concept of ''secondary education'', which involves the education of 14 to 16-year-olds. In Finland, there is comprehensive basic education from age 7 to 16, which is why the Finnish tradition of classifying statistics contradicts the OECD definition. This is only one example of the many difficulties in publishing a Finnish version of *Education at a Glance.*

The second part of the Finnish version consists of seven articles with a twofold focus: the Finnish situation with respect to each indicator is highlighted, discussed, and compared with background information that is not available in the text of the first part. Also, the objectives and background of the work that has been done in INES are discussed more thoroughly than is done in the original *Education at a Glance* publications (1992).

Future Plans

Preparation of national education indicators has just started in Finland. The National Board of Education, in fact, has a plan to prepare sets of indicators for comprehensive schools, upper secondary education, and adult education, the first examples of which were ready in late 1994.

There are also plans in some municipalities to prepare and publish municipal indicators, but these publications are not yet ready. The definition of the indicators was decided upon by municipal administrators and principals of schools. The use of the sets of indicators is motivated by the taxpayers' need and right to know, and by the importance of providing new ways of giving relevant information to municipal boards of trustees.

Statistics Finland has already developed, with funding from the Ministry of Education, provisional indicators to reflect profiles of educational attainment of the population in the municipalities. These indicators have not been published as a single report, but the municipalities have an opportunity to buy an analysis of their own profiles from Statistics Finland. All this documentation is available only in Finnish.

7. Conclusion

Most of the reports represented and commented upon above are similar in format to *Education at a Glance.* Some make use of the same indicators, while others include indicators to address additional educational topics, or to measure differently a topic which is already covered. As reflected in the mini-case studies, all of the countries represented realised that there was a need for indicator comparisons that were of direct relevance to their main educational policy-making bodies. The result in each nation was, or will be, an indicator set that authorities can use to gauge progress in education on the basis of disparate national data.

A similar impetus for all of the reports was the desire of the developers to increase the relevance and impact of the OECD's work. Consequently, the books that resulted are largely fine-tuned versions of *Education at a Glance,* specific to each country, and designed to be used for policy-making. The mini-case studies illustrate a desire to make use of *Education at a Glance* data and format for the presentation of such data, each in its own way. Finland, for example, translated and commented on the OECD indicators; the United States produced an ''offshoot'' of *Education at a Glance;* Switzerland endeavoured to develop a comparison of cantonal education systems; and the Flemish Community in Belgium made use of multiple sources of data (40 per cent on its own). In future, these types of publication are likely to become more common.

Notes

1. The explicit mission of the commission that wrote *A Nation at Risk* was to study ''the quality of learning and teaching in our nation's schools''. Since then, education reformers have often employed the language and methods of the historically parallel quality management movement. Indicators are needed in order to monitor processes and measure progress towards goals. Outcome measures are as important as input measures. Goals and standards should be universally accepted by stakeholders, clear enough to serve as a common focus, measurable, and challenging. Standards, or benchmarks, from outside one's own organisation serve to ground plans in a reality not defined by vested interests.

2. Altogether, over 90 per cent of funding for American public schools is generated at the state and local levels, with the states, on average, now outspending the local districts by a small margin. There is, however, considerable variation among the states in their state-level support for education.

3. Beginning in 1984, and for the next several years, the Department of Education published state education performance charts, or ''wall charts''. Described as a collection of ''education indicators'', the charts compared states in areas such as student achievement and education finance. They used data that were readily available, such as the Scholastic Aptitude Test (SAT) and American College Test (ACT) scores, by state, as measures of average statewide student achievement. Although the charts were criticised for using measures that some considered inappropriate to judge states' performance, they did seem to increase the demand for more or for better indicators.

International Comparisons of Student Achievement: Problems and Prospects
Comparaisons internationales de la réussite scolaire : problèmes et perspectives

by

Thomas Kellaghan
St. Patrick's College, Dublin, Ireland

and

Aletta Grisay
University of Liège, Belgium

This chapter focuses on the preconditions for obtaining meaningful comparisons of student achievement. By measuring the output of education system(s), national and international assessments can contribute to policy formation. Because of the difficulties of long-term comparative analysis of different countries, the OECD INES group has considered making international comparisons using national assessment data. However, national assessments raise problems of validity and feasibility in the OECD context because of the variation in their methods of measuring achievement. There are also technical problems with administration, scoring and reporting procedures, as well as variation in students' perceptions of the testing process. Meaningful comparisons require that the populations being compared are adequately represented in the study, and that sufficient information is available about the contexts in which the data were obtained.

Several alternative approaches to measuring student achievement are discussed in a concluding part of the chapter. These include: 1) replacing international assessments based on a common set of curricular items by assessments of curriculum domains, which allow for differences in national curricula; 2) incorporating a set of identical items into all national assessments; and 3) creating an assessment of cross-curricular competencies.

Recognising that the provision of education is meaningful only if students actually acquire useful knowledge, reasoning ability, skills, and values, Article 4 of the World Declaration on Education for All (1990), which was adopted by the World Conference on

Education for All held in Jomtien, Thailand, in March 1990, states that the focus of education must be "on actual learning acquisition and outcome, rather than exclusively upon enrolment, continued participation in organised programmes and completion of certification requirements" (p. 5). In line with this view, recent years have witnessed increasing interest in adding indicators of student achievement to the information that is normally collected about education systems.

Although for a long time countries have routinely collected and published data on inputs to systems (relating, for example, to the number of students enrolled, student-teacher ratios, and perhaps progression and retention rates), it has not been common to obtain data on the outputs of systems, though such data might be considered a prerequisite for assessing the extent which an education system achieves its goals (Bottani and Tuijnman, 1994). Interest in obtaining data on the outcomes of students' educational experiences has been attributed to a number of factors, including an increase in public concern about school failure and the standard of education of school-leavers. The increasing cost of education has also led to demands, in the interest of accountability and increased efficiency, for information on the performance of education systems.

In this chapter, we shall describe two major approaches to obtaining information on the outputs of education systems – *national assessments* and *international surveys*. We shall then consider a proposal to use national assessment data for international comparisons of achievement, categorising the factors that have to be taken into account in determining whether or not comparisons between the achievements of countries are meaningful. These factors are: the extent to which measured targeted achievement is similar in each country; the extent to which the conditions surrounding the collection of data are similar from country to country; and the characteristics of participants in the samples for whom data are obtained.

*

* *

Note de synthèse

Ce chapitre examine les conditions à satisfaire pour disposer de comparaisons sérieuses des résultats scolaires. En mesurant les résultats des systèmes d'enseignement, les évaluations nationales et internationales peuvent contribuer à l'élaboration des politiques éducatives. Étant donné les difficultés de l'analyse comparative à long terme des différents pays, le projet de l'OCDE sur les indicateurs internationaux des systèmes d'enseignement (INES) a envisagé de faire des comparaisons internationales au moyen des données nationales d'évaluation. Cependant, les évaluations nationales sont, elles aussi, problématiques dans la mesure où elles soulèvent pour l'OCDE des questions d'exactitude et de faisabilité étant donné les différentes méthodes de mesures des résultats. C'est dans les domaines de l'administration, et des méthodes de notation et d'enre-

gistrement que les problèmes techniques risquent de se poser, ainsi que dans l'idée que les élèves se font de la situation d'évaluation. Pour obtenir des comparaisons valables, il faut aussi que les populations comparées soient bien représentées dans les études et que l'on dispose d'informations suffisantes sur les contextes dans lesquels les données ont été obtenues.

Ce rapport se termine par la description de plusieurs méthodes permettant de mesurer la réussite scolaire, à savoir 1) remplacer les évaluations internationales qui contiennent les mêmes éléments de programme pour tous les pays participants par l'évaluation de divers domaines du programme, pour tenir compte des différences entre les divers programmes nationaux ; 2) inclure un ensemble d'éléments identiques dans les évaluations nationales de tous les pays participants ; et 3) mettre au point l'évaluation des compétences transdisciplinaires.

*

* *

1. National Assessments and International Studies

The first major approach to obtaining information on the levels of achievement generated in education systems involves collecting data at a national level in an individual country. This approach, following the United States terminology, is often referred to as national assessment. It involves the administration of a measure of achievement to all students at a particular age or grade level, or more usually to a representative sample of such students. Furthermore, information is usually collected at different points in time so that trends in the performance of the system can be monitored. The best known national assessment systems are those which have operated in the United Kingdom in one form or another since 1948, in the United States since 1969, and in France since 1979. Several other countries, both industrialised (*e.g.* Australia, Canada, Finland, the Netherlands, and New Zealand) and developing (*e.g.* Chile, Costa Rica, and Egypt), have also developed a capacity for monitoring and assessing education.

The second approach to examining the educational outputs of systems is to be found in international comparative studies of achievement. In this approach, representatives of a number of countries (usually research organisations) agree on an instrument to assess achievement in a curriculum area that is common to the countries, the instrument is administered to a representative sample of students at a particular age or grade level in each country, and comparative analyses of the data obtained are carried out. Both the range of achievements that were assessed and the grade levels at which they were assessed have been more limited in international surveys than in national assessments. Since 1959, the International Association for the Evaluation of Educational Achievement (IEA) has been carrying out studies of school achievement, attitudes, and curricula in a variety of countries. For the most part, the surveys have been limited to reading, mathematics, and science, and have focused on grades 3 or 4 at the primary level, grades 7 or 8 in the lower secondary school, and the terminal grade in the upper secondary school. Other areas of achievement that have been studied include writing, literature, French as a foreign language, English as a foreign language, civic education, and computer literacy. From the twelve countries that initially participated in a pilot project between 1959 and 1961 (Foshay, 1962), the number of participating countries grew to 32 for the reading literacy survey which was carried out in 1990-91 (Elley, 1992, 1994).

Two international studies in the areas of mathematics and science have also been carried out in a smaller number of countries in 1988 and 1991 by the International Association for Educational Progress (IAEP). Though more limited in scale than the IEA studies, the IAEP surveys are of particular interest because of the attempts that were made to link international studies to a national assessment programme, in particular the United States National Assessment of Educational Progress (NAEP) (see Pashley and Phillips, 1993). The use of US NAEP items, however, may also have meant that the achievements of other participating countries were inadequately represented.

The participation of countries in international studies of achievement, as well as the fact that several countries now have their own systems of national assessment, or are in the course of developing them, would seem to indicate that there is considerable interest in obtaining both data on the performance of students in national systems and information that will allow judgements to be made about national performance relative to the performance of students in other countries. The interest lies in the belief that such data provide valuable objective information about the state, quality, or performance of the education system that can be used to guide policy-making, to serve an accountability function by informing the public, and to drive educational practice by monitoring education systems, evaluating programmes, diagnosing problems, and suggesting solutions for reform (Bottani and Tuijnman, 1994; Bryk and Hermanson, 1994; Burnstein *et al.*, 1992; Oakes, 1986; OECD, 1992).

The potential contribution of international studies to policy formation has been enunciated on numerous occasions. For example, the proposal for the IEA survey on reading literacy set policy issues at the forefront and listed the following questions which would be addressed in the survey:

"To what extent do students who leave school for work or further education read well enough to undertake their economic and societal roles? What proportion of students at particular levels have difficulty reading at a given level? What are the major facts that are associated with reading success or failure? How can reading achievement for all students be improved? What changes in educational programmes will improve reading achievement (Postlethwaite, 1988)?"

In less specific terms, the IAEP study on achievement on mathematics and science also pointed to policy implications, as follows:

"In truth, the only justification for the disruption of student and professional lives caused by an international assessment is the improvement of learning. Results should provide teachers, school administrators, policy-makers, and taxpayers with information that helps to define the characteristics of successful student performance and suggests areas for possible improvement and change (Lapointe *et al.*, 1989, p. 7)."

These statements could apply equally well to national assessments. Additional arguments are made in favour of international studies. Firstly, international comparisons illustrate what is possible and feasible. The fact that students in some countries perform relatively well indicates that it is not unrealistic to expect improvement from students in countries with lower levels of achievement. Thus, the findings of international studies may be used to support an optimistic view of education, underpinning a belief that systems can be improved significantly. A further advantage of cross-national studies is that they provide data which expand the range of variation to be found in such factors as curricula, amount of time spent in school, teacher training, class size, and expenditure, thus providing opportunities to examine the relationships between these factors and achievement that might not be possible with data that is confined to one country. Arguments for obtaining cross-national data have also been based on recent evaluation of the relationship between a nation's knowledge and skills and its economic competitiveness. In this context, the study of the Industrial Research and Development Advisory Committee of the Commission of the European Communities concluded that "the output of education and training systems (...) in terms of both quantity and quality of skills at all levels is the prime determinant of a country's level of productivity and hence competitiveness" (p. iii). Finally, the claim is also made that "skilled people become the only sustainable competitive advantage" in a world in which natural resources, capital, and new technologies can rapidly move from country to country (Thurow, 1992, p. 52). If this is so, then it would seem reasonable to monitor the level of skills produced by the education system of one's own country relative to those of others.

Interest in indicators that measure the output of education systems in terms of student achievement, at national as well as at state levels, increased during the 1980s (Bryk and Hermanson, 1994; Smith, 1988). The interest received a boost in 1987 when the United States government supported a cross-national indicator effort – the International Indicators of Education Systems (INES) project – in the OECD (Bryk and Hermanson, 1994). In its two editions to date of *Education at a Glance* (OECD, 1992, 1993), data from both IEA and IAEP studies were used to provide comparative data on the performance of students in OECD Member countries in mathematics, science, and reading literacy. The availability of these unique data was crucial in getting the project started. However, the political visibility of the OECD output indicators also served to reignite controversies which had existed since initiation of the risky enterprise of international comparisons. Questions were raised about the extent to which available data were reliable, the "fairness" of comparisons, and the ways in which the many disadvantages associated with data from international studies could be overcome.

One of the disadvantages associated with the available international data which needs to be addressed is the fact that data are not available for all OECD countries since all did not participate in the international surveys. A second disadvantage is that surveys were not carried out on a regular basis, as is common in national assessments (*e.g.* every four or five years). Thus, in the publication *Education at a Glance* (OECD, 1992), some of the data used for mathematics were collected in the early 1980s. Thirdly, reporting of the IEA studies has until recently been slow. Fourthly, procedures from one study to another did not always provide data that would allow comparisons to be made over time. Finally, while data from non-OECD countries (which have participated in IEA studies) provide an interesting basis for comparisons, at the same time, their inclusion increases constraints in defining common sets of domains to be assessed and may also lead to delays in the execution of studies (*e.g.* in agreeing common sets of items and in analysing data).

For these reasons, the OECD INES group has been considering the possibility of using data collected in the national assessment programmes of individual countries to provide information for international comparisons. This would appear to have several advantages relating, for example, to the topics on which data could be collected and the timing and frequency of data collection. However, the use of data from national assessments also gives rise to a number of problems. Not all OECD countries carry out national assessments, at present. To reach a situation in which all did so, and agreed on the details of such assessments, including the aspects of the education system about which information would be gathered, would, of course, require political will. However, this is not the topic that will be addressed in this chapter. While it is acknowledged that indicator design and development, including choice of indicators and basic logistical and technical issues that arise in collecting data, involve a dynamic interplay of both technical and policy concerns (Burnstein *et al.,* 1992), in this chapter the focus is on the conditions that must be fulfilled to obtain meaningful comparisons about students' achievements (whether those comparisons are based on national or international surveys), and on a series of problems that arise in those comparisons. Some of the problems are specific to national assessments, some are specific to international surveys, while others are common to both types of study. Issues of validity and feasibility are of particular concern and will be illustrated with reference to the experience of both international studies and national assessments.

2. Targeted Achievement

If we go by the names applied to the subjects that are taught in school, there is great similarity between countries in their curricular offerings at the elementary level. For example, a world-wide review of primary-school curricula in approximately 125 countries revealed that language, mathematics, natural science, and social sciences were specified at some grade level in all countries, while 96 per cent of countries specified physical education, 95 per cent aesthetic education, and 75 per cent religious or moral education (Benavot *et al.,* 1991). This agreement on what may be regarded as the "basics" of education is reflected in national assessments, which in all countries include assessment of students' first language and mathematics. This may suggest that these are regarded as the most important areas of achievement, though it may also be that they are more easily measured than other outputs of schooling (Johnstone, 1981). Science is included in some and, in a small number, a second language (*e.g.* in the Netherlands and Sweden), art, music, and social studies (*e.g.* in Sweden and the United States). While the practice is to assess students in a relatively small number of areas of achievement, it is also recognised that it would be desirable if assessments were not so limited (Bottani and Tuijnman, 1994). In this context, consideration is being given in France to including civic education and study skills at grade 6 and perhaps grade 9.

There is also considerable agreement that national assessment is appropriate at the primary level. In practically all countries that carry out national assessments, these take place at that level. They are also carried out in most countries at some points in the secondary school, more usually in lower grades during the period of compulsory schooling. There is, however, considerable variation in the grade at which an assessment is first carried out. It can begin at kindergarten (Canada), first (France), second (Ireland and Sweden), third (Finland) or fourth grade (Scotland). There are also differences between countries in the number of grades at which an assessment is carried out, which can vary from two grade levels to all. There would obviously have to be some harmonisation of practice if national assessment data were to be used for international comparisons.

While there may be similarities in the names of subjects and in the ages at which students are assessed in national assessments, one cannot assume on that basis that comparisons between performances in different countries will be justifiable. The fact that the contexts of education differ between countries means that different goals are posited and different emphases are attached to the various domains of the curriculum in different countries (Bottani and Tuijnman, 1994). Many examples can be provided of differences between countries in curricular goals, organisation and emphasis. Firstly, some subjects (*e.g.* philosophy and statistics) are taught in secondary school in some countries, but not in others. Secondly, similarity of the title of a subject (*e.g.* mathematics and science) does not ensure similarity of curriculum content or achievement. For example, science in elementary school can mean environmental studies, social studies, natural history, or life experience. Even when science is taken to mean physical science, curricula can vary in the topics that are presented and emphasised as well as in the order in which they are presented (Rosier and Keeves, 1991). Thus, it is difficult to define concepts such as "achievement in science" or "achievement in mathematics" that will be equally appropriate in a number of countries since different countries will choose different skills applied to different facts and concepts to constitute what they regard as scientific or mathematical achievement. Thirdly, a particular domain of a subject may be taught at different grade levels in different countries. For example, the grade at which specific topics in addition and subtraction are introduced in arithmetic has been found to vary (Fuson *et al.*, 1988). Fourthly, domains that are considered in some countries to form a single subject (*e.g.* civics) are spread across many subjects in other countries (*e.g.* history and social studies). Fifthly, even when the same domain is taught under the same title and at the same grade in different countries, the perspective from which it is taught may vary. For example, some countries emphasise an experimental approach in the study of optics, while others adopt a more mathematical approach. Finally, there may be variation between countries in the level of cognitive processes which receives emphasis. For example, while 30 per cent of items were devoted to recall in a comparison of items in the IAEP international mathematics assessment, which was mainly American, this figure was 40 per cent in a national assessment in Ireland. Conversely, 45 per cent of items in the international test, but only 15 per cent of items in the Irish test, covered so-called higher-order skills (routine and non-routine applications and problems) (Greaney and Close, 1989).

Specification of achievement is the first step but only part of the problem facing anyone interested in national or international assessments. The second step involves the construction of instruments on the basis of which indicators of achievement will be obtained. These instruments will be designed not to discriminate between individuals but to measure the extent to which a given body of knowledge and skills has been transmitted and goals achieved in a system of education. The process of constructing instruments, however, lacks precision, not only because the goals of learning are vague and the universe of achievement incompletely defined, but also because criteria for the construction of the instruments lack explicitness. Item writing is essentially an art, dependent on the judgement of subject-matter experts, in which large margins for interpretation are left to the test constructors (Kvale, 1990). Hence, we cannot be certain that any assessment procedure is entirely accurate in its representation of a curriculum or body of knowledge.

A further problem in the development of assessment procedures is that curriculum representation and balance may be affected by scaling after tests have been administered. For example, in attempts to set achievement levels (basic, proficient, and advanced) for the United States 1990 NAEP mathematics test at grades 4, 8, and 12, the group involved in the National Assessment Governing Body exercise was struck by the inadequacy of the item pool and, in particular, by the lack of what they described as ''sufficiently challenging'' items. What had happened was that more difficult items which did not meet Item Response Theory scaling criteria had been excluded from the item pool, thus reducing the congruence between the assessment procedure and the curriculum domain it was designed to represent.

Additional problems arise in constructing measures of achievement for international studies. The general procedure has been to seek a consensus among educators and others from a number of countries concerning knowledge and skills that are appropriate for a particular age or grade level and then to construct items to measure the knowledge and skills. However, obtaining such a consensus has often proved illusive, given the differences among countries. Items can be considered appropriate either because they reflect curricular material that is common across countries or because they measure knowledge and skills that, according to social criteria, are regarded as important for all to learn. Items will normally be tried out with students and reviewed by panels representing participating countries to determine the extent to which they are appropriate in a particular country. It is extremely unlikely, however, whatever criteria are used to select items, that the final test will accurately reflect the curricula of all participating countries and indeed some aspects of a national curriculum might not even find a place in the final measure.

The lack of congruence between measures used in international studies and those used in national studies can be illustrated by comparing the IAEP mathematics test (Lapointe *et al.,* 1989) with a mathematics test used in a national assessment in Ireland. The first thing that one finds is that certain areas of the Irish curriculum (calculation of simple interest, co-ordinates, symmetry, and indices) are not covered in the international test. Secondly, the balance of curriculum representation in the international test differs considerably from the balance in the Irish test. In a comparison of the content of the tests, 50 per cent of items in the international test, compared to 65 per cent of items in the Irish test, involved operations with whole numbers, fractions, and decimals. It is clear that if different weights had been applied in the international test, the overall score, and ranking, of Ireland would have differed from what was achieved. Thirdly, even when a sub-test had the same title (dealing with charts and graphs) in the national and international assessments, the skills covered in the two assessments were quite different (Greaney and Close, 1989). It could be argued that the international test failed to represent adequately the goals and curricula of Irish schools, and no doubt the same argument could be made for other countries.

It would seem to be extremely difficult, perhaps impossible, as Nuttall (1994) has pointed out, to devise a single test that is an equally valid measure of different countries' definition of, for example, "achievement in mathematics or science" (Nuttall, 1994, p. 85). The task in curricular areas that are more culturally laden than mathematics or science would appear to be even more difficult. While there is no easy way round this problem, there is a minimum set of conditions that must be met if international comparisons are to be made, whether those comparisons are based on national assessments or international surveys. Firstly, groups of experts from participating countries should carefully examine their curricula and reach agreement on the domains that are to be accepted as a common basis for comparison. In this, one must rely on the informed judgements of individuals who are familiar with their education systems in order to reach a conclusion that the domains, and the items selected to represent those domains, are acceptable as a basis for comparison. Secondly, in addition to developing output indicators, it is also necessary to develop indicators of curriculum coverage and opportunity to learn. These indicators will help to identify the extent to which the curricula of individual countries are represented in the agreed assessment procedure. Thirdly, while there may be advantages for policy-makers in keeping the number of indicators used to describe an education system within manageable proportions, aggregating data to produce composite indicators may not only obscure important information, but may also give rise to misrepresentation. Thus, the provision of information on sub-domains rather than overall scores is thought to discourage the use of indicators for "cognitive olympics" (Maddison, 1975). Indeed, this may be the most useful kind of information which indicators representing scholastic achievement can provide for policy-makers, since it helps to identify areas of relative strength and weakness in output. In the light of this information, which a single measure cannot provide, judgements can be made about the appropriateness of curricular emphases within a country.

3. Conditions Surrounding the Collection of Data

Care is taken in international studies (which may include a quality control component) that the conditions surrounding the collection of data are as similar as possible from one country to another. Deviations in conditions are inevitable, however, as, for example, when an achievement test has to be provided in different languages. In this case, procedures are used, involving the translation of items by a number of translators, backtranslations, and an examination of how students perform on the items, to ensure as far as possible the equivalence of tests in the different languages (Elley, 1992). However, problems relating to the establishment of the equivalence of tests when used in different countries may still remain. For example, is what might be termed "equivalence in meaning'' more important than literal equivalence? And what is the effect of adapting test items to reflect local usage and environments, by changing units of measurement, the names of children, or the species of plants and animals, as occurred in IAEP and IEA studies? While a reasonable standardisation may be achieved in international surveys, the problems in using national assessment data would appear to be more intractable.

No attempts have been made to date to establish equivalence between the data-gathering procedures of national assessments of individual countries, beyond the equivalence that would be implied in, for example, the use of standardised tests. That major differences exist is clear from an inspection of procedures in a number of countries. Further, the differences are so great and in some cases so entwined with ideological positions about measurement and accountability that the promotion of standardisation in procedures would appear to be a formidable task.

Two areas seem of particular importance in considering differences between countries in the conditions surrounding the collection of data on student achievement. The first relates to the standardisation of administration, scoring, and reporting procedures of the assessments; the second relates to participants' perceptions of the assessment situation.

Administration, Scoring and Reporting Procedures

When multiple-choice tests are used to collect data on student achievement in national assessments, the administration follows clearly laid-down and accepted procedures. While the method of scoring can vary depending, for example, on whether corrections are made for guessing, and while various methods for reporting data also exist, any variation in scoring or reporting will follow clearly defined rules. If countries follow similar procedures, then standardised multiple-choice tests will provide data that will be comparable from the point of view of administration, scoring, and reporting.

However, there have been many criticisms of multiple-choice tests over the past two decades, particularly in the context of their use in evaluating the output of schools (Madaus et al., 1980; Madaus and Kellaghan, 1992), leading to efforts to develop more ''authentic'' methods of testing which would involve the direct assessment of complex performance. While such methods might have several advantages – for example, in providing clear models of acceptable outcomes, positively influencing learning and instruction, and encouraging the teaching and learning of higher forms of mental functioning – they present serious problems when used in national or international assessments because of the possibility of variation in their administration and scoring procedures. Nevertheless, several countries use methods other than standardised tests, though often in conjunction with them, to obtain information on student achievements in national assessments. These include short-answer tests, essays, practicals (e.g. setting up an experiment in science), and portfolios of student achievement.

In French-speaking countries, where open-ended or essay items are used, several problems have arisen. One relates to the accuracy of scoring which is generally done by teachers, with the help of a scoring manual but often without special training. Because of doubts about scoring accuracy, it is sometimes necessary to discount the results from particular schools. A further problem arises from the burden which scoring places on teachers, which may affect the rate of return of assessment data from schools. It may also give rise to claims for additional payment, increasing the cost of data gathering.

The most comprehensive approach to the use of performance testing in national assessment is to be found in the British national assessment system. The key to the system, as it was originally envisaged, were Standard Attainment Tasks (SATs), which were designed to provide information on students' performance on a cluster of attainment targets which had been set for a range of curriculum areas. The tasks were designed to use a wide range of modes of presentation (*e.g.* oral, written, pictorial, video), operation (mental only, written, practical oral), and response (*e.g.* choosing an option in a multiple-choice question, writing a short prescribed response, open-ended writing, a practical product). Teachers were required to integrate the tasks into their normal classroom practice, thus avoiding the artificial separation of assessment and teaching. They would also score the students' performance (United Kingdom Department of Education and Science, 1988).

Experience with the first major assessment of 7-year-old children in 1991 brought to light serious inconsistencies in the administration and scoring of the SATs (see Broadfoot *et al.,* 1991; Gipps *et al.,* 1991; Madaus and Kellaghan, 1993). The lack of standardisation that was a feature of administration and scoring must call into question the use of the data obtained, not only for international comparisons but even for comparing individual pupil scores or aggregated school scores. As a result of the problems experienced in administration of SATs relating to topic effect, rater effect, and the generalisability of scores, assessment procedures have been greatly modified and will in future involve more streamlined and conventional tests (see Kellaghan, 1994). The lesson from the British experience would seem to be that data from performance testing, in its present state of development, would not be suitable for international comparisons.

Participants' Perceptions of the Assessment Situation

We may assume that the choice of indicators in all national assessment systems reflects assumptions about the nature and purposes of education and is often based on beliefs about the direction that reform should take (Bottani and Tuijnman, 1994). However, there is evidence both that assessment systems have very little impact on policy or practice (see Gipps and Goldstein, 1983) and that they influence curricula and teaching styles to bring them into line with the demands of the assessment (see Madaus and Kellaghan, 1992). Whether or not assessment systems and indicators do in fact push an education system towards the assumptions and beliefs they embody (Burnstein *et al.,* 1992) would seem to depend to some extent on participants' perceptions of the assessment situation and, in particular, the perceived consequences of their performance.

Cohen and Spillane (1994) distinguish between indicator systems that monitor the education system in current terms and those that lead policy and practice, identifying the former with the use of standardised multiple-choice tests and the latter with the use of performance or "authentic" measures. However, the association of the distinction with different types of assessment would seem to be coincidental rather than essential. It is true that much of the rhetoric surrounding "authentic" testing relates to the beneficial effect which such testing could have on practice. However, it would be incorrect to assume that standardised tests do not also affect practice. Indeed, one of the major criticisms of such tests is that they encourage teachers to concentrate on the relatively low-level skills which many standardised tests measure (Madaus and Kellaghan, 1992). It would also be correct to assume that performance-based measures might have a negative impact on educational practice. Evidence from the use of public examinations, which sometimes contain performance elements, indicates that negative as well as positive effects can be anticipated (Kellaghan and Greaney, 1992; Madaus and Kellaghan, 1992).

A crucial factor in determining whether or not a system of assessment will have an impact on practice would appear to be not the method of measurement but rather whether or not high stakes are attached to test performance. Attaching high stakes to a test in the form of important rewards or punishment for performance (*e.g.* publishing and ranking the performances of schools or teachers) can have a number of consequences. Firstly, since the test operationally defines the "valid" knowledge of a discipline (Kvale, 1990), the curriculum taught in the school will be narrowed to focus on the test's requirements. Secondly, such narrowing leads to the neglect of other areas of the curriculum. The areas of a subject that are likely to be examined will receive time and attention while subjects on the curriculum which are not examined will receive little attention. Thirdly, as a result of all this, as well as of efforts to develop the test-taking skills of students, students' test scores will be boosted, but it will not be possible to interpret the improved performance as evidence of real gains in "achievement" or learning. A number of empirical studies provide evidence that improved scores on tests used for high stakes purposes are not matched by increases on other measures of achievement (Koretz *et al.,* 1991; Linn *et al.,* 1990).

From the point of view of international comparisons, what is important is that some countries attach high stakes to performance in national assessments while others do not. For example, in the United States, the tradition has been for national assessments to provide unobtrusive measures of the performance of the education system, focusing on what students know and can do. The assessments were not designed to influence directly what goes on in schools. On the other hand, in the United Kingdom, high stakes are attached to the post-1988 national assessment system through the publication of results for individual schools. Even if all other conditions of administration were constant, the fact that in one country high stakes are attached to performance, while in another they are not, would raise issues about the validity of comparisons.

Even when high stakes are not attached to performance, students in different cultures may vary in their approach to an assessment, which may affect the effort that they invest in it and ultimately their performance. In some cultures, students may perform indifferently if they know that they are not going to get any feedback from the assessment. In other cultures, students appear to attach great importance to an assessment situation and will give of their best. In the former situation, of course, performance on the assessment is likely to underestimate students' level of achievement. Differences in attitudes towards assessment cannot readily be dealt with either in the administration of the assessment or in data analysis.

4.   Characteristics of Participants

If one is to make meaningful comparisons in international studies, it is necessary to ensure that the populations being compared are adequately represented in the studies and that sufficient information, including information on students' educational experiences, is available about the contexts in which data were obtained. Much of this information will probably have been collected anyhow for within-country analysis to provide an interpretative framework consisting of links between indicators and other features of schooling, student background, and cultural context (Burnstein *et al.,* 1992; Mol and Kaiser, 1994; Nuttall, 1992). However, additional information may be required if the indicators are going to be used for international comparisons rather than for just describing or even monitoring the performance of an individual system.

Level of Data Collection and Reporting

For both national and international comparisons, it is necessary to define the level for which instruments will be constructed and indicators reported. In many countries, for both national and international studies, data are collected and reported at the national level. However, there are several countries within which there is considerable variance between jurisdictions in their education systems and in their arrangements for political responsibility. For example, education is organised at a state rather than a national level or in autonomous or semi-autonomous regions in Australia, Belgium, Canada, Germany, Italy, Spain, and Switzerland. Approaches to system assessment vary between countries, even ones with federal arrangements for government. In Germany and the United States, data for international studies have been reported at the national level. The same was true until recently for the reporting of national assessment data in the United States, partly for political reasons and partly because of cost (Tyler, 1985). On the other hand, the Canadian provinces carry out separate provincial assessments and participated as individual entities in the IAEP studies, without aggregating data to the national level. A similar situation exists in the United Kingdom, where the arrangements for both national and international assessments in Scotland differ from those in England and Wales.

The approach that is adopted in dealing with within-country variation is obviously a matter for concern in international comparisons. Firstly, it affects the number of units (countries, states, regions) that have to be accommodated. Secondly, the issue of validity is relevant since instruments constructed at a national level might not adequately represent the curricula of individual states or regions within a country. However, this may be the case whether or not data are aggregated at the national level.

Target Populations

If comparisons are to be made between the indicators derived from individual countries, defined target populations should be comparable or, at any rate, those sections of the population that are comparable should be identifiable. While national and international assessments may purport to describe the performances of education systems, in practice elements may be excluded from the assessment. In international studies, students with handicapping conditions enrolled in special schools are almost always excluded. However, difficulties arise in comparisons between countries when definitions of a handicapping condition vary and when there are differences in national policies relating to provision of special schools or the integration of all students in mainstream schools.

Categories of students other than those with handicapping conditions may also be excluded. In international studies, students in certain areas of a country, students in private schools, and students in a school who would have been unable to take a test because the language of instruction in the school differed from the language used in the test have all been excluded (Elley, 1994). The effect of such exclusions is that in the IAEP science and mathematics studies, seven countries had limited participation at the 9-year-old level and a further three at the 13-year-old level (Lapointe *et al.*, 1992*a* and 1992*b*). Although the IEA reading literacy survey achieved much better coverage, more than 10 per cent of populations were excluded in two countries at the 9-year-old level and in three countries at the 14-year-old level (Elley, 1994). Further attrition from a sample may occur during testing. In the IEA literacy study, for example, the percentage excluded at this stage ranged from zero to 2.98 for 9-year-olds but only from zero to 0.80 at the 14-year-old level.

Experience from international studies indicates that inadequacies in the representation of populations can be a major focus of attention when results are published. While concerns may also be raised about the adequacy of curriculum coverage or conditions of administration, the extent to which results can be said to represent the achievements of the total education system (or, at any rate, the part of it that was targeted for study) seems to be paramount. To address this concern, there would seem to be a clear need, if assessment data are to be used for international comparisons, to specify, agree, and implement criteria for exclusion relating, for example, to special needs students, students with limited familiarity with the school's language of instruction, and students who are absent on the day of assessment.

A further factor that could affect comparisons between indicators derived from different countries is whether students are targeted for assessment on the basis of their age or their grade level. The majority of countries select on the basis of grade level for their national assessment. An exception to this is the United Kingdom, within which practice actually varies. Students are assessed by age (7, 11, 14, and 16) in England and Wales and in Northern Ireland (8, 11, 14, 16) but by grade (4, 7, and 9) in Scotland. In the national assessment of the United States, students have been selected on the basis of age (9, 13, and 17) but, since 1984, samples from the relevant modal grades (*i.e.* the grade level of the majority of the students in a particular age group) have also been included (Johnson, 1992). A preference for age rather than for grade arises when some students repeat grades (Tyler, 1985) since one would expect the retention of lower-scoring students on a large scale to have the effect of boosting the mean scores of students in higher grades. On the other hand, unqualified comparisons based on age may be inappropriate if the age of starting school varies from country to country. The limitations for international comparisons of adopting either age or grade would seem to point to the need for information on both the age and grade level of students.

Sampling

Most countries work with samples of students rather than with total populations at the relevant age or grade level. An exception is the United Kingdom, where all students are assessed. There are several advantages in sampling compared to census testing: reduced costs in gathering and analysing data, greater speed in data analysis and reporting, and greater accuracy due to the possibility of providing more intense supervision of fieldwork and data preparation (Ross, 1987).

When sampling is employed in national assessments and in international studies, it invariably involves stratification and clustering (*e.g.* schools and classrooms). Since the characteristics of complex sample designs (*e.g.* the way clusters are formed) affect the value of sample means and other statistics, it is important when designs vary from country to country that their effects be taken into account. In the past, because of differences between countries in sampling design, some countries (England and Switzerland) have had to be excluded from some comparisons (involving the intra-class correlation coefficient) in the OECD's *Education at a Glance* (1993).

An important issue in sampling within schools, if it is envisaged that estimates of within-school and between-school variance are to be calculated, is whether to select one class at the relevant grade, a random sample of students from all classes at the grade, or all classes at the grade. Practice on this matter has varied in international surveys, giving rise to problems in interpreting differences between countries in the extent of between-school variance which was manifested in achievement measures.

In international studies, problems in achieving equivalence of sampling design have occurred more often in industrialised than in developing countries. This is because developing countries, in the absence of local expertise, have relied more heavily on the recommendations of an international co-ordinator than have industrialised countries, in which reliance on national tradition and judgement may serve to endanger common designs. To date, international organisations have not been able to overcome this problem entirely in industrialised countries with the result that it has not been possible to achieve universal equivalence of sampling. One would expect even greater diversity of approach to sampling in national assessments. If it is envisaged that data from national assessments will be used to make international comparisons, it is clear that problems relating to the equivalence of sampling between countries will need to be addressed.

While at first blush, there might not appear to be any major problem in comparing census data with sample data, in practice a number of problems could arise. Firstly, the quality of the census data may suffer from inadequate supervision. Secondly, the data derived from a sample would be subject to sampling error whereas the census data would not. And thirdly, it is likely that data are collected on a census rather than a sample basis so that findings can be used for purposes other than national assessment. It may be, for example, that census information is collected so that data can be published on the performance of individual schools or local authorities or can be used for other accountability purposes. If this is so, one would expect higher performance for the census group which, as we saw in considering the conditions surrounding the administration of the assessment procedure, would probably be spurious.

Participation

The participation rates of schools in recent international studies has been quite high. In the IEA reading literacy survey, it ranged from 82.5 to 100 per cent for 9-year-olds and from 80.9 to 100 per cent for 14-year-olds (Elley, 1994, Tables B.1 and B.2). One might expect even higher participation rates in national assessments since they are likely to be supported by stronger political commitment and effort.

Students' Educational Experiences

Data on sub-populations of students, especially data on students' educational experiences, would seem essential if one is to make meaningful comparisons between student performance in different countries. At any level (national, regional, or state), within-group variability can be considerable with the result that comparisons between total populations may not be meaningful. However, it may be possible to identify sub-populations that may be comparable, though implementation of a design that would provide the necessary information on a variety of such populations is likely to be costly and may be the source of political difficulties (Cohen and Spillane, 1994).

Sub-populations of students are most readily identifiable in education systems which have a differentiated structure, such as is found at the secondary level in many European countries where students attend different types of school and follow different curricula. They may be less obvious, but still exist, in countries in which a comprehensive system of secondary education exists. In the latter situation, the educational experiences of students can be overlooked in making comparisons. The best efforts to deal with this have been made in IEA studies in which estimates have been obtained of students' opportunity to learn material that appears in tests.

However, the identification of students who have taken similar courses may not in itself allow unambiguous interpretation of similarities or differences that may be found in the achievements of students. This becomes clear when we consider that in some countries whole populations of students take a course that is taken by only a minority in another country. This was the case for certain areas in mathematics in the Second International Mathematics Study (SIMS). For example, some courses were taken by all students at the relevant grade level in Japan but by only a quarter of students in the United States. In such a situation, interpretation of the performances of students following similar courses in the two countries in terms of the ''effectiveness'' of their school systems (Baker, 1993; Westbury, 1993) is obviously confounded by the selective nature of the American sample.

5. Conclusion

In this chapter, a variety of problems have been considered that arise in international comparisons of achievement, particularly in the context of using national assessments to make international comparisons. The problems are not trivial. And yet the political will seems strong, not only to continue with national assessments to monitor the output of education systems, but also, if one is to judge from the number of countries participating in international studies at the moment, to obtain data that will be comparable with the output of other education systems. If we are to proceed towards the goal of developing a system in which national assessment data can be used for comparisons among OECD countries, then it is clear that we are faced with a number of problems, some of which may be taken care of by co-ordination of effort and advanced planning and others of which are less tractable.

The more tractable issues relate to the broad areas of achievement that are to be measured (*e.g.* mathematics and science), the age or grade level at which students will be assessed, the timing of assessments, definition and identification of populations, sampling design, and whether or not high stakes will be attached to performance. The most intractable issue, and of course it is a central one, is the way in which achievement is defined and measured.

A number of suggestions may be made for dealing with the measurement of achievement. One could follow the course taken in IEA studies which would involve all countries agreeing to use a common test. Given the differences in curricula which exist between countries, this would involve compromise and an acceptance of the fact that the test would not fully represent the curriculum of any individual country. However, if the assessment procedure is divided into sections which would represent different domains of a curriculum, there is a probability that there will be congruence for individual countries between sections of the assessment procedure and some areas of its curriculum. Such an approach could be useful in identifying relative strengths and weaknesses of a country's performance across curriculum domains.

If countries do not agree to a common assessment instrument but wish to continue to use their own, there are a number of approaches which might be used to establish links between the performances of students in different countries. In the first approach, each country could incorporate into its own procedure a number of items which would be common to all countries. The precise location of such items in an assessment instrument would be important, since the context in which items are embedded can affect response success rate (see Beaton and Zwick, 1990). Furthermore, generalisation to other aspects of achievement would be problematic, since it would involve the use of information obtained from test items based on specifications derived from one domain to make inferences about another domain (see Nitko, 1989; Schmidt, 1983). In the second approach, a sample of students in each country would take the assessment instrument being used in another country. Thus, a sample in country B would take the test administered in country A, a sample in country C would take the test administered in country B, and so on. This approach would provide wider opportunities for linkages.

Another alternative might involve adding to the conventional achievement measures based on surface features of curriculum-specific domains an assessment of cross-curricular competencies or ''life skills'' (*e.g.* problem-solving, information processing) (Trier, 1994). This possibility, which is at present being explored by the OECD INES group, will involve the definition of *a priori* domains by using social criteria to judge what it is important for all to learn.

Finally, data from national assessments, even if they could not be used to provide direct comparisons between levels of achievement, could help to inform policy decisions about a number of educational matters. If data for each country were expressed in standard scores they could, for example, be used across countries to explore gender differences, urban-rural differences, differences between grades, differences related to grade retention, between-school differences, and differences over time.

The experience of international studies to date should serve to undermine any hope, if such hope survives, that unambiguous ranking of countries in terms of "overall" achievement is possible. The options that we have just considered, which may not be exhaustive, all involve compromise of such an ideal for international comparisons, and indeed one of them does not involve direct comparisons of performance at all. Whether or not individual countries will accept the compromise and maintain and develop further their interest in international comparisons is likely to be influenced by two factors: the political will to obtain comparative cross-national data and the value which is placed on the kind of information which such data can provide.

References

BAKER, D.P. (1993), "Compared to Japan, the US is a poor achiever (...) really. New evidence and comment on Westbury", *Educational Researcher*, Vol. 22 (3), pp. 18-20.

BEATON, A.E., and ZWICK, R. (1990), *The Effect of Changes in the National Assessment: Disentangling the NAEP 1985-86 Reading Anomaly*, Educational Testing Service, Princeton, NJ.

BENAVOT, A., CHA, Y.-.K, KAMENS, D., MEYER, J.W., and WONG, S-Y. (1991), "Knowledge for the masses: world models and national curricula, 1920-1986", *American Sociological Review*, No. 56, pp. 85-100.

BOTTANI, N., and TUIJNMAN, A. (1994), "International education indicators: framework, development and interpretation", in *Making Education Count. Developing and Using International Indicators*, OECD, Paris.

BROADFOOT, P., ABBOTT, D., CROLL, P., OSBORN, M., and POLLARD, A. (1991), *Look Back in Anger? Findings of the PACE Project Concerning Primary Teachers' Experiences of SATs*, unpublished paper, University of Bristol.

BRYK, A., and HERMANSON, K. (1994), "Observations on the structure, interpretation and use of education indicator systems", in *Making Education Count. Developing and Using International Indicators*, OECD, Paris.

BURNSTEIN, L., OAKES, J., and GUITON, G. (1992), "Education indicators", in M.C. Alkin (ed.), *Encyclopedia of Educational Research* (6th ed.), Macmillan, New York.

COHEN, D.K., and SPILLANE, J.P. (1994), "National education indicators and traditions of accountability", in *Making Education Count. Developing and Using International Indicators*, OECD, Paris.

Commission of the European Communities, Industrial Research and Development Advisory Committee (n.d.), *Skills Shortages in Europe*, Brussels.

ELLEY, W.B. (1992), *How in the World do Students Read? IEA Study of Reading Literacy*, International Association for the Evaluation of Educational Achievement, The Hague.

ELLEY, W.B. (ed.) (1994), *The IEA Study of Reading Literacy: Achievement and Instruction in Thirty-two School Systems*, Pergamon, Oxford.

FOSHAY, A.W. (ed.) (1962), *Educational Achievements of 13-year-olds in Twelve Countries: Results of an International Research Project 1959-61*, UNESCO Institute for Education, Hamburg.

FUSON, K.G., STIGLER, J.W., and BARTSCH, K. (1988), "Grade placement of addition and subtraction topics in Japan, mainland China, the Soviet Union, Taiwan and the USA", *Journal for Research in Mathematics Education*, No. 19, pp. 449-456.

GIPPS, C., and GOLDSTEIN, H. (1983), *Monitoring children. An Evaluation of the Assessment of Performance Unit,* Heinemann, London.

GIPPS, C., MCCALLUM, S., MCALLISTER, S., and BROWN, M. (1991), *National Assessment at Seven: Some Emerging Themes,* Paper presented at the annual meeting of the American Educational Research Association, Chicago, April 1-5.

GREANEY, V., and CLOSE, J. (1989), "Mathematics achievement in Irish primary schools", *Irish Journal of Education,* No. 23, pp. 51-64.

JOHNSON, E.G. (1992), "The design of the national assessment of educational progress", *Journal of Educational Measurement,* Vol. 29, pp. 95-110.

JOHNSTONE, J.N. (1981), *Indicators of Education Systems,* UNESCO, Paris.

KELLAGHAN, T. (1994), "National assessment in England and Wales", in P. Murphy *et al.,* (eds.), *National assessment,* The World Bank, Washington DC.

KELLAGHAN, T., and GREANEY, V. (1992), *Using Examinations to Improve Education. A Study in Fourteen African Countries,* The World Bank, Washington DC.

KORETZ, D.M., LINN, R.L., DUNBAR, S.B., and SHEPARD, L.A (1991), *The Effects of High Stakes Testing on Achievement. Preliminary Findings about Generalisation across Tests,* Paper read at the annual meeting of the American Educational Research Association, Chicago, April 1-5.

KVALE, S. (1990), "Evaluation and decentralisation of knowledge", in M. Kogan and U.P. Lundgren (eds.), *Evaluation as Policymaking. Introducing Evaluation into a National Decentralised Educational System,* Jessica Kingsley, London.

LAPOINTE, A.E., ASKEW, J.M., and MEAD, N.A. (1992*a*), *Learning Science,* Educational Testing Service, Princeton, NJ.

LAPOINTE, A.E., MEAD, N.A., and ASKEW, J.M. (1992*b*), *Learning Mathematics,* Educational Testing Service, Princeton, NJ.

LAPOINTE, A.E., MEAD, N.A., and PHILLIPS, G.W. (1989), *A World of Differences. An International Assessment of Mathematics and Science,* Educational Testing Service, Princeton, NJ.

LINN, R.L., GRAUE, M.E., and SANDERS, N.M. (1990), "Comparing state and district test results to national norms: the validity of claims that 'everyone is above average'", *Educational Measurement Issues and Practice,* Vol. 9 (3), pp. 5-14.

MADAUS, G.F., and KELLAGHAN, T. (1992), "Curriculum evaluation and assessment", in P.W. Jackson (ed.), *Handbook of Curriculum Research,* Macmillan, New York.

MADAUS, G.F., and KELLAGHAN, T. (1993), "British experience with 'authentic' testing", *Phi Delta Kappan,* Vol. 74, pp. 458-469.

MADAUS, G.F., AIRASIAN, P.W., and KELLAGHAN, T. (1980), *School Effectiveness. A Reassessment of the Evidence,* McGraw Hill, New York.

MADDISON, A. (1975), "Commentary", in A.C. Purves and D.U. Levine (eds.), *Educational Policy and International Assessment,* McCutchan, Berkeley, CA.

MOL, N.P., and KAISER, F. (1994), "Interpretation and analysis of cost-per-pupil indicators in international comparisons of education systems", in *Making Education Count. Developing and Using International Indicators,* OECD, Paris.

NITKO, A. (1989), "Designing tests that are integrated with instruction", in R.L. Linn (ed.), *Educational Measurement (3rd ed.),* American Council on Education/Macmillan, New York.

NUTTALL, D. (1992), ''The functions and limitations of international education indicators'', in *The OECD International Education Indicators: A Framework for Analysis,* OECD, Paris.

NUTTALL, D. (1994), ''Choosing indicators'', in *Making Education Count. Developing and Using International Indicators,* OECD, Paris.

OAKES, J. (1986), *Educational Indicators: A Guide for Policymakers,* Rand Corporation, Santa Monica, LA.

OECD (1992), *Education at a Glance. OECD Indicators* (bilingual), 1st edition, CERI, Paris.

OECD (1993), *Education at a Glance. OECD Indicators* (bilingual), 2nd edition, CERI, Paris.

OSBURN, H.G. (1968), ''Item sampling for achievement testing'', *Educational and Psychological Measurement,* Vol. 28, pp. 95-104.

PASHLEY, P.J., and PHILLIPS, G.W. (1993), *Toward World-Class Standards. A Research Study Linking International and National Assessments,* Educational Testing Service, Princeton, NJ.

POSTLETHWAITE, T.N. (1988), ''The IEA project on reading literacy: a proposal'', mimeo, International Association for the Evaluation of Educational Achievement, IEA Secretariat, the Hague.

ROSIER, M.J., and KEEVES, J.P. (1991), *The IEA Study of Science 1: Science Education and Curricula in Twenty-three Countries,* Pergamon, Oxford.

ROSS, K.N. (1987), ''Sample design'', *International Journal of Educational Research,* Vol. 11, pp. 57-75.

SCHMIDT, W.H. (1983), ''Content bias in achievement tests'', *Journal of Educational Measurement,* Vol. 20, pp. 165-178.

SMITH, M.S. (1988), ''Educational indicators'', *Phi Delta Kappan,* Vol. 69 (7), pp. 487-491.

THUROW, L. (1992), *Head to Head. The Coming Economic Battle among Japan, Europe, and America,* Morrow, New York.

TRIER, U. (1994), *Establishing Indicators for Cross-curricular Competencies (CCC) in a Comparative Setting,* Paper presented at the annual meeting of the American Educational Research Association, New Orleans, April 4-8.

TYLER, R. (1985), ''National assessment of educational progress (NAEP)'', in T. Husén and T.N. Postlethwaite (eds.), *The International Encyclopedia of Education,* Pergamon, Oxford.

United Kingdom Department of Education and Science, Group on Assessment and Testing (1988), *National Curriculum. A Report,* Department of Education and Science, London.

WESTBURY, I. (1993), ''American and Japanese achievement (...) again. A response to Baker'', *Educational Researcher,* Vol. 22 (3), pp. 21-25.

Réflexions sur quelques indicateurs inaboutis
Reflections on Some Unsuccessful Indicators

par

Aletta Grisay
Université de Liège, Belgique

Ce chapitre passe en revue quelques-uns des indicateurs que le Réseau A du projet INES a envisagé de construire, mais qu'il n'a pas développés (ou qu'il a développés, mais sans les calculer, ou encore qui n'ont pas été publiés).

Comme les non-anniversaires d'Alice au pays des Merveilles, les indicateurs inaboutis sont en effet des non-événements méritant bien plus d'attention qu'on veut bien leur en prêter : ils dressent un inventaire sans complaisance des difficultés conceptuelles posées par la mise au point d'indicateurs d'acquis des élèves, et peuvent alimenter la réflexion sur les dispositifs susceptibles d'améliorer l'entreprise.

*

*   *

Summary

This report investigates and discusses in turn all the indicators that were to be set up by Network A of the INES project but for some reason or other, were never implemented. The unsuccessful indicators were based on data culled from international surveys conducted by independent bodies (IEA, IAEP). In view of the relatively large number of failed attempts, it seems that the quality of the data available from international surveys is often deficient. It is therefore important to find out why the above-mentioned indicators were discarded, as this may help the network to assess whether alternative arrangements can reasonably be expected to improve the quality of the information obtained.

Learning/teaching ratio: *there are several different reasons why this indicator is not performing as well as expected. Besides conceptual and technical considerations, the main difficulty is that the indicator is outdated. The only survey for which the indicator could be developed was the 1981 IEA SIMS survey (Second International Mathematics Study). The data contained in the latter showed a significant correlation between teaching and learning and (partly) explained the international classification observed. However, time was against this indicator. Because of curriculum reforms, it proved difficult to create a current "Opportunity-To-Learn" indicator because by the time the creation process was completed the data no longer matched the current education system. Nevertheless, it would be useful to use the data in order to compare the successive states of curricula over time.*

Between-schools and within-schools variance in mathematics scores: *although this indicator is useful, it remains crude. It seems that performance disparities between schools are less significant than those between classes. There is also a feeling that the indicator is too complex. There were problems with data that were incomplete, or not comparable because of the methods of calculation used and the need to carry out more detailed technical checks than those performed on other indicators. Nevertheless, this indicator does have potential and seems to be worth investigating and developing in future.*

Trend in reading skills between 1970 and 1991: *the development of this indicator would have required the difficult task of reanalysing the data in the 1970 IEA Reading Comprehension Study. The items used twenty years ago are so outdated and out of line with "modern" practices in this field that it would hardly have been possible to compare them with more recent items. Only five or so items were considered re-usable, and no new indicator can be based on so few outmoded items. In order to obtain time series in future, it will be necessary to ensure that the new test carries forward an adequate number of old items selected on the basis of good psychometric performance.*

Reading handicap of students whose home language differs from the school language: *this indicator shows that cost-cutting in science infrastructure may have adverse effects on the subsequent processing of data. Many countries have very few students belonging to a linguistic minority, so that the assessment of their reading performance becomes technically unstable. The contextual variables available do not allow any distinction to be made between different types of linguistic "minorities" (because fewer variables are used). If this indicator is to be improved in future, the scientific basis of the indicators to be developed should not be jeopardised for the sake of cost-cutting.*

Computer literacy: *the conflicting needs of comparability, flexibility, adaptability to requirements, and resources are apparent in this indicator. For a start, there were only six countries participating in the second part of the survey used (IEA Computer Education). Some of these adjusted the survey to local constraints and the survey ended up with one unusable sample and four other sample designs that failed to fully meet the INES technical standards. In spite of the data failures, the information supplied was interesting and potentially useful. The challenge arising from this indicator is that of international co-ordination and the common rules to be adopted by the partner countries. Even one single failure might jeopardise the work of all countries involved.*

In conclusion, this report definitely shows that all the unsuccessful indicators were (potentially at least) vectors of important information for improving our understanding of OECD school systems. The common thread that seems to run through the discarded indicators is deficient survey planning and international control. In order to achieve better data quality for future indicators of performance of INES students, the network should reflect on ways of ensuring international coherence.

*

* *

1. Introduction

Jusqu'ici, les données utilisées par le Réseau A pour élaborer des indicateurs d'acquis des élèves ont toujours été empruntées à des enquêtes internationales menées par des organismes indépendants (IEA : International Association for the Evaluation of Educational Achievement et IAEP : International Association for Educational Progress).

Le rôle du Réseau A, dans ce contexte, relève donc essentiellement du *contrôle de qualité* (les données recueillies sont-elles conformes aux standards fixés ?) et de la *mise en forme* (comment présenter les résultats de manière à en faciliter, autant que possible, la lecture ?). Lorsque, après avoir envisagé la possibilité d'élaborer un indicateur donné, le groupe décide en définitive de l'écarter, c'est donc, en principe, parce que les données prises en considération n'offrent pas les garanties techniques indispensables.

Les tentatives inabouties sont relativement nombreuses (tableau 3.1), du moins si on les rapporte aux indicateurs effectivement publiés (une quinzaine jusqu'ici). Cela a

Tableau/Table 3.1.

Indicateurs d'acquis des élèves non inclus dans *Regards sur l'éducation*

Indicators of student attainment not included in **Education at a Glance**

	Source des données
Ratio matières enseignées/matières apprises	IEA/SIMS (1981)
Variance entre écoles et entre classes du rendement en mathématiques	IEA/SIMS (1981)
Évolution des scores en lecture entre 1970 et 1991	IEA/RC (1970) et IEA/RL (1991)
Handicap en lecture des élèves parlant une autre langue que la langue d'enseignement	IEA/RL (1991)
Familiarité avec l'ordinateur	IEA/COMPED (1992)

contribué à alimenter, au sein du groupe, l'impression fâcheuse que les données rendues disponibles par les enquêtes internationales sont souvent de qualité médiocre. L'on s'interroge dès lors sur la nécessité éventuelle de fonder les indicateurs internationaux des systèmes d'enseignement sur des sources plus rapides et plus «sûres».

Ces dernières sont généralement gérées par les autorités scolaires des divers pays et sont menées à des fins de pilotage éducatif; par leur origine, leur conception, le type de public auquel elles sont destinées et la nature des besoins auxquels elles répondent, ces enquêtes sont sensiblement plus proches du projet INES que ne le sont les enquêtes internationales à finalité scientifique. On en conclut volontiers qu'elles conviendraient mieux aux exigences posées par ce projet.

Examinons cependant de plus près les raisons qui ont conduit à l'abandon des différents indicateurs énumérés dans le tableau 3.1, et demandons-nous quelles conditions il eût fallu réunir pour éviter ces échecs. Cela peut éventuellement aider à comprendre si des modalités alternatives ont des chances raisonnables d'améliorer la qualité de l'information recueillie.

2. Ratio matière apprise/matière enseignée

L'échec (que l'on espère provisoire) de cet indicateur est d'autant plus gênant qu'il constituait, dans le schéma initialement envisagé par le Réseau A, un des quatre «piliers de base» de l'information à fournir pour chacune des disciplines scolaires prévues. Ces piliers étaient les suivants :

1. comparaison des résultats moyens obtenus par les élèves des divers pays;
2. relation entre les résultats obtenus par les élèves et leur «exposition à l'apprentissage» (ratio matière apprise/matière enseignée);
3. disparité des résultats entre élèves;
4. disparité des résultats entre établissements.

Alors que les indicateurs 1, 3 et 4 ont pu être fournis régulièrement pour les matières abordées jusqu'ici dans *Regards sur l'éducation* (mathématiques, sciences et lecture), il n'en a pas été de même pour l'indicateur 2, du moins jusqu'à présent. Les raisons en sont diverses.

D'une part, la technique utilisée pour recueillir auprès des enseignants des informations sur l'«exposition à l'apprentissage» (*Opportunity-To-Learn,* OTL) dont ont bénéficié leurs élèves, ne convient guère à un domaine qui, comme la *lecture,* relève d'une compétence globale bien davantage que de l'apprentissage de contenus spécifiques. L'enquête Reading Literacy de l'IEA de 1991 a comporté, de ce fait, des questionnaires sur les *activités de lecture* des élèves et non un relevé classique d'OTL.

D'autre part, lors des enquêtes IAEP de 1991 sur les mathématiques et les sciences, aucun relevé ''Opportunity-To-Learn'' n'a été effectué.

Un indicateur intéressant, mais trop âgé

La seule enquête pour laquelle un ratio matière apprise/matière enseignée pouvait être développé (et a effectivement été calculé) est la Second International Mathematics Study de l'IEA (1981). Comme le montre le tableau 3.2 (extrait d'un des documents préparatoires utilisés lors des débats du Réseau A portant sur cet indicateur), les données recueillies ne manquaient pas d'intérêt.

Les variations de pays à pays de l'indice OTL (pourcentage moyen d'items du test dont les professeurs affirment avoir enseigné le contenu à leurs élèves) apparaissent en effet liées de manière significative avec les résultats obtenus (pourcentage moyen d'items effectivement réussis par les élèves) ; la corrélation est de 0.59 (pour N = 15 pays).

Ces données permettaient, dès lors, d'expliquer (en partie) le classement international observé. Les bons résultats en mathématiques du Japon, des Pays-Bas ou de la Hongrie pouvaient probablement être attribués – entre autres causes – à un curriculum de mathématiques plus exigeant, ou plus complètement parcouru qu'ailleurs. La Suède, la Finlande ou la Nouvelle-Zélande, qui obtenaient des résultats plus modestes, semblaient mettre en œuvre, au moment de l'enquête (1981), un curriculum de mathématiques sensiblement moins ambitieux.

Tableau/Table 3.2.

Scores des élèves au test de mathématiques et réponses des maîtres relatives à l'exposition à l'apprentissage

Student scores in the mathematics test

	Score au test (% d'items réussis)	OTL (% d'items abordés)	Efficience éducative (ratio score au test/OTL)
Japon	62.1	76.7	81
Pays-Bas	57.1	70.5	81
Hongrie	56.0	90.1	62
Belgique (Communauté flamande)	53.2	60.6	88
France	52.5	72.3	73
Canada (Colombie britannique)	51.6	72.0	72
Belgique (Communauté française)	51.3	n.d.	n.d.
Canada (Ontario)	49.0	71.7	68
Écosse	48.4	n.d.	n.d.
Angleterre et pays de Galles	47.3	68.4	69
Finlande	46.8	61.0	77
Nouvelle-Zélande	45.5	64.1	71
États-Unis	45.3	68.6	66
Suède	41.8	53.8	78

n.d. : non disponible.
OTL : Opportunity-To-Learn.
Note : Le calcul porte sur l'ensemble du test (157 items).

Les résultats de pays comme les États-Unis ou la Belgique (Communauté flamande) mettaient en outre en évidence le rôle joué par l'efficience proprement dite du système. Les enseignants flamands étaient apparemment ceux qui abordaient le moins de contenus (61 pour cent d'items vus), mais en obtenant le plus souvent de leurs élèves que la matière vue soit effectivement apprise. Cela se traduisait, pour ce pays, par un résultat global honorable et un très bon ratio matière apprise/matière enseignée (en moyenne, 88 pour cent des items enseignés étaient effectivement réussis par les élèves). Aux États-Unis, non seulement la proportion d'items abordés en classe était plus faible que la moyenne internationale, mais, en outre, les items enseignés l'étaient de manière apparemment peu efficace (indice d'efficience : 66 pour cent).

Parmi les raisons qui ont conduit à l'abandon de cet indicateur, certaines sont de nature conceptuelle (en particulier le fait que le questionnaire OTL s'adressait aux seuls maîtres du grade 8, alors que les apprentissages visés par certains items pouvaient avoir été réalisés plus tôt dans le cursus de l'élève), d'autres de nature technique (en particulier, le fait que dans plusieurs pays le taux de retour des questionnaires OTL était inférieur à 80 pour cent, mettant en cause la fiabilité des résultats).

Cependant, l'objection principale (et déterminante) relève d'un tout autre ordre de considérations. Des réformes importantes des programmes de mathématiques ont pris place dans plusieurs des pays ayant participé à cette enquête, si bien que l'indice d'exposition à l'apprentissage relevé en 1981 paraissait beaucoup trop vieux pour être publié en 1992.

Et à l'avenir ?

On peut, certes, espérer qu'une amélioration interviendra à ce propos lors des prochaines éditions de *Regards sur l'éducation*. En particulier, les démarches d'analyse du curriculum enseigné ont fait l'objet d'un soin particulier dans la Third International Mathematics and Science Study (TIMSS) actuellement en cours (Schmidt, 1993) et donneront lieu à des indicateurs d'exposition à l'apprentissage en mathématiques et en sciences fondés sur une prise d'information beaucoup plus récente.

Rendons-nous cependant à l'évidence : aucun indicateur OTL ne pourra jamais être tout à fait «à jour». Il faut du temps pour créer une grille de contenus acceptable internationalement ; il faut du temps pour l'appliquer aux curriculum mis en œuvre par les divers pays ; et il faut du temps pour mener l'analyse des résultats. Les réformes des programmes étant un des exercices auxquels les systèmes scolaires se livrent avec le plus d'entrain, il y a fort à parier qu'entre le début et la fin de l'enquête TIMSS (pour ne prendre que cet exemple) plus d'un des pays impliqués sera en droit de dire que les données OTL *«ne correspondent plus à la réalité»*, le curriculum ayant été modifié.

Le problème est sans doute plus psychologique que réel. Il tient à une incompatibilité de rythme : pour le décideur pressé (et confiant en ses mesures d'innovation), l'ancien curriculum n'existe plus dès lors qu'il est remplacé par un nouveau. Il oublie volontiers que le temps de réaction des systèmes scolaires est beaucoup plus lent qu'il ne le voudrait, et que plusieurs années s'écoulent parfois entre le moment où un nouveau curriculum est inauguré et celui où il est effectivement appliqué dans toutes les écoles du pays. Les relevés OTL de la TIMSS porteront sans doute la trace des réformes de curriculum intervenues durant la décennie 1980-90, comme le relevé SIMS de 1981 portait probablement la trace des réformes intervenues durant la décennie 1970-80 : c'est à ce rythme-là que «respirent» les systèmes scolaires. Il faut se résigner à ce que les indicateurs OTL aient surtout une valeur rétrospective ; ils ne permettent de mesurer les modifications intervenues qu'après un délai relativement long – et à condition que l'on dispose de points de repère antérieurs.

Au lieu de céder à la pression, en exigeant une «actualisation» pratiquement hors d'atteinte, il serait probablement plus avisé, en matière d'indicateurs OTL, de s'assurer que les outils mis au point permettent effectivement de comparer, à travers le temps, les états successifs des curriculum. Il n'est pas évident que cet objectif soit actuellement prioritaire. A cet égard, le Réseau A pourrait jouer un rôle utile, en élaborant des spécifications, ou une description des besoins relative à cet indicateur.

3.   Variance entre écoles et entre classes des scores en mathématiques

Regards sur l'éducation a fourni régulièrement, jusqu'à présent, une estimation des disparités de rendement existant entre écoles pour les diverses disciplines prises en considération.

Cet indicateur demeure grossier. L'entité «école» est, certes, une des subdivisions importantes du système éducatif ; mais ce n'est ni la seule, ni, probablement, celle à laquelle sont associées les disparités de rendement les plus significatives. Les unités «classe» constituent, dans tous les systèmes scolaires, les «cellules» élémentaires probablement les plus déterminantes, en raison des divers phénomènes d'agrégation qui leur sont liés (qualité des maîtres enseignant dans telle ou telle classe ; influence du groupe de pairs ; conséquences des dispositifs utilisés pour répartir les élèves dans les diverses classes d'un même niveau, etc.).

Un indicateur fournissant une estimation des disparités entre écoles et entre classes a pu être calculé à partir des données de la Second International Mathematics Study (tableau 3.3), dans la mesure où, lors de cette enquête, les échantillons testés par plusieurs pays comportaient plus d'une classe par école.

Les résultats, fort intéressants malgré le nombre limité de pays pour lesquels ils étaient disponibles, montraient de manière tout à fait éloquente que les deux indications (école *et* classe) sont indispensables si l'on veut se faire une idée plus correcte de la manière dont les disparités de rendement se distribuent dans les divers systèmes scolaires. On constate, par exemple, que des pays connus pour leurs très faibles taux de disparité entre *écoles* (Suède, Finlande) semblent en fait gérer au niveau des *classes* les problèmes d'hétérogénéité de compétences entre élèves. De ce fait, l'indice global d'agrégation (addition des disparités entre classes et entre écoles) n'y est en définitive pas très différent de celui observé dans des pays comme l'Écosse ou le Luxembourg, où on sait que les clivages entre écoles sont plus importants – mais où les disparités entre classes s'avèrent moindres.

69

Tableau/Table 3.3.

Inégalités de rendement liées aux différences entre classes et entre écoles

Efficiency: between-class and between-school variance

	Composante de variance liée à la classe fréquentée	Composante de variance liée à l'école fréquentée	Total (proportion de variance liée à l'école et à la classe fréquentée)
Belgique (Communauté flamande)	–	–	0.50
Belgique (Communauté française)	–	–	0.64
Canada (Colombie britannique)	–	–	0.27
Canada (Ontario)	0.18	0.09	0.27
Finlande	0.45	0.002	0.452
France	0.17	0.06	0.23
Japon	–	–	0.08
Luxembourg	0.29	0.15	0.44
Pays-Bas	–	–	0.67
Nouvelle-Zélande	0.45	0.01	0.46
Écosse	0.34	0.12	0.46
Suède	0.45	0.00	0.45
États-Unis	0.46	0.10	0.56

Source : Réanalyse des données *IEA Second International Mathematics Study* effectuée par Scheerens *et al.* (1989).

Un indicateur «trop complexe»

Cet indicateur soulevait cependant plus de questions qu'il n'apportait d'informations, ce qui a conduit à son abandon :

- Les données sont justement incomplètes pour les trois systèmes scolaires où la valeur de l'indice global est la plus élevée (les communautés flamande et française de Belgique et les Pays-Bas : plus de 0.50) et pour le pays où elle est la plus faible (Japon : 0.08), ce qui paraît particulièrement frustrant.
- Par la manière dont elles sont calculées, les valeurs obtenues ne peuvent pas être comparées avec les indicateurs de variance entre écoles fournis par les autres sources disponibles (IAEP, Reading Literacy Study de l'IEA) et publiés dans *Regards sur l'éducation*. Les indicateurs publiés sont, en fait, légèrement «impurs» : l'indice fourni amalgame l'effet «école» avec tout ou partie de l'effet «classe»; il est donc surévalué. Les risques de confusion eussent été considérables si l'on avait permis la coexistence des deux modes de calcul dans la même brochure, ou dans deux brochures successives.
- La qualité de cet indicateur (et, plus généralement, celle de tout indicateur de disparité) est extrêmement dépendante des procédures d'échantillonnage mises en œuvre. Des dérapages mineurs dans tel ou tel pays, sans grave conséquence pour le calcul du score moyen, peuvent défigurer entièrement son indice de disparité

entre écoles. Le contrôle de la comparabilité de pays à pays nécessiterait donc des vérifications techniques encore plus approfondies que celles consacrées aux autres indicateurs.

Et à l'avenir ?

De manière plus diffuse, les indicateurs de disparité mis au point par le Réseau A (qu'ils soient publiés ou non) souffrent de trois « maladies » :

- Ils sont « scientifiquement jeunes » : les chercheurs ne disposent pas, à leur propos, d'archives importantes, qui pourraient aider à comprendre leur fonctionnement.
- Le dispositif d'enquête doit reposer sur un plan d'échantillonnage particulièrement coûteux si l'on veut qu'il fournisse une bonne estimation de la variance entre écoles et entre classes – ce qui explique que très peu des enquêtes disponibles permettent effectivement d'obtenir ces deux estimations.
- Ils sont considérés comme difficiles à interpréter par des utilisateurs peu familiers avec la statistique.

Il y a pourtant de solides raisons d'être optimiste pour l'avenir.

De tous les indicateurs du Réseau A, l'indice de disparité est, en effet, celui qui gagnerait le plus à s'appuyer sur les recueils *nationaux* de données. Rien ne s'oppose (en principe tout au moins) à ce qu'il soit calculé à partir de scores d'examens, ou de tests utilisés dans les enquêtes nationales : il peut se fonder sans inconvénient sur des instruments dont les items diffèrent d'un pays à l'autre, ce qui n'est le cas d'aucun des autres indicateurs d'acquis[1].

A noter qu'en raison du caractère très élémentaire du calcul requis et des paramètres sur lesquels il se fonde (voir le détail de la formule utilisée dans le chapitre 4), il est probable que des séries temporelles pourraient être reconstruites sans difficulté majeure (ni coût prohibitif) dans tous les pays où existe un système de recueil récurrent d'informations sur les acquis des élèves.

Une méta-analyse prenant pour objet la variance entre écoles et entre classes, et portant sur l'ensemble des enquêtes standardisées ayant pris place dans les pays de l'OCDE au cours des dix ou quinze dernières années, balaierait probablement d'un seul coup les obscurités qui gênent aujourd'hui l'interprétation de cet indicateur, tout en apportant une contribution décisive à l'histoire des mouvements de massification et de démocratisation des études dans nos pays industrialisés.

Un tel afflux d'informations rétrospectives aurait probablement d'heureux effets sur la prétendue « difficulté de lecture » de l'indicateur de disparité. Celui-ci n'est, à vrai dire, guère plus difficile à comprendre que bien d'autres indicateurs couramment utilisés (taux de chômage corrigé des variations saisonnières, ou PIB en standard de pouvoir d'achat). S'il paraît « difficile », c'est surtout parce qu'il n'a (encore) que très peu servi.

L'exploitation des enquêtes nationales pour le calcul de l'indicateur de disparité entre écoles et classes présenterait un autre avantage important : celui de réduire les contraintes, déjà très lourdes, qui pèsent sur les enquêtes internationales. Il ne serait plus indispensable que l'échantillon testé lors de ces enquêtes ait partout les (coûteuses) caractéristiques nécessaires au calcul de la variance entre écoles et classes : ce surcoût demeurerait nécessaire dans les seuls pays ne disposant pas d'enquêtes nationales.

4. Évolution des compétences en lecture entre 1970 et 1991

Cet indicateur, envisagé lors de la préparation de la troisième version de *Regards sur l'éducation* (1995) n'a pas été calculé. Les difficultés techniques qu'il soulevait n'étaient pas insurmontables, tout en paraissant importantes. La mise au point de l'indicateur aurait en effet exigé une réanalyse des données de la Reading Comprehension Study de l'IEA de 1970 (entreprise délicate, s'agissant de fichiers vieux d'une vingtaine d'années). D'autre part, la définition de l'échantillon testé en 1970 (fondée sur l'âge) différait de celle de 1991 (fondée sur le grade), ce qui eût exigé une procédure d'ajustement statistique des résultats, toujours discutable.

Mais le vrai problème posé par cet indicateur est, ici encore, lié à une question d'impatience et de méconnaissance des «durées» propres aux systèmes éducatifs.

Un effet de mode

L'impatience n'est pas cette fois le fait des décideurs. Souvent confrontées à mille récriminations concernant une prétendue «baisse du niveau» des élèves, les autorités scolaires des divers pays seraient en réalité très heureuses de savoir si le niveau en lecture a, oui ou non, «baissé» depuis vingt ans. Ce sont plutôt les spécialistes de la discipline – didacticiens, pédagogues, chercheurs – qui trouvent à redire à la comparaison : les items utilisés il y a vingt ans leur paraissent si vieillis, si peu conformes aux tendances «modernes» en leur domaine qu'ils doutent de la possibilité de comparer quoi que ce soit sur cette base.

Cette attitude de rejet a joué une première fois au niveau de la conception même de la Reading Literacy Study de 1991 : le comité scientifique de cette étude n'a jugé «réutilisables» qu'un très petit nombre d'items de l'enquête de 1970[2].

Le rejet a joué une seconde fois au sein du Réseau A sur les indicateurs, lorsqu'il a fallu décider si un indicateur d'évolution des compétences en lecture pouvait ou non être fondé sur cette poignée d'items vieillots ; la réponse ne pouvait être que négative.

Ironiquement, les analyses statistiques montrent que ces items prétendument «démodés» fonctionnent dans le test de 1991 aussi bien que les items plus «modernes». En particulier, ils discriminent les bons des mauvais lecteurs de 1991 tout aussi efficacement qu'ils le faisaient en 1970. Cependant, *parce qu'il n'en reste qu'une poignée,* l'indicateur d'évolution envisagé aurait effectivement eu une fiabilité technique insuffisante : si la censure avait été moins sévère, il aurait pu être construit.

Et à l'avenir?

La situation de ce type d'indicateurs a-t-elle des chances de s'améliorer dans le futur? En principe, oui : si les recueils de données deviennent plus fréquents et plus réguliers, il sera moins malaisé de prévoir des ancrages solides d'une enquête à l'autre.

Sur le fond cependant, le problème restera probablement inchangé. S'il porte sur une durée limitée (trois, cinq ans), l'ancrage n'enregistrera vraisemblablement que des fluctuations insignifiantes. Sur de plus longues durées (quinze, vingt ans), des évolutions significatives pourraient être observées, mais la crédibilité pédagogique des items d'ancrage risque d'être très fortement critiquée.

Pour obtenir des séries temporelles, il faudra donc être à même d'*imposer,* de manière quelque peu autoritaire, des plans de recherche permettant de les constituer : faire en sorte qu'en toute circonstance, et quelle que soit la mode du jour, le nouveau test comporte une section d'ancrage contenant un nombre suffisant d'items anciens, sélectionnés *d'abord* en fonction de leur bon fonctionnement psychométrique, et en second lieu seulement, en fonction des caprices didactiques de l'époque.

5. Handicap en lecture des élèves parlant en famille une autre langue que la langue d'enseignement

On reproche parfois aux enquêtes internationales d'être d'imposants navires, que leur gréement trop lourd empêche de manœuvrer facilement; et il est vrai que le cahier des charges scientifique des enquêtes IEA de ces dernières années a souvent été très complexe.

En conclure qu'il suffirait de revenir à des dispositifs beaucoup plus simples pour réduire à la fois le coût et la durée de ce type d'entreprise est cependant plus aisé à dire qu'à réussir, comme en témoigne la relative indigence des données obtenues à travers les enquêtes de l'IAEP, où pratiquement aucun recueil d'informations contextuelles ne permet d'éclairer les résultats.

Se voulant goélette plutôt que paquebot, l'enquête Reading Literacy Study de l'IEA de 1991 a soumis à une sélection très sévère l'inventaire des instruments embarqués, ce qui a grandement facilité sa navigation. Parmi les variables qu'il a ainsi fallu renoncer à recueillir, il en était cependant dont on doit, *a posteriori*, regretter l'absence. Le cas de l'indicateur «Handicap des élèves parlant en famille une autre langue que la langue d'enseignement» illustre bien cette situation : il montre que les «économies» réalisées en matière d'infrastructure scientifique peuvent avoir des effets négatifs sur l'exploitation ultérieure des données.

Dans le cadre de l'enquête Reading Literacy Study, il avait été demandé aux élèves d'indiquer s'ils parlaient à la maison, avec leurs parents, la même langue que celle utilisée à l'école. On constate que, dans tous les pays, les élèves appartenant à ces minorités linguistiques (ceux qui affirment parler *«parfois»*, *«souvent»* ou *«toujours»* en famille une langue différente de celle de l'enseignement) obtiennent au test de lecture un score moyen inférieur à celui de leurs camarades dont la langue maternelle est la même que la langue d'enseignement.

L'ampleur de ce handicap diffère cependant beaucoup d'un pays à l'autre (tableau 3.4), ce qui invite à se demander si certains systèmes scolaires ne sont pas plus efficaces que d'autres dans l'intégration de leurs minorités linguistiques.

Afin de mieux comprendre les différences observées, il a paru utile de s'intéresser au milieu d'origine de ces minorités. Un indice de «handicap socio-économique» a donc été

Tableau/Table 3.4.

**Handicap en lecture et handicap socio-économique des élèves
ne parlant pas la langue d'enseignement**

*Reading handicap and socio-economic handicap of students speaking a language
other than the language of instruction*

	Pourcentage d'élèves parlant en famille une autre langue que la langue d'enseignement	Handicap en lecture des élèves parlant une autre langue que la langue d'enseignement	Handicap socio-économique des élèves parlant une autre langue que la langue d'enseignement
Italie	26.1	−.50	−.77
Suisse	15.0	−.62	−.70
Espagne	11.4	−.16	n.d.
Pays-Bas	9.1	−.38	−.38
Belgique			
(Communauté française)	8.7	−.70	−.71
Allemagne (ex-RFA)	8.3	−.96	−.90
Canada			
(Colombie britannique)	7.6	−.21	−.58
Nouvelle-Zélande	5.6	−.86	−.56
Suède	5.1	−.60	−.50
France	3.9	−.52	−.50
États-Unis	3.8	−.71	−.89
Grèce	2.8	−.36	+.19
Danemark	2.5	−.74	−.63
Norvège	1.9	−.62	−.39
Portugal	1.6	−.35	+.08
Irlande	1.2	−.35	+.02
Allemagne (ex-RDA)	0.8	−.05	−.49
Hongrie	0.6	−.56	−.14
Finlande	0.6	−.51	+.82
Irlande	0.4	−.36	+.10

Note : Les deux indicateurs de handicap sont des scores réduits (moyenne : 0 ; écart-type : 1). Une valeur nulle ou proche de 0 indique qu'il n'y a pas de différence significative entre le groupe d'élèves appartenant à des minorités linguistiques et le reste de la population. Un indice *négatif* indique que le résultat moyen de ce groupe d'élèves est *inférieur* à celui du reste de la population. Un indice *positif* indique le contraire.

Source : Réanalyse des données *IEA Reading Literacy Study,* effectuée par Jungclaus (1994).

calculé pour ce groupe d'élèves, en comparant leurs scores et ceux de leurs camarades à un indice socio-économique (fondé sur le niveau d'éducation des parents et sur une échelle d'aisance économique : la famille possède-t-elle une voiture, un magnétoscope, un lave-vaisselle, etc. ?).

L'indice de « handicap social » obtenu, exprimé sur une échelle réduite ayant la même métrique que l'indice de « handicap en lecture » permet de constater que la position sociale des élèves appartenant aux minorités linguistiques paraît beaucoup plus défavorisée dans certains pays : par exemple, l'Allemagne (ex-RFA) et les États-Unis. Dans d'autres (Finlande, Grèce), les « minorités » paraissent plutôt appartenir, en moyenne, à un groupe socialement privilégié.

L'ampleur du handicap en lecture semble liée, dans de nombreux cas, à celle du handicap social (comparer, par exemple, les résultats des Pays-Bas, de la Belgique francophone et de l'Allemagne ex-RFA). Il existe cependant des exceptions intéressantes : à handicap social pratiquement identique, les élèves des minorités linguistiques de la Colombie britannique présentent un handicap en lecture bien moindre que celui observé chez leurs équivalents en Nouvelle-Zélande.

L'abandon de cet indicateur est dû à deux difficultés :

- De nombreux pays ne comptent que très peu d'élèves appartenant à une minorité linguistique (moins de 2 ou 3 pour cent) ce qui rend techniquement instable l'évaluation de leurs performances en lecture : sur de si faibles sous-échantillons, l'erreur de mesure est trop importante. En Grèce, au Portugal, dans les pays scandinaves, dans les pays de l'Est ou en Irlande, il eût fallu prévoir de sur-échantillonner ce groupe d'élèves pour obtenir des résultats suffisamment fiables.
- D'autre part, les variables contextuelles disponibles ne permettent pas d'effectuer une distinction (importante et politiquement très sensible) entre différents types de « minorités » linguistiques. En particulier, on n'a pas relevé la nationalité des élèves ; on ne leur a pas demandé s'ils étaient bi ou trilingues, ni quelle était leur langue maternelle. L'économie de variables est ici compréhensible : en pratique, il eût fallu mettre en œuvre un questionnement (et un traitement de données) spécifique à chacun des pays participants pour obtenir les renseignements pertinents. Mais l'absence de ces informations contextuelles interdit de distinguer, parmi les élèves qui parlent une autre langue que la langue d'enseignement, ceux qui parlent une *langue étrangère* (élèves issus de familles immigrées) de ceux qui parlent une *langue seconde* ou un *dialecte* (et qui sont le plus souvent des nationaux, généralement bilingues). Le problème se pose notamment pour des pays comme l'Italie, l'Espagne, la Suisse, où la confusion entre ces catégories rend tout à fait impubliable l'indicateur tel qu'il est présenté par le tableau 3.4.

Et à l'avenir ?

La leçon à tirer de cet échec est qu'il y a lieu de planifier les indicateurs que l'on souhaite obtenir et de le faire en tenant compte de l'information contextuelle indispensable à leur mise au point. Il est certainement possible de concevoir des enquêtes relativement «légères». Encore faut-il éviter qu'elles soient, pour tel ou tel aspect déterminant, «légères» au point de compromettre l'assise scientifique des indicateurs que l'on souhaite produire.

6. Familiarité avec l'ordinateur

Le cas de cet indicateur (ou plutôt de ce bloc d'indicateurs) illustre à merveille une des sources de difficulté les plus communément rencontrées dans les enquêtes internationales : le conflit entre un *impératif de comparabilité* (réclamant que tous les pays impliqués se plient rigoureusement au même schéma de recueil de données) et un *impératif de souplesse, d'adaptation aux besoins et aux ressources* (impliquant que certains pays puissent ajouter des options nationales sur des points qu'ils jugent cruciaux pour eux ou s'abstenir de participer à tel volet de l'étude qu'ils jugent plus coûteux qu'intéressant dans leur cas, etc.).

Un indicateur victime des options nationales

Le projet Computer Education (COMPED) de l'IEA a eu ainsi un objectif «prioritaire» : la comparaison internationale des ressources et des processus mis en œuvre par les divers pays lors de l'introduction de l'informatique dans les systèmes scolaires.

Un second volet de l'étude, *facultatif,* impliquait l'administration à un échantillon représentatif d'élèves de 14 ans d'une trentaine d'items destinés à évaluer leur *familiarité avec l'usage de l'ordinateur.* Parmi la vingtaine de pays ayant participé à l'enquête COMPED, six seulement ont accepté de prendre en charge ce (lourd) complément d'enquête. De plus, certains l'ont fait – comme il arrive souvent lorsqu'il s'agit d'un volet secondaire de l'enquête – en «simplifiant» quelque peu le plan d'échantillonnage ou en l'adaptant à des contraintes locales. En particulier, il n'a pas été mis en place de dispositif permettant de remplacer les établissements qui refusaient leur coopération.

La conséquence en est qu'un des six échantillons est entièrement inutilisable pour la comparaison internationale (la Grèce n'a sélectionné que des écoles possédant un équipement informatique) et qu'un seul des cinq autres (celui du Japon) répond aux normes techniques du projet INES de l'OCDE sur les indicateurs internationaux des systèmes d'enseignement (le taux de retour y est de 94 pour cent, contre des valeurs de 73 pour cent à 25 pour cent dans les autres pays).

Les résultats observés (tableau 3.5) ont dès lors toutes chances de paraître suspects. Le Japon, dont l'échantillon est irréprochable, arrive en queue de classement, précédé de peu par les États-Unis (où le taux de retour, pourtant insuffisant, reste meilleur que dans les pays venant en tête). Bien que des contrôles *a posteriori* menés en Autriche, aux Pays-Bas et aux États-Unis aient montré qu'aucun biais significatif ne paraît avoir été introduit par les non-retours, l'indicateur demeure beaucoup trop boiteux pour être publié, compte tenu des standards d'INES.

En pareil cas, l'échec est purement et simplement irrémédiable. L'occasion a été perdue d'analyser comment une innovation aussi importante que l'introduction de l'ordi-

Tableau/Table 3.5.

Familiarité avec l'ordinateur des élèves de 14 ans (grade 8)

Computer familiarity, age 14 (grade 8)

	Score moyen	Erreur standard	N	Taux de retour (%)	Âge	Délai intervenu depuis l'introduction	% de variance entre écoles
Allemagne (ex-RFA)	532	7.4	1 486	52	14.3	4 ans	32
Autriche	532	3.2	5 473	46	14.7	4 ans	22
Pays-Bas	523	3.7	4 911	25	14.5	5 ans	32
États-Unis	487	4.5	3 704	73	14.4	7 ans	24
Japon	425	6.1	5 404	94	14.2	2 ans	15

Source : Réanalyse des données *IEA Computer Education,* effectuée par Steen (1994).

nateur à l'école (qui s'est produite à peu près au même moment dans l'ensemble des pays industrialisés, mais selon des modalités différentes et avec une mobilisation inégale des ressources) a pu se traduire concrètement dans les acquis des premières générations d'élèves qui en ont bénéficié.

Les informations fournies par les quelques pays impliqués dans la phase 2 de COMPED sont, en dépit des défaillances décrites ci-dessus, si intéressantes qu'elles font regretter le peu d'empressement mis par les autres pays à tester leurs élèves.

Justement parce que les *processus* (et non l'*output*) ont été le centre d'intérêt de l'enquête, COMPED apparaît ainsi comme une des rares enquêtes à avoir fourni des informations réellement éclairantes sur les facteurs susceptibles d'expliquer les différences de résultats observées de pays à pays. Le faible score du Japon se comprend par exemple fort bien, lorsqu'on apprend que dans ce pays l'introduction de l'ordinateur avait pris place seulement deux ans avant la date de l'enquête (contre quatre en Allemagne et en Autriche, cinq au Pays-Bas, sept aux États-Unis) et que l'équipement des écoles, ainsi que l'exposition des élèves à l'apprentissage y étaient encore, au moment de l'enquête, de très loin inférieurs à ceux relevés dans les quatre autres pays. Le système éducatif japonais, habituellement «performant», se voyait donc pris en flagrant délit de retard technologique.

Dans ces résultats, on peut encore mettre en évidence deux autres tendances.

L'une concerne le «profil» des apprentissages réalisés, qui tend à se modifier au fil du temps. Dans les pays où l'innovation est la plus récente, les élèves acquièrent surtout des connaissances sur l'ordinateur lui-même. Dans les pays où elle date déjà quelque peu, un changement d'objectif s'est produit; et l'on enseigne plutôt aux élèves à se servir de l'ordinateur pour acquérir des connaissances dans d'autres disciplines.

L'autre tendance est relative aux disparités entre écoles. Celles-ci paraissent être plus amples lorsque l'innovation est plus ancienne dans un pays – suggérant donc que le passage du temps joue, dans l'implantation d'une nouvelle discipline, un rôle de différenciation progressive. L'hypothèse inverse aurait pu paraître plausible (forte différenciation entre écoles en période initiale, quand le nouveau programme est encore inégalement implanté ; homogénéisation progressive, au fur et à mesure que les écoles s'équipent, que les maîtres se forment).

Et à l'avenir ?

Pour que des aventures aussi cuisantes ne se reproduisent plus dans le futur, le défi posé est celui de la *coordination internationale* et de la *discipline commune* que doivent savoir s'imposer les pays partenaires. Personne ne peut forcer un pays à participer à une enquête, ni, s'il y participe, à se plier à toutes les conditions prévues par le dispositif international. La tentation d'aménager le dispositif à sa convenance peut être extrêmement forte pour des équipes dont le budget est souvent très étroit et les préoccupations diverses. Pour qu'elles y résistent, il faut sans doute qu'elles aient appris *à leurs dépens* combien sont désastreuses, dans un plan de recherche international, les dérogations apparemment les plus anodines.

L'existence du projet INES de l'OCDE ajoute désormais une donnée supplémentaire. Chaque défaillance n'a plus seulement des conséquences pour le pays en cause : elle risque aussi de compromettre le travail des autres, puisque un indicateur ne pourra être calculé que lorsque des données effectivement comparables existent pour un nombre suffisant de pays.

7. Conclusion

Nous espérons avoir montré, au fil des pages qui précèdent, l'intérêt très réel des indicateurs auxquels le Réseau A a dû renoncer (provisoirement pour certains). Tous étaient, au moins potentiellement, porteurs d'informations importantes pour une meilleure connaissance des systèmes scolaires de l'OCDE : c'est ce qui nous a conduit à pointer ici et là quelques résultats (choisis parmi ceux que les défauts de l'indicateur ne sont pas de nature à avoir affecté).

Peut-on trouver un fil commun reliant ces cinq histoires d'indicateurs inaboutis ? Il en existe un, évident à nos yeux : la plupart de ces échecs ont peu ou prou pour origine une *défaillance de la planification et du contrôle international* de l'enquête.

Malgré l'expérience accumulée à ce propos depuis une trentaine d'années, il reste toujours extrêmement difficile, pour l'équipe assurant le pilotage d'une enquête, d'obtenir un consensus solide de la part de pays que ne lie aucune contrainte, sinon celles qu'ils acceptent de s'imposer eux-mêmes. Qu'il s'agisse d'assurer qu'un nombre suffisant de pays participe à l'opération ; qu'il s'agisse de définir les objectifs, l'inventaire des informations à obtenir et le plan de recherche ; qu'il s'agisse de contenir des dogmatismes théoriques chez les uns, des effets de mode chez d'autres, des ambitions impraticables chez pratiquement tous ; qu'il s'agisse enfin d'empêcher les dérives techniques en cours d'exécution, l'autorité du groupe de coordination n'est jamais que celle qu'on veut bien lui reconnaître.

Dans ces conditions, on peut penser que pour améliorer la qualité des données sur lesquelles se fonderont les futurs indicateurs d'acquis des élèves, l'enjeu principal n'est *pas* de savoir, par exemple, s'il faut confier le recueil des données dans les divers pays aux autorités scolaires plutôt qu'à des instituts de recherche. On ne voit pas, en tout cas, en quoi le fait de confier le recueil des données à un organisme plutôt qu'à un autre (surtout lorsque l'organisme choisi a moins d'expérience que le précédent en matière de coopération internationale) atténuerait les problèmes posés par les particularismes nationaux, la réticence à reconnaître le point de vue d'autrui et la pénurie de ressources (qui sont les trois causes principales des défaillances relevées).

Mieux vaudrait réfléchir aux démarches qui pourraient être mises en œuvre pour *consolider la cohérence internationale.* A cet égard, une des tâches les plus utiles auxquelles le Réseau A pourrait s'atteler serait la mise au point de véritables *cahiers des charges relatifs aux indicateurs souhaités,* pouvant servir de référence internationale incontestable lors du lancement de futures enquêtes.

Notes

1. Sa comparabilité internationale est, en revanche, fortement dépendante de la manière dont sont constitués les échantillons. Ne pourraient être considérés comme fiables que des indices de disparité issus de recensements intéressant l'ensemble de la population du pays (par exemple des examens nationaux) ou d'échantillons nationaux constitués de manière strictement comparable (écoles et classes intactes).

2. Des difficultés de même nature ont été rencontrées lors de la sélection d'items d'ancrage pour la Third International Mathematics and Science Study (TIMSS), et s'annoncent déjà pour le projet Second Foreign Language Study.

Références

JUNGCLAUS, H. (1994), «Reading achievement by "use of language" and index of social background», miméo, Institute of Comparative Education, Université d'Hambourg, Hambourg.

SCHEERENS, J., VERMEULEN, C.J., et PELGRUM, W.J. (1989), «Generalizability of instructional and school effectiveness indicators across nations», *International Journal of Educational Research,* n° 13, (7), pp. 789-799.

SCHMIDT, W.H. (1993), «Curriculum content: defining the parameters of educational opportunity», rapport présenté à la réunion du Réseau A du projet INES à Stockholm, 30 août-1er septembre 1993.

STEEN, R. (1994), Contribution proposée pour *Regards sur l'éducation 1994* par l'étude IEA «Computers in education study», miméo, OCTO, Université de Twente, Enschede.

SUTER, L.S. (1989), «A synthesis of research results from the IEA Second International Mathematics Study», miméo, National Centre for Education Statistics, US Department of Education, Washington DC.

Calculation and Interpretation of Between-School and Within-School Variation in Achievement *(rho)*
Calcul et interprétation des variations de la réussite entre écoles et à l'intérieur d'un même établissement (rho)

by

T. Neville Postlethwaite
Institute of Comparative Education,
University of Hamburg, Germany

Rho is an indicator of variance between clusters relative to variance within clusters. In education, clusters are usually regions or schools or classes. The most frequent use of *rho* is for variance between schools and within schools or between classes and within classes. The extreme values of *rho* are typically 0.0 and 1.0. If one is examining the scores on a reading test, for example, a *rho* of 0.30 means that 30 per cent of all variation is between schools and 70 per cent between students within schools. When the *rho* is high, the difference between schools is high and, in this case, the level of a student's reading score will very much depend on which school he or she attends. However, when *rho* is low, it does not matter much which school a student attends. This chapter presents an explanation of *rho*, with an example. It then presents the *rhos* calculated for the IEA Reading Literacy Study.

*

*   *

Note de synthèse

La détermination des variations de la réussite entre écoles et à l'intérieur d'un même établissement joue un rôle essentiel dans la production des indicateurs de la réussite scolaire. Grâce à l'exploitation d'une technique statistique, le rho *offre cette possibilité aux chercheurs. On trouvera dans ce chapitre une explication détaillée de cette technique, ainsi que plusieurs exemples de son utilisation.*

Comme nous l'avons vu, le rho *sert à mesurer la variation entre deux groupes distincts et à l'intérieur de chacun d'eux, et se fonde sur une échelle de 0 à 1.0 dans laquelle l'augmentation du* rho *répond à celle de la variation correspondante entre les groupes comparés. Si par exemple le* rho *de deux groupes comparés est de 0.8, 80 pour cent de leur variation peuvent être attribués à la variation entre eux et 20 pour cent à leur variation interne. Du fait que le réseau s'intéresse aux résultats scolaires, son utilisation du* rho *porte sur les différences entre groupes d'élèves, classes, écoles et collectivités.*

Par exemple, un complexe tel qu'une école contient diverses variables qui pourraient contribuer aux notes des élèves. Certaines, telles que le programme d'études de l'école, les bâtiments, les équipements et les fournitures, relèvent de différences entre écoles et pourraient sans doute avoir une influence non négligeable sur les résultats scolaires si l'analyse faisait apparaître un rho *important. Ces facteurs, associés aux différences internes à l'école, telles que les regroupements des élèves de même force, correspondraient plus vraisemblablement aux résultats scolaires si la valeur du* rho *était faible. Dans ce cas, la politique adoptée par chaque pays participant à l'analyse en matière de regroupement des élèves selon les aptitudes pourrait jouer un rôle dans le niveau de réussite scolaire. C'est ainsi que l'application du* rho *permet au chercheur de tirer de groupes aussi complexes que le sont les écoles les variables qui sont susceptibles d'être étroitement associées à la réussite scolaire et celles dont la corrélation semble plus faible.*

Les exemples de l'utilisation du rho *cités dans ce chapitre comprennent deux scénarios hypothétiques qui font des différences de niveau d'instruction scolaire et de résultats scolaires des variables qui démontrent les nombreuses applications possibles du* rho *à la recherche. Des représentations graphiques du* rho *sont comprises pour aider le lecteur à visualiser les incidences des résultats produits par cette technique.*

Dans le dernier exemple, on applique cette technique aux notes obtenues par les élèves des pays de l'OCDE dans l'étude sur la maîtrise de la lecture (Reading Literacy Study) *de l'International Association for the Evaluation of Educational Achievement (IEA). Avec les graphiques du* rho *pour la Suède et les Pays-Bas, cet exemple montre que dans les pays où le* rho *est élevé, l'école fréquentée par les élèves a une influence plus forte sur leur maîtrise de la lecture que dans les pays ayant un* rho *faible. Ce résultat démontre que le* rho *est un outil statistique important pour la production de comparaisons internationales de la réussite scolaire.*

*

*   *

1. Introduction

Within any one age or grade group, there are differences among pupils. Those differences have to do with various factors, including: the personal characteristics of students; the sorts of homes from which students come; the areas in which students live; the types of schools students attend; the teachers students have; the curriculum to which students are exposed; and student levels of achievement in given subject areas.

Rho, or the intra-class coefficient, is a measure of the homogeneity of pupils within clusters, or, to put it another way, how much of the variation (differences) on any one attribute is between pupils within schools and how much of the variation is between schools (in other words, *between clusters and within clusters*). A high value of *rho* means that there is wide variation between schools and a low value means that there is little variation between schools, relative to the variation within schools. Thus, a value of 0.50 means that 50 per cent of the variation is between schools and 50 per cent is between pupils within schools. A value of 0.10 means that 10 per cent of the variation is between schools and 90 per cent of the variation is between pupils within schools.

2. Types of Difference

Differences among Communities

In some countries, social policy has sought to make communities similar in terms of access to health facilities, public libraries, sports centres, and so on. Indeed, in some countries there is a policy of redistributing wealth in order to minimise the differences between communities or regions. Some of the Nordic countries are good examples of this. However, in other countries, there are considerable differences among communities and among people within communities. There are large differences, too, between rural and urban areas, and between ordinary rural areas and isolated rural areas.

Differences between Schools

Between schools, there are two major categories of differences, as described in the following paragraphs.

Buildings, Equipment and Supplies

Some systems of education have a deliberate policy of having basic norms apply to every school in terms of the condition of school buildings, the provision of equipment (such as blackboards, cupboards, shelving, overhead projectors, and the like), and of supplies (such as textbooks, pencils, ball-point pens, classroom libraries, school libraries, and so on); and, there is a strict policy of ensuring that norms are adhered to. The result is that there is virtually no difference between schools in terms of provision. In other systems of education, either there are no norms, or norms are not observed, either because of negligence or because of variations in the levels of public and private spending on education. In those systems, there can be fairly large differences between schools.

Structure of Schooling and Curricula

Some systems have instituted comprehensive schools up to the end of compulsory schooling (say, from grade 1 to grade 9), whereby all students are exposed to a similar curriculum, albeit allowing for differences in interests and abilities, up to the end of grade 6 or 7. About 80 to 90 per cent of the curriculum will continue to be the same for all, with some minor specialisation allowed, even for the last two grades. In other systems, there may be three or four different types of secondary schooling, whereby the "best" *x* per cent go to the "best" school, and so on. In this latter kind of system, there is often a different curriculum, with the "lowest" type of school having the least demanding curriculum. It is also often the case that the teachers at the "best" type of school have to have more preservice training than the teachers at the "lower" type of school.

Differences within Schools

In some schools, homogeneous ability grouping (whether it be for all subjects together or for separate subjects) is not allowed until the age of 13 or 14. In other countries, homogeneous ability groups are formed at some point in the primary school. These homogeneous groups are often called classes, hence there can be differences between classes within schools in terms of provision, teachers, and, often, the level of achievement.

3.   Two Hypothetical Examples

As can be seen from the above, for any one characteristic of a student, class, school, or community, there may be differences among students, classes, schools, or communities. Take two examples: parental education and achievement.

Parental Education

Assume that the measure of parental education is:
- not completed lower secondary education = 1;
- completed lower secondary education   = 2;
- completed upper secondary education   = 3;
- completed some tertiary education   = 4.

If, in an educational survey, every child were to answer the question, say, about his or her father's education, then each child would have a value ranging from 1 to 4. Let us assume that the mean and standard deviation for all pupils are: Mean = 2.5 and Standard Deviation = 0.95. However, pupils are clustered into classes, and classes are clustered into schools, and schools are clustered into communities.

If the mean for every class is calculated, the resulting means might range from 1.5 to 3.5. In other words, some classes have children whose fathers nearly all have a very low level of education (1.5) and some classes contain children with fathers with a high level of education (3.5). If the means of all class means are calculated, this will be the same as for the mean of all children given (about 2.5), but the standard deviation will be smaller (say, 0.4). The reason why the standard deviation is not as high as for all children is that children are clustered into classes and the range of class means will not be as great as for all children.

In most schools there are several classes at a particular grade level. It is therefore possible to calculate the mean fathers' educational level for all children in the grade in the school. Each school in the survey is likely to have a different mean level for fathers' education. Again, the mean of all schools will be the same as the mean of all classes and the mean of all pupils, but the standard deviation will be smaller for schools than for classes, because some of the variation occurs between classes within schools. As has been explained above, the clustering into classes and the clustering of pupils and classes into schools will be different according to the education policy of the individual system.

Differences in Achievement

The second example is the same as the first, but for a different measure. Assume that a reading test has been administered and that the test has 100 items. Table 4.1 sets out the reading scores for ten pupils in each of the two classes in each of three schools.

In Figure 4.1, the reading scores for each student in each class are given. First, the mean score and standard deviation for each class are presented. Each of the class means is different and the standard deviations are also different. The standard deviation for Class 2 in School 3 is low and the standard deviation for Class 1 in School 2 is high, which reflects the spread of scores in each class. (It should be noted that in the example given in Table 4.1 the data are assumed to contain the whole population, and not a sample. Hence, n and not n − 1 has been used as the denominator for the calculation of the standard deviation.)

Finally, the mean and standard deviation for all pupils are given, as well as the mean for all classes, and then for all schools. It can be seen that the mean is 45.73, and the standard deviation is 28.10. It follows that the mean of all classes and of all schools is also 45.73. However, the standard deviation of all classes is 26.11; and between the three schools it is 25.19. In each case in Table 4.1, the variance of scores is also presented. The variance is the same as the standard deviation squared. However, as will be seen at the end of this chapter, it is the variances that are used in the calculation of the *rho*, and hence they have been presented.

Table/Tableau 4.1.

Hypothetical example of reading scores of pupils, classes and schools

Résultats en lecture des élèves, des classes et des établissements – exemple hypothétique

Pupil	School 1		School 2		School 3	
	Class 1	Class 2	Class 1	Class 2	Class 1	Class 2
1	36.00	8.00	45.00	60.00	90.00	96.00
2	38.00	6.00	35.00	64.00	70.00	98.00
3	17.00	10.00	55.00	66.00	80.00	82.00
4	15.00	14.00	25.00	56.00	78.00	78.00
5	20.00	17.00	10.00	50.00	84.00	84.00
6	25.00	21.00	30.00	52.00	66.00	90.00
7	8.00	19.00	40.00	48.00	70.00	70.00
8	12.00	4.00	20.00	32.00	64.00	76.00
9	10.00	26.00	10.00	54.00	62.00	80.00
10	6.00	24.00	50.00	42.00	60.00	86.00
Class Mean	18.70	14.90	32.00	52.40	72.40	84.00
Within Class						
a. Standard Deviation	10.61	7.31	15.03	9.71	9.58	8.34
b. Variance	112.61	53.49	226.00	94.24	91.84	69.60
School Mean	16.80		42.20		78.20	
Within School						
a. Standard Deviation	9.31		16.25		10.69	
b. Variance	86.66		264.16		114.36	
Pupils:						
Mean			45.75			
Standard Deviation			28.10			
Variance			789.63			
Class Means:						
Mean			45.73			
Standard Deviation			26.11			
Variance			681.67			
School Means:						
Mean			45.73			
Standard Deviation			25.19			
Variance			634.57			

Using the formula at the end of this chapter, the *rhos* for classes and for schools were calculated. The *rho* for classes was 0.84, which means that for the six classes in Table 4.1, 84 per cent of the variance of scores was between classes and 16 per cent was between pupils within classes. The *rho* for schools was 0.74, showing that 74 per cent of the variation was between schools and 26 per cent between classes within schools. Sometimes researchers undertake statistical analyses to determine which variables or

Figure/*Graphique* 4.1. **Graphical representation of class and school standard deviations**
Représentation graphique de l'écart-type entre les classes et entre les établissements

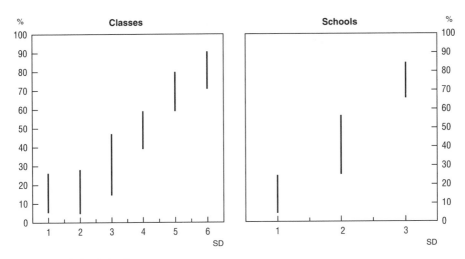

Source: T. Neville Postlethwaite.

indicators account for variance between students, between classes, or between schools; that is the difference in scores between students, or between the mean scores of all classes, or the mean scores of all schools; or, they may try to account for the differences between students within schools (*i.e.* each student's score as a deviation from their school mean), or differences between classes within schools (*i.e.* each class mean score as a deviation from the school mean score in particular class areas).

4. A Graphical Presentation

Figure 4.2 presents an extreme example that one would never find in practice. The overall variance (all pupils) is given in the middle of the diagram. On the left-hand side there is System A, in which there is no overlap of scores between schools, and all of the variance is between schools. In this case, the *rho* would be 1.00 (100 per cent of the variance is *between* schools). On the right-hand side there is System B, in which all of the variation is within schools, and there is no variation between schools. In this case, the *rho* would be 0.00, because there is zero per cent variation between schools.

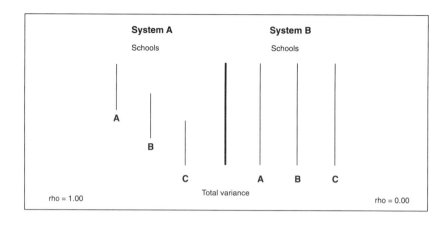

Figure/*Graphique* 4.2. **Graphical representation of an extreme situation**
Représentation graphique d'une situation extrême

Source: T. Neville Postlethwaite.

5. The *rhos* for the OECD Countries

Rhos for the total reading achievement scores for the OECD countries that participated in the IEA Reading Literacy Study are presented in Table 4.2 for the modal 9-year-olds' grade (Population A) and the modal 14-year-olds' grade (Population B).

It can be seen that the *rhos* at Population A level range from 0.05 in Norway to 0.35 in Greece. Six of the 19 systems have *rhos* that are 0.10 or lower, eleven of the systems are in the range 0.11 to 0.20, and only three systems have *rhos* that are higher than 0.20. In other words, at the primary school level, nearly all of the variation is within schools. However, at Population B level, the *rhos* range from 0.03 in Finland to 0.50 in the Netherlands. At the Population B level, thirteen of the systems have *rhos* higher than 0.20, and eight of them have *rhos* higher than 0.30. Clearly, whereas some systems allow for little differentiation between schools, others allow for a great deal.

In countries with large *rhos,* the school a child attends will be highly related to his or her achievement in reading. In countries with very low *rhos,* it really does not matter which school in the country a child attends.

Figures 4.3 and 4.4 present a graphical picture of the results for Sweden and the Netherlands, for Population B, where the *rhos* are 0.08 and 0.50, respectively. In each

Table/Tableau 4.2.

**Estimates of the intra-class coefficients for IEA reading literacy scores
for populations A and B**

*Valeurs estimées des coefficients intra-classes relatifs aux résultats en lecture
dans l'enquête de l'IEA, pour les populations A et B*

	Population A	Population B
Belgium (French Community)	0.16	0.40
Canada (British Columbia)	0.20	0.27
Denmark	0.12	0.09
Finland	0.08	0.03
France	0.14	0.35
Germany (FGDR)	0.15	0.10
Germany (FTFR)	0.13	0.49
Greece	0.35	0.22
Iceland	0.09	0.08
Ireland	0.16	0.48
Italy	0.33	0.28
Netherlands	0.13	0.50
New Zealand	0.19	0.41
Norway	0.05	0.06
Portugal	0.29	0.27
Spain	0.18	0.22
Sweden	0.09	0.08
Switzerland	0.10	0.48
United States	0.19	0.42

case, every third school has been presented in order not to overcrowd the graph. However, it can be seen that in Sweden (Population B) the variance is nearly all within schools, whereas in the Netherlands (Population B) it is 50: 50.

Word of Warning

A word of warning is required. The sampling design of the IEA Reading Literacy Study assumes that schools were drawn with a probability proportional to size, as the first stage of sampling. However, at the second stage of sampling, an intact class was drawn at random within each school that had more than one class at the chosen grade level. In other words, it was not a random sample of all pupils within the modal grade and hence the total within-school variance was not necessarily covered, so that the *rho* might be an overestimate. On the other hand, the size of *rho* will not be far wrong, if pupils within schools are allocated to classes at random.

Figure/*Graphique* 4.3. **Between-school and within-school differences in reading achievement**
Sweden population B
***Résultats en lecture : différences entre établissements d'enseignement et à l'intérieur
d'un même établissement***
Population suédoise B

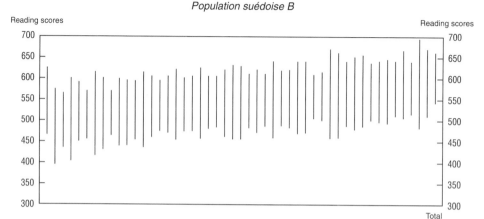

Note: rho = 0.08.
Source: T. Neville Postlethwaite.

Figure/*Graphique* 4.4. **Between-school and within-school differences in reading achievement**
Netherlands population B
***Résultats en lecture : différences entre établissements d'enseignement et à l'intérieur
d'un même établissement***
Population hollandaise B

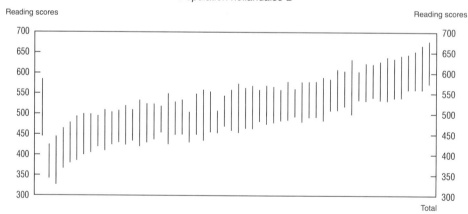

Note: rho = 0.50.
Source: T. Neville Postlethwaite.

Some Formulae

The most commonly used method of calculating *rho* is:

$$Rho = \frac{\dfrac{A-1}{A}V_a - \dfrac{1}{\bar{n}}V_b}{\dfrac{N-1}{N}V(y)}, \qquad [1]$$

where A is the number of schools (or classes), N is the number of students, V(y) is the population variance, n the cluster size, and V_a and V_b are the between and within-cluster variance components, that is:

$$V_a = \frac{1}{A-1}\sum_{a}^{A}(\bar{y}_a - \bar{y})^2 \qquad [2]$$

$$V_b = \frac{1}{A(B-1)}\sum_{a}^{A}\sum_{\beta}^{B}(\bar{y}_{a\beta} - \bar{y}_a)^2 \qquad [3]$$

References

GUILFORD, F.P. and FRUCHTER, B. (1987), *Fundamental Statistics in Psychology and Education,* McGraw-Hill, New York.

KISH, L. (1965), *Survey Sampling,* Wiley, New York.

KISH, L. (1987), *Statistical Design for Research,* Wiley, New York.

Developing an Indicator of Cross-Curricular Competencies
Mise au point d'un indicateur de compétences transdisciplinaires

Introduction

by

Jules Peschar
Department of Sociology,
University of Groningen, the Netherlands

In examining the options for Network A, Member countries felt that subject-related indicators of student achievement, while essential, needed to be complemented by new indicators that would offer a broader perspective on the outcomes of education, not specifically referring to particular subjects or curricula but related to what is needed for adult life. The network agreed to follow this direction in February 1993, at a meeting held in Vilamoura, Portugal. The decision was taken after an extensive discussion of various background papers. A first set of domains was chosen, and for each domain an expert review was commissioned. Secondly, a background paper was written to document whether, and to what extent, the education goals of countries refer to specific subject-related competencies, for example mathematics achievement, or whether such goals tend to refer to broad skills and knowledge required for adult life. On the basis of these documents, the Cross-Curricular Competencies (CCC) project was launched in late 1993.

In Part 2, three papers are included that document the thinking in the CCC domain. In Chapter 5, Uri Peter Trier and Jules Peschar describe the background of the CCC project and the planning of the feasibility study that is under way. This chapter summarises various earlier documents, among them the 1991 discussion paper by Trier and the 1993 background paper on education goals by Peschar. Chapter 6, by Loek Halman, was originally commissioned as an expert paper for the 1993 conference in Vilamoura. The chapter addresses the question whether it is feasible to develop indicators on (the knowledge of) democratic values. This is a difficult area, especially from a comparative point of view. Chapter 7, by Helmut Fend, discusses the possibility of applying measures of self-concept and self-perception for the construction of comparative indicators. Finally, Chapter 8, by Douglas Hodgkinson and Michelle Crawford, describes some of the difficulties that were encountered in developing an instrument designed to measure student performance in the CCC domain.

Introduction

par

Jules Peschar
Département de sociologie,
Université de Groningue, Pays-Bas

Durant l'étude des orientations à donner au Réseau A, les pays Membres ont estimé que des indicateurs de réussite scolaire par disciplines, pour essentiels qu'ils soient, avaient besoin d'être complétés par de nouveaux indicateurs offrant une perspective plus large, qui ne se référeraient pas précisément à des disciplines ou à des programmes particuliers mais concerneraient les éléments nécessaires à la vie des adultes. A la réunion organisée à Vilamoura, au Portugal, en février 1993, le réseau a convenu de suivre cette orientation. Une première série de domaines a été retenue et, pour chacun d'eux, il a été décidé de faire procéder à une étude d'expert. Ensuite, un document de base a été rédigé pour montrer si, et jusqu'à quel point, les objectifs éducatifs des pays faisaient référence à des compétences particulières liées aux disciplines – par exemple les résultats en mathématiques – ou si de tels objectifs se référaient plutôt à des compétences et connaissances générales nécessaires à l'âge adulte. Sur la base de ces documents a été lancé le projet sur les compétences transdisciplinaires (CCC) à la fin de 1993.

Dans la deuxième partie figurent trois articles illustrant les opinions en matière de compétences transdisciplinaires. Au chapitre 5, Uri Peter Trier et Jules Peschar décrivent la genèse du projet CCC et la planification de l'étude de faisabilité actuellement en cours. Ils résument certains documents précédents, dont le rapport de base rédigé par Trier en 1991 et le document d'information sur les objectifs éducatifs rédigé par Peschar en 1993. A l'origine, le chapitre 6, que l'on doit à Loek Halman, était une étude d'expert commandée en vue de la conférence de Vilamoura en 1993. Il s'interroge sur la possibilité de mettre au point des indicateurs concernant les valeurs démocratiques (et leur connaissance). Cette question est délicate, en particulier vue sous l'angle comparatif. Au chapitre 7, Helmut Fend évalue la possibilité d'appliquer des mesures de l'image et de la perception de soi à la construction d'indicateurs comparatifs. Enfin, dans le chapitre 8, Douglas Hodgkinson et Michelle Crawford décrivent quelques-unes des difficultés rencontrées en mettant au point un outil conçu pour évaluer la performance des élèves dans le domaine des compétences transdisciplinaires.

Chapter/Chapitre 5

Cross-Curricular Competencies: Rationale and Strategy for Developing a New Indicator
Les compétences transdisciplinaires : raison d'être et stratégie de mise au point d'un nouvel indicateur

by

Uri Peter Trier
National Research Programme, Bern, Switzerland

and

Jules L. Peschar
Department of Sociology, University of Groningen, the Netherlands

The question of how well schools perform against their own standards is only part of the larger question of what educational indicators should stand for. Firstly, not all that is learned in childhood and youth is learned at school. Secondly, not all that is taught at school is needed in later life. Thirdly, not all that is needed in social life is taught at school. An important aspect is missing, the crucial question being: What do young men and women at the end of school require in order to be able to play a constructive role in the society, and according to what criteria? Are the basic knowledge and skills – we call them parts of a "survival kit" – which are essential to live an individually worthwhile and socially valuable life provided through education? The Cross-Curricular Competencies (CCC) project aims to develop a complex indicator for this vast domain. The project focuses on aspects such as problem-solving and critical thinking; communication skills; political, democratic, economic and social values; self-perception and self-confidence. The aim is to develop a "basket" of measures that can be tapped using existing instruments. These instruments should reflect challenges in the "real life" situations of young people. This ambitious project is intended to eventually yield an indicator that can show the proportion of a determined age group which is above a certain criterion that is considered to represent a minimum level of competencies. Six countries (Austria, Belgium, Canada, Italy, Switzerland and the United States) have agreed to undertake a joint pilot study to explore the feasibility of this new achievement indicator. This chapter discusses the background of this initiative, as well as a strategy for developing the new indicator.

*

*   *

Note de synthèse

De caractère plus général que les compétences qui font simplement partie du programme d'études, les compétences transdisciplinaires (Cross-Curricular Competencies ou CCC) sont enseignées dans l'optique d'un apprentissage qui s'étend sur toute la vie, et doivent être utiles aux élèves au fil des années. La mise au point d'indicateurs des compétences transdisciplinaires permettrait d'étendre le débat sur l'enseignement de façon à couvrir des objectifs et des thèmes nouveaux, et notamment l'impact de ces objectifs et de ces thèmes sur les gains du travail et l'adéquation de l'enseignement à la vie en société dans son ensemble. Le principal effort de recherche en matière de compétences transdisciplinaires consiste à définir les domaines pertinents et à élaborer des indicateurs des connaissances théoriques et pratiques qui permettent à chacun de bien fonctionner au sein de la société. On cherche à mesurer le niveau des compétences transdisciplinaires à un stade plus tardif, au moment du passage de l'enseignement secondaire au supérieur, et de l'école au travail. La justification d'une recherche nouvelle sur les compétences transdisciplinaires est l'insuffisance de l'information fournie par les études internationales actuelles sur les mesures de la réussite scolaire – des études qui portent principalement sur certains domaines et sujets du programme, et ne concernent les résultats que de certains élèves d'âge scolaire.

Le projet pilote sur les compétences transdisciplinaires a pour objet d'établir un ensemble d'indicateurs concis, afin de voir dans quelle mesure l'enseignement contribue à l'acquisition des compétences transdisciplinaires. Il est possible de faire des comparaisons valables entre pays dans le domaine des compétences transdisciplinaires si les finalités de leur enseignement comprennent aussi les objectifs propres aux compétences transdisciplinaires. Il ressort d'un inventaire récent des objectifs de l'enseignement dans les pays de l'OCDE qu'ils comportent une dimension de compétences transdisciplinaires assez forte pour que des comparaisons valables puissent être effectuées. L'inventaire a aussi montré que la mise en œuvre des objectifs propres aux compétences transdisciplinaires varient considérablement entre pays et qu'il n'existe pas de moyen normalisé de vérifier que ces compétences ont bien été acquises par les élèves.

Une fois établie la possibilité de faire des comparaisons valables entre pays, la recherche sur les compétences transdisciplinaires a été divisée en trois étapes. Au cours de la première étape, dite étape préliminaire, il s'agit avant tout de définir l'ampleur des problèmes de recherche et des questions qui s'y rattachent. La deuxième étape, ou étape de faisabilité, qui comprend une étude pilote, a pour objectif principal de mener à bien un tour d'horizon complet de la documentation spécialisée et de choisir les outils de recherche. Enfin, l'étude principale, qui n'est pas encore mise en place, pourrait comprendre deux activités distinctes: la première serait une étude des pays de l'OCDE, destinée à déterminer l'équivalence et l'exactitude des outils mis au point; la seconde serait une enquête menée dans ces pays pour obtenir les données nécessaires à l'élaboration des indicateurs de compétences transdisciplinaires.

Le développement ultérieur des indicateurs de compétences transdisciplinaires dépend des résultats de l'étude pilote et peut nécessiter un long travail. Cependant, comme l'on peut s'attendre à ce que les objectifs de l'enseignement fassent l'objet de réformes portant sur l'adéquation sociale de l'enseignement, il se pourrait que les indicateurs de compétences transdisciplinaires revêtent un intérêt nouveau pour les décideurs.

*

*　　*

1. Background

One of the main activities in the project of International Indicators of Education Systems (INES) is the establishment of standards and criteria to compare educational output between OECD countries and eventually to compare these as developments over time. The choice of available empirical indicators for educational output is rather restricted, as the first two versions of *Education at a Glance* (1992, 1993) have shown. There may be various reasons for the rather restricted number of outcome characteristics in these publications. One reason may be that there are not many large-scale data bases available, on the basis of which indicators can be constructed and compared. Another reason may be that new data collection at an international level will be very costly, so that the strategy is to rely on existing data. This, however, has the disadvantage that these data have not been collected for indicator purposes, *per se.*

In the international comparisons that focus on outcome measures, such as those of the OECD, three aspects are relevant. Firstly, available indicators could mainly be found in the domain of school-related learning outcomes, especially in mathematics, science or reading comprehension. These domains are considered the least difficult to measure and compare, but large surveys need to be conducted in order to establish reliable indicators. The OECD itself has so far not sought to raise the resources needed for conducting such large surveys. Instead, the INES project has relied on international surveys carried out by the International Association for the Evaluation of Educational Achievement (IEA) and the International Assessment of Educational Progress (IAEP). Secondly, it is unfortunate that the IEA and IAEP studies have mainly been carried out for certain age groups, mostly at an early stage in the educational career. Presently, findings for the 13- and 14-year-old students have been applied for indicator construction, an age which reflects only partially the outcomes of secondary education. Thirdly, the international assessments have been mainly, if not only, focused on particular subjects taught at school, *e.g.* mathematics, science or reading. No effort has yet been undertaken to measure skills that are developed in several subjects, or are only formulated as implicit goals for a certain subject. Such cross-curricular competencies are most relevant, however, as they indicate the achievement of a student in a broader sense, namely whether he or she is "prepared for real life"(similar arguments are mentioned by Halpern, 1992, and Perkins *et al.*, 1993).

Measuring "preparedness" is a daunting task. First of all, the available comparative evidence on the non-cognitive aspects of school outcomes is extremely limited. Secondly, even within countries, there are only a few reviews that give attention to non-cognitive aspects.[1] An interesting overview of Japanese cognitive and non-cognitive issues is given by Burstein and Hawkins (1992). The non-cognitive aspects reviewed by these authors are: self-concept; locus of control and attributions; school and subject matter interests; educational expectations; certain attitudes; and creativity. The conclusion is that the picture of non-cognitive outcomes is puzzling. For comparative research the implication is that information on cultural context cannot be excluded.

Eckstein and Noah (1993) reviewed the secondary education examination systems in eight countries. It appears that there is wide variety in these examination systems. Some have standardised tests, while other countries have examinations which take the form of essays. Some systems have a school-based examination, while in other systems a standard national examination is in place. Most of the examinations are *in a particular subject*. It appears that in Sweden there has been a practice of cross-curricular testing (see Eckstein and Noah, 1993, pp. 119, 120, 257). One week before the examinations are to take place, the candidates received a booklet with various information (timetables, poems, and so on). The examination referred directly to the information given.

2. Policy Issues and Relevance of Cross-Curricular Competencies (CCC)

The development of CCC indicators is relevant for at least three reasons. Firstly, present discussions on the quality of education can be extended to important goals of education that have not yet been measured. Secondly, discussions on the impact of education on labour market variables and earnings are usually restricted by the fact that only subject-bound measures are available. Finally, the relevance of formal education for social life is subject to discussion in many countries, among which are Canada and the United States. For example, the national education goals in the United States emphasise competencies that are not related to one specific subject. Similar developments may be seen elsewhere, for example in Austria and Norway.

This chapter focuses on the development of international indicators of cross-curricular competencies. It builds on Trier (1991), who asked: "What do young adults who complete their formal education need in terms of skills so as to be able to play a constructive role as a citizen in society?" In previous discussions in Network A, broad support was found to elaborate indicators that could help to answer this question. The elements of the "survival kit" are rarely to be found in *one specific* subject, but may be seen as CCCs. The main *research effort,* therefore, is to identify relevant areas and to develop indicators for such knowledge and skills as are needed to be able to function in society.[2]

On the basis of the preceding, several questions may be asked:

- Are CCCs an integral part of the education goals of OECD countries?
- If CCCs are identified, is there enough commonality to allow comparisons across countries? Which dimensions are relevant?
- Are instruments for the measurement of these dimensions available?

3.   Cross-Curricular Practices in OECD Countries

We focus first on the question to what degree CCC goals are defined or formulated as education goals.[3] If CCC measures are to be used for comparative purposes, one must be sure that they are relevant for the countries under study. It makes no sense to compare countries on criteria that might not be accepted as goals. A similar point is made by Wyatt (1992, point 5a).

In order to be able to compare aspects of countries' education goals, one needs to know at what level such goals are effectively formulated. For this reason an inventory study was undertaken (Peschar, 1993). Table 5.1 gives an overview of the main findings.

The results show a large variation in the levels at which education goals are formulated. While some countries seem to set curriculum guidelines at the central level, others apparently leave the formulation of goals to lower levels in the system. The question is to what degree this will be reflected in outcomes – both cognitive and non-cognitive – at the different levels of the education system. If CCC-related goals feature among the goals specified for the education system, then logic suggests that valid CCC comparisons may be made, provided that appropriate instruments and assessment procedures can be developed.

The question therefore is whether the education goals which countries have formulated include CCC goals. The questions included in the survey refer mainly to non-cognitive aspects, but the information given is clear enough to indicate that CCC goals are indeed distinguished in all the countries surveyed. Some focus on attitudes, while others support particular skills. It appears that the scope of education goals is – with no exception – much wider than the domain suggested by the curricula of schools. This finding lends some support for the relevance of CCC-indicators. There appears, however, to be wide variety in practice. Whereas one country leaves the implementation of higher-order goals to the school or community, another country's central authorities draw up a detailed curriculum that includes statements of the higher-order goals to be achieved.

The next question is whether the countries that have CCC-related goals also employ procedures to assess and evaluate their attainment. Some countries indeed have a standardised (or standardisable) practice of testing. Other countries evaluate the progress through

Table/Tableau 5.1.

Level of formulation of education goals

Question 1: Where are education goals formulated?

Niveaux auxquels sont définis les objectifs en matière d'enseignement

Question 1 : A quels niveaux les objectifs en matière d'enseignement sont-ils définis?

	National Level	State Canton Land Province	District	Local Community	School Level
Austria	X	X			
Belgium	X				
British Columbia		X			
Denmark	X				
Finland	X			X	
France	X				
Germany	(X)				
Ireland	X				
Italy	X				
Netherlands	X				X
New Zealand	X			X	X
Norway	X			X	X
Spain	X				
Sweden	X				
Switzerland		X			
United States	X	X	X	X	X

teacher ratings at the school level. In the area of CCC, however, no systematic test programme is in use in any country surveyed.

Although not always framed in that sense, the curricula of most countries appear to emphasise the importance of competencies that arch over those associated with specific subjects. The above-mentioned inventory shows that all OECD countries surveyed distinguish CCC. It also appears that there are no standardised ways of assessing whether these competencies are acquired by students. The necessity and usefulness of an approach which uses CCC indicators may have been demonstrated above; but the inventory has not led to the discovery of relevant assessment practices that can be applied internationally.

4. Towards CCC Indicators

Cross-Curricular Competencies include knowledge and skills needed to live an individually worthwhile and socially valuable life in society. There are many possible domains that could be considered relevant for private life and functioning in society. In principle, several questions must be answered before deciding which areas should receive priority. These questions include:

• Which CCCs can be distinguished?

- Which are currently acceptable?
- Which are measurable?
- Which can be considered good indicators?

In identifying the possible CCC areas to be assessed, a modest approach is the most appropriate. It would be over-ambitious to define the area of CCC too broadly. A practical approach was therefore chosen by the network. A preliminary selection of *possible areas* was made by a CCC Steering Committee in September 1992, at a meeting in Zurich, Switzerland, and the following five areas were seen as *first targets* for indicator development:

- basic knowledge of the social, political and economic system;
- problem-solving capacity;
- communication skills;
- self-perception; and
- (knowledge of) democratic values.

For each of the five initial domains, expert reviews were commissioned, on the basis of which the feasibility of developing indicators was judged. In addition, it will be clear that the selected domains do not represent five independent dimensions. One might prefer to specify a knowledge dimension (areas 1 and 5, touching on "civics"), a skills dimension (areas 2 and 3, through all curriculum areas) and an attitudes dimension (area 4, mostly self-concept and self-confidence).

5. Aims and Purposes of the CCC Project

The CCC pilot project extends the basic INES model, which follows the linear input-process-output sequence of variables that is presented in *Education at a Glance*. The currently available indicators for education outcomes concentrate on two domains: grades/diplomas and achievement measures.[4] In contrast, the pilot project aims at measuring CCC for students at the transition between secondary and tertiary education, and between school and the workplace. Two modalities are in principle possible:

- *Option 1* is to measure CCC at the end of compulsory education. This would facilitate the design of appropriate samples, although drop-out and other selection mechanisms could still distort the picture.
- *Option 2* is the assessment of CCC at the age of 18.

The choice between *Option 1* and *Option 2* depends first and foremost on survey objectives. Resources are another factor that must be considered. For CCC pilot survey, *Option 1* was selected.

As part of the project, a set of indicators that represent CCCs will be developed. In the first stage, the focus is on areas that appear to be the most feasible in *the short term*. In the longer run, indicators for all five areas distinguished should be developed. However, for the moment the CCC project does not aim for extensive coverage of all possible dimensions of CCC, but mainly seeks to establish a relatively concise set of broad indicators. A most challenging question is the degree to which the school has contributed to the CCC acquired by the students at the end of compulsory education. This issue can be tested empirically when the indicators are available.[5]

There may be some discussion whether the indicators should be criterion-referenced or norm-referenced. Setting a minimum level of competencies which need to be acquired possibly relates most nearly to educational or social practice, but may prove difficult in a comparative perspective. A comparison of distributions of CCC measures may serve the intended goals as well. A decision on this point may, however, be delayed until the testing stage has been completed.

6. A Work Plan

The process of developing CCC indicators can be divided into three stages. The preliminary stage covers the initial reviews and feasibility judgements: the main target is the identification of problems and issues. In the next stage, that of a feasibility or pilot study, various tasks must be performed: comprehensive reviews of literature and national practices, preliminary selection of instruments, and a feasibility study in several countries with a small sample. The stage of the main study, which is still to be planned, might involve two separate activities. The first is a national study in the participating OECD countries to establish the equivalence and validity of the instruments developed. This stage must be rounded off with an evaluation of the results for indicator purposes. The next step will be to carry out national surveys that will provide the information for constructing the indicators for all countries. The different stages are discussed in more details below.

The Preliminary Stage

The preliminary stage has already been concluded. A first step was to identify what knowledge is available [see, for instance, Burstein and Hawkins (1992) for a report on comparisons of CCC-related issues between Japan and the United States]. A review of the relevant literature in each of the five areas was commissioned. In the reviews, the following issues were discussed:

- theoretical and conceptual issues, in particular dimensionality;
- methodological and measurement issues, *e.g.* the choice of instruments and their quality and reliability;
- possibilities for national and international comparisons;
- utility, *e.g.* what possibilities are there for policy actions?
- proposal for further review of the issues identified by the experts; and
- overview and synthesis of the relevant research literature.

The conceptual design of the pilot survey needs to be elaborated during this stage. The following activities are envisaged:

- a review of concepts and measures of civic competencies, democratic values and political/economic knowledge insofar as these have been developed for the IEA surveys;
- a critical assessment of the instruments developed by IEA, and if necessary, modification;
- a study of materials and instruments related to political competencies;
- a study on national practices of inclusion of CCC in curricula;
- a study on problem-solving in everyday life; and
- a symposium where ideas can be discussed and recommendations made for the main stage of the study.

The main goal of the pilot project will be to demonstrate that the chosen approach is possible and leads to relevant results. To this end, the following steps might be envisaged:

- selection of areas for which indicators are to be developed;
- selection of instruments that may possibly be used for indicator construction;
- selection of 4-6 countries, where these instruments will be fielded in a restricted sample of 20-30 schools (N about 700 students per country); and
- planning for field work, data collection, and centralised data analysis.

Presently, six countries have expressed their interest in participating in the feasibility phase of the study: Austria, Belgium (Flemish and French Communities), Canada, Italy, Switzerland and the United States. Both from a geographical viewpoint, and from a language perspective, there is sufficient variety for a feasibility project. Its results should offer a basis for deciding whether it is useful to continue with the CCC initiative.

7. Conclusions and Further Steps

The purpose of this chapter was to review the education goals of OECD countries, to see whether CCC activities are distinguished, and to propose a strategy for developing CCC indicators. Valid comparisons between countries in the CCC domain may be made, if education goals include CCC. It is concluded that the education goals in OECD countries contain enough CCC dimensions to allow meaningful comparisons. This also applies to countries with a federal structure (Canada, Germany, Switzerland and the United States), where national comparisons may be broken down to the level of *Land,* province, canton, or state. The primary question raised in this chapter can therefore be answered affirmatively.

It will take some time before sufficiently valid constructs of the CCC domain can be elaborated and concrete measures proposed. The pilot study in six countries will have to provide evidence to support the idea that it would be useful to continue. Fortunately, a few instruments already exist in some countries. Detailed inspection of such instruments from, say, Canada (British Columbia), France or the United States, may provide relevant suggestions for future work.

Notes

1. China, England and Wales, France, Germany, Japan, Sweden, the Soviet Union (Russia) and the United States.

2. At the meeting of the INES project in Oslo (June 1992), it was decided to work as set out above.

3. These issues were raised before another group within Network A had begun work in this area. Presently, the Goals Orientation and Attainment in Learning Systems (GOALS) project is examining the issue of intended curriculum, realised curriculum, and achieved curriculum and may cover this issue more comprehensively in the future.

4. Labour market position is a third indicator area. But the position in the labour market depends both on education and the state of the economy, and thus reflects more than educational outcomes.

5. This has also been done by Wittebrood (1992) on a limited set of civics indicators for the Netherlands and in the Adult Literacy Studies in Canada (1994) and the United States (1993).

References

Bundesministerium für Unterricht und Kunst (1991/92), *Fachübergreifende Fähigkeiten fur Berufsbildende Schulen. Experimentalfassung: 1. Teil: Komponenten der Problemlosung. 2. Teil: Komponenten der Erziehung,* Wien.

BURSTEIN, L., and HAWKINS, J. (1992), "An analysis of cognitive, noncognitive, and behavioral characteristics of students in Japan", in R. Leestma and H.J. Walberg (eds.), *Japanese Educational Productivity,* The Center for Japanese Studies at the University of Michigan, Ann Arbor, MI, pp. 173-224.

CASSIDY, W., and BOGNAR, C.J. (1991), *More than a Good Idea: Moving from Words to Action in Social Studies,* Ministry of Education, Victoria, Province of British Columbia.

Department of Education (1971), *Primary School Curriculum. Teacher's Handbook Part 1,* Dublin, Ireland.

ECKSTEIN, M.A., and NOAH, H.J. (1993), *Secondary School Examinations. International Perspectives on Policies and Practices,* Yale University Press, London.

FEND, H. (1993), *Self-Concept and Social Competence*, Paper prepared for the meeting of Network A of the OECD INES project on educational indicators, February 1993, Vilamoura, Portugal.

HALPERN, D.F. (1992), *A National Assessment of Critical Thinking Skills in Adults: Taking Steps towards the Goal,* Department of Psychology, California State University, San Bernardino.

Ministère de l'Éducation nationale, Direction des écoles, (n.d.), *Les cycles à l'école primaire,* Paris, France.

Ministry of Education and Ministry Responsible for Multiculturalism and Human Rights (1991), *British Columbia Assessment of Science 1991. Technical Report I: Classical Component. Technical Report II: Student Performance Component. Technical Report 1990: Mathematics Assessment. Technical Report 1989: Social Studies Assessment. Technical Report III: Socio-scientific Issues Component. Technical Report IV: Context for Science Component,* Ministry of Education, Victoria, Province of British Columbia.

Ministry of Education and Science (1990), *Richness of the Uncompleted. Challenges facing Dutch Education,* Report to the OECD, Zoetermeer, the Netherlands.

Ministry of Education, Research and Church Affairs (1990), *Curriculum Guidelines for Compulsory Education in Norway,* Oslo.

PERKINS, D., JAY, E. and TISHMAN, S. (1993), *Assessing Thinking: A Framework for Measuring Critical Thinking and Problem Solving Skills at the College Level*, Harvard University, Cambridge, Mass.

PESCHAR, J.L. (1993) *Educational Goals, the Curriculum and Non-Curriculum Bound Objectives in OECD Countries,* Inventory study prepared for the meeting of Network A of the OECD INES project on educational indicators, February 1993, Vilamoura, Portugal.

TRIER, U.P. (1991), *Non Curriculum Bound Outcomes,* Proposal presented at the Network A meeting of the OECD INES project on educational indicators, Paris.

US Department of Education (1992), *The National Education Goals,* Washington, DC.

WITTEBROOD, K. (1992), *Do Schools Make a Difference? The Impact of Social Class Composition of Schools on Individual Political Involvement,* Department of Political Administration, Nijmegen University.

WYATT, T. (1992), *Thinking about Indicators of Non-Curriculum Bound Outcomes,* National Center for Education Statistics, memorandum, Washington, DC.

Measuring and Comparing Democratic Values[1]
Mesurer et comparer les valeurs démocratiques

by

Loek Halman
Tilburg University, the Netherlands

This brief review will explore the concept of values – in particular, the concept of democratic values. The methodological pitfalls and obstacles to understanding such a theoretical concept will also be discussed. The exact nature of democratic values is not clearly defined, but some suggestions for measuring values that are associated with democracy will be put forward here. Where values are studied and compared across several countries or cultures, questions concerning the legitimacy and various possibilities of comparing values between countries or cultures will be discussed. Also discussed are some of the problems a comparative researcher has to face when dealing with the difficult task of comparing values.

*

* *

Note de synthèse

La définition des valeurs varie d'une discipline à l'autre. Mais en général, on dit que les valeurs sont des motivations ou des orientations profondément ancrées qui déterminent ou expliquent certaines attitudes, normes et opinions, lesquelles, a leur tour, donnent leur sens à l'action humaine. On utilise un modèle de structure latente comme cadre théorique des valeurs, ce qui revient à adopter une hiérarchie de cette conceptuali-

sation des valeurs : les attitudes, les opinions et les normes servent à expliquer les comportements, et les valeurs servent à expliquer les attitudes, les opinions et les normes.

Plusieurs méthodes ont été utilisées pour mesurer les valeurs (notamment les questions directes quant aux valeurs de chacun, l'analyse du contenu des discours, l'observation et les enquêtes). Si l'on admet que les valeurs constituent une orientation solidement enracinée, un indicateur portant sur un seul élément ne suffit pas à cerner le caractère stable de ce concept. Il est nécessaire de disposer d'indicateurs multiples qui mesurent une large gamme de comportements.

Le concept plus spécifique des valeurs démocratiques n'est pas clairement défini, même s'il a été proposé de faire de la participation politique la caractéristique qui définit ces valeurs. Par ailleurs, on n'a pas tenté de mesurer les valeurs démocratiques, bien que deux grands projets menés aux Pays-Bas et ailleurs mesurent des concepts proches (c'est-à-dire le matérialisme et le_ post-matérialisme). Ces projets sont intitulés «Développement social et culturel aux Pays-Bas» (SOCON) et «Étude européenne des valeurs» (EVS). L'EVS a pour particularité de procéder à l'évaluation empirique des valeurs dans des domaines divers en utilisant la recherche par enquêtes ; des enquêtes ont été conduites dans plus de vingt pays.

Les études de ce type donnent des indications quant aux moyens permettant d'élaborer des indicateurs des valeurs démocratiques. Au stade théorique, il faut utiliser des concepts transnationaux, ce qui risque d'être difficile car nombre de concepts sont interprétés en fonction d'une culture donnée. Au stade de la mise en œuvre, les mesures doivent être comparables, mais pas nécessairement identiques, entre pays. Il faudra en outre tenir compte de l'existence possible de différences culturelles entre les modes de réponse. Au moment de la collecte des données, il sera peut-être nécessaire d'évaluer la fiabilité d'un entretien selon ce que l'on sait de l'aptitude des personnes interrogées à donner des réponses inexactes. Au stade de l'analyse, le problème principal est celui de la comparabilité des résultats. Il faut au minimum que les mêmes variables manifestes soient liées aux mêmes variables latentes, même s'il n'est pas nécessaire de disposer de mesures identiques (telles que des traductions mot à mot).

Bien que l'on n'ait pas tenté de mesurer les valeurs démocratiques, de nombreux éléments qui s'y rapportent sont connus et ont été étudiés. Quelques études ont mesuré diverses valeurs, dont certaines peuvent être considérées comme démocratiques et deux études ont porté sur des concepts liés aux valeurs démocratiques. Les mesures existantes pourraient d'ailleurs servir à guider l'étude directe des valeurs démocratiques.

*

* *

1. Values

The sociological and psychological literature concerning values reveals a jungle of terminology and a definition of values that varies throughout disparate disciplines. In moral philosophy or aesthetics, for instance, the concept of value is given a normative meaning (*i.e.* values are criteria by which to discriminate between good and evil, between beauty and ugliness, between right and wrong). Such a normative connotation is also prevalent in social, political, and educational circles (*i.e.* one hears talk of a decline in values, a crisis of values, or an education in values).

In the many sociological and psychological efforts to define values, it is almost universally accepted to refer to the study by Lautmann (1971), who propounded no fewer than 180 different value definitions. To a large extent, Lautmann's definitions demonstrate that conceptual confusion is grounded in the very nature of values. One obvious problem in social research is that values can only be postulated or inferred because they are not directly visible or measurable. As a consequence, values are more or less *open concepts*. They are both conceptual and theoretical, and hardly based on empirical evidence, which in turn yields a speculative theoretical approach that causes much confusion (Brandsma, 1977, p. 62).

In general, however, values are defined as deeply rooted motivations or orientations guiding or explaining human action. Holding a specific value means having a disposition or a propensity to act in a particular way. The same, though, can be said of attitudes, opinions, norms, and so on, which are also theoretical notions (Kluckhohn, 1959; Friedrichs, 1968; Williams, 1968; Rokeach, 1973; Scholl-Schaaf, 1975; Kmieciak, 1976). One might, therefore, raise the question whether it makes any sense at all to distinguish between values and others of these theoretical concepts. The main argument in answer to such a question is that attitudes, norms, and so forth refer to a more restricted complex of objects and behavioural situations than do values (Reich and Adcock, 1976, p. 20). Common to the different value theories seems to be the notion that values are somehow more basic, more fundamental, and more *existential* than all similar concepts.

In structuring a value-based theoretical argument, one assumes a more or less hierarchical structure in which values are viewed as *dispositions* underlying other theoretical notions (*i.e.* attitudes, norms, and so on). "A value is seen to be a disposition of a person just like an attitude, but more basic than an attitude, often underlying it" (Rokeach, 1968, p. 124). Thus, regularities of behaviour may be explained by attitudes, and a complex of attitudes may be explained by values. Values, therefore, are to be seen as deeply rooted motivations or orientations guiding or explaining certain attitudes, norms, and opinions, which, in turn, direct human action. Following Ajzen and Fishbein (1980, p. 88), one can argue that the number of children in a family, the use of birth control, a visit to a family planning clinic, and the signing of a petition on legalised abortion are results of one's attitude towards family planning. In turn, this and other attitudes may be explained by the underlying values one holds with respect to sexuality, marriage, and family.

Theoretically, two different steps may be distinguished in explaining such human behaviour. Firstly, different attitudes may be postulated to explain several behavioural acts. For instance, one can assume a particular attitude to explain behaviour regarding euthanasia, another attitude to explain pre-marital or extra-marital behaviour, and yet another attitude towards, say, homosexuality. Taken one step further, the argument can be used to postulate theoretically that all attitudes are guided by a more general underlying

Figure/*Graphique* 6.1. **Hypothesised relationship between values and behaviour**
Lien hypothétique entre les valeurs et les comportements

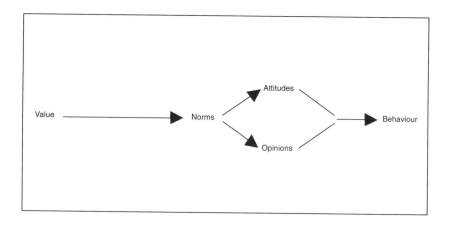

Source: Loek Halman.

disposition with a much wider scope; and that such an underlying disposition is, in fact, a *value* (see Figure 6.1).

Unfortunately, a firmly based, elaborate theory on values and related concepts rarely exists in the social sciences and, as a consequence, there is a lack of criteria to distinguish between values and attitudes. Similarly, it is difficult to distinguish between values and other related theoretical concepts, such as norms and opinions. Although such concepts are not directly observable, in general, values may be regarded as basic, more deeply rooted, and less specific than attitudes, norms, and opinions. To state this concept simply, values lie behind and appear within attitudes, norms, and opinions.

2. Measuring Values

The theoretical and conceptual nature of values makes empirical assessment difficult. As is true of other theoretical concepts, values are not easily reduced to elements specified in terms of indicators and measures. "Yet if social sciences are to exploit the explanatory potential of large-scale survey research, using representative sampling and quantitative techniques (...) this is a necessary step along the road. Theoretical terms have to be translated into research instruments" (Bulmer, 1984, p. 44); and several approaches to do just that have been attempted.

McLaughlin's (1965) rather naive approach is simply to ask people what their values are. Another simple approach is to distill values from what people say they want or need (see van Deth, 1984, p. 85). Such approaches are far too simple, for people may not be aware of the values they adhere to, or be able to express clearly why they behave as they do. Furthermore, asking people to express their values in such a direct way is largely meaningless because "a person might not be willing or able to tell us about them, or he might be highly selective in what he chooses to tell us" (Rokeach, 1973, pp. 26-27). Given the inaccuracy of direct approaches, values can be investigated only indirectly.

Indirectly, values can be traced in documents (*i.e.* articles, letters, and speeches) by applying a standard content analysis, such as that used by White (1951), Rokeach (1968), Becker and Nauta (1983), Klingemann (1984), and Segers (1988). Values also can be investigated by observing actual behaviour or by asking complex and revealing questions. According to Kluckhohn, any indirect measure of values implies a careful analysis of selections made in situations of *choice* (Kluckhohn, 1959, p. 408).

Indirect approaches have advantages and disadvantages. If the aim of a research project is to discover a variety of values, beliefs, and attitudes reflected by a great number of the population (and to discover whether such values and beliefs constitute patterns or systems), one possible approach is the *survey method.*[2] This chapter will be limited to this approach, and begins by discussing the manner in which values can be measured in survey research. We shall then turn to the problems that must be confronted when dealing with large numbers of people.

Values as dispositions underlying behaviour can be detected by exploring the basic principles underlying a wide variety of behaviours; and dispositions can only be traced to values if the answers to several questions are found to refer to the same disposition. In a questionnaire, for example, if someone says that it is important to have fun, to enjoy life, to do what you want to do, to experience new sensations, one may be safe in denoting *hedonism* as a basic, underlying feature of that person's discourse (Felling *et al.*, 1983, p. 68). In other words, the common feature in several behavioural responses (*i.e.* the answers to the questions) can be detected; and this common feature will be called a *value.* In empirical terms, this approach demands a search for latent variables or factors.

Thus, it is clear that a single indicator will not be sufficient to measure a value, because any value is much broader than any single item may indicate. A value, simply put, is indicated by multiple items. This strategy implies, of course, that the content of the theoretical construct of a value is sufficiently determined by the behaviours (the items) included in a questionnaire, which may be arguable. The questions asked in an interview, for example, will be a small collection of all possible questions that could refer to the latent variable that may be found. On the other hand, although this argument may be correct, such an argument could be raised against all statements of a theoretical nature, in all of science. The only conclusion to be drawn is that scientific knowledge is of a hypothetical nature and therefore open to revision.

What should be clear from all of the above is that in order to measure values as reliably as possible, one has to use several indicators. Single items for a value are not sufficient. The more indicators and the more aspects covered by those indicators, the more reliable the measure will be.

Figure/*Graphique* 6.2. **A generic latent structure model**
Modèle général de structure latente

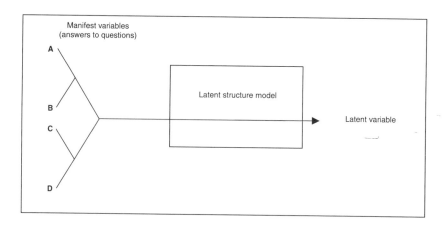

Source: Loek Halman.

Numerous statistical techniques are available and widely used to trace underlying factors, such as factor analysis, latent class analysis and latent trait analysis, Guttman scaling, cluster analysis, multidimensional scaling and so on. All such techniques, well known under the name of *latent structure models,* are used to identify latent variables that can explain the correlations between different behaviours, attitudes, opinions, and so on. See Figure 6.2 for the general model.

3. Democratic Values

Despite the fact that the general idea of values has been discussed, as well as the way in which they can be investigated, the exact meaning of *democratic values* is still unclear. Questions remain: How are values related to democracy? Are democratic values related to personal freedom or individualism?

As far as is known, no one has ever made an attempt to measure democratic values, making referral to earlier research impossible. However, since democratic values are used to define democracy in terms of "rule by the people" (Kaase and Marsh, 1979, p. 28), *participation* must be one of the issues measured in any investigation of democratic values. As Kaase and Marsh wrote, "The notion of political participation is at the centre of the concept of the democratic state''; and any instrument for measuring what Midden-

dorp (1979, p. 188) called a *democratic attitude* would have to consist of four requirements regarding participation. That is, people must have a voice in government, compa-
nies, universities, and schools. However, democracy is not limited to participation in
those areas alone. Democracy also has to do with issues such as freedom and equality,
solidarity, tolerance, and legitimacy (Dogan, 1988).

Interestingly, democratic values appear typical of advanced and wealthy Western
cultures, particularly after the American Revolution, and seem, too, to be characteristic of
modern welfare states. Dogan, for instance, observes that "the list of the thirty richest
countries in the world overlaps almost exactly with the list of the thirty pluralist democracies" (Dogan, 1988, p. 11). His conclusion is that: "Historically, democracy has grown
on capitalist soil".

In less advanced, non-welfare states, people seem more concerned with individual,
short-term interests than with the collective, long-term and negative side-effects caused
by promoting such interests. Democratic values are favoured, then, by people who do not
have to focus on their very existence in order to survive. The modern welfare state, for
example, provides people with certain social securities that allow room for fulfilling
needs that transcend the need for material well-being (Inglehart, 1977; 1990). In such
welfare states, people have become increasingly concerned about what is often called
quality of life, or, to use Inglehart's expression, the modern welfare state has shifted from
materialist to postmaterialist value preferences.

It is, then, the modern and democratic welfare state that must serve as a model for
the study of democratic values. Personal happiness, individual freedom, and equality
have a place in welfare state governmental decisions, as well as in individual participation, solidarity, and anti-authoritarianism.[3]

There have been several efforts to arrive at measurements for attitudes and values
regarding such topics, although these attempts have not always been guided by the idea of
measuring *democratic* values. For instance, measurement of the well-known materialist-
postmaterialist concept contains indicators that refer to democratic values. However,
indicators not related to democracy are also present.[4] This measurement of materialism
and postmaterialism is often used, and was part of two large-scale projects in the
Netherlands and abroad: Social and Cultural Development in the Netherlands (SOCON)
and the European Values Study (EVS).[5] SOCON 1990 also contained an extended
version of the measurement of three basic issues: materialism, libertarianism, and authoritarianism (Eisinga *et al.,* 1992). (Efforts to measure authoritarianism were undertaken
earlier by Hagendoorn and Janssen, 1983, and Eisinga and Scheepers, 1989, who
developed *authoritarianism scales.*)

Various instruments have also been developed to measure political participation.
Usually, three different kinds of participation are distinguished: *electoral, conventional,*
and *unconventional.* For an overview of the indicators of such orientations, one can refer
to the relevant literature (Barnes *et al.,* 1979; Elsinga, 1985; Castemiller, 1988; Halman,
1991). However, the three types of participation are measured in terms of *behaviours*
(*i.e.* taking part in electoral, conventional, or unconventional political activities). To this
list, one must add topics more directly linked to democratic value orientations, such as

interest in politics, political efficacy, accessibility of the political system, and confidence in the effectiveness of politics (Eisinga *et al.*, 1992).

All measurements mentioned here consist of *scales* or *dimensions,* and thus are in line with the reasoning that values cannot be measured by a single indicator, but must be measured by several indicators, tapping as wide a variety of behaviours as possible. Only if several indicators are used, can one be certain that a basic value orientation is being tapped. Whatever one defines as democratic values, scales or dimensions must be developed to measure the relative nature of such values.

4.   Comparing Values

As is clear by now, international comparative research into democratic values is rather scarce. The European Values Study (EVS) is, as far as is known, a unique enterprise in at least two ways. It is a first attempt empirically to assess basic values in a wide variety of domains (*e.g.* religion and morality, society and politics, primary relations and labour), using survey research (Almond and Verba, 1965; Barnes *et al.,* 1979; Inglehart, 1977). EVS is also attempting to survey many countries. In fact, more than twenty countries are participating in the project, which enables comparisons to be made as never before.

However, the sheer number of countries causes some difficulty, as comparative research is a "tricky business" at every stage (*i.e.* conceptualisation, operationalisation, data collection, and data analysis). Briefly, this review will describe the pitfalls in cross-cultural research and explain how to avoid them in the European Values Study.

Firstly, as was concisely and simply stated by Frey: "Cross-cultural research demands cross-cultural concepts" (Frey, 1970, p. 187). Occurrences of phenomena may be country-specific or universal (Warwick and Osherson, 1973; Malpass and Poortinga, 1986). However, even if their occurrence is universal, they may need interpretation that is specific to a country or culture. *Being a liberal,* for example, has one meaning in the United States and another in Western Europe (Klingemann, 1979; Halman, 1991). Other examples of concepts with culture-specific interpretations include "deviant", "unemployed", "unskilled", and "old" (Armer, 1973, p. 55).

The first problem of cross-cultural research, therefore, has already to be solved when translating a standard version of a questionnaire into several languages. A word-for-word translation may not always be the best approach. Instead, it is necessary to define accurately the phenomena that one wishes to study and to determine whether these phenomena appear universally in countries participating in the survey. However, as long as the study is confined to countries characterised as belonging to Western democratic culture, and as long as the design of the questionnaire is the co-operative endeavour of researchers who have intimate knowledge of the societies involved, one might assume this first demand to be sufficiently met.

Subsequently, the operationalisation of the concepts needs to be carefully considered. Comparability demands that valid indicators of a concept be used and that such indicators be comparable between countries. Comparability does not *demand* identical measures, for "phenomenally identical measures do not necessarily provide equivalent measurement, different indicators are often needed to tap equivalent concepts in different settings" (Armer, 1973, p. 65). For instance, indicators of the level of education, political parties, or even religious preferences are "nation-specific". National education systems differ considerably. Therefore, whereas community colleges are part of the higher education system in the United States, many of their curricula are provided in the secondary school system of European countries. Similarly, the concept of university education is not quite the same in all countries. Even apparently similar items such as "income", "degree of urbanisation", and even "age" are not simply comparable (Verba, 1969; 1971). Therefore, one can never give a fool-proof guarantee that the same element, even though it bears the same name, has been measured in all the countries.

A further problem at the stage of operationalisation is to be found in culturally different appraisals of scale points. In some countries, for example, the tendency to choose extreme answer categories may be stronger than in other countries; and differences in answers may be caused by what has been called "response style" or "differential loquacity". A response style is a tendency to choose a response category, such as "yes" or "agree", regardless of item content (Warwick and Osherson, 1973, p. 25). Differential loquacity implies that one population is more eager to respond than others (the Chinese, for example, prefer to remain rather silent).

At the stage of data collection, the question becomes whether an interview yields reliable data. That question may be resolved, however, if interviews are done frequently. Furthermore, there is no clear reason to expect respondents in particular countries to give unreliable answers.

Finally, there are obstacles to cross-cultural comparison at the analytical stage. In part, these obstacles have been discussed previously as differences in response styles, a reluctance to answer sensitive questions reliably, and translation errors. To these must be added the possibility of culturally determined reticence to admit one has no opinion on certain issues (see Brislin *et al.,* 1973, p. 61, and Brislin, 1986, p. 163).

The crucial question to be answered at the data analysis stage is whether the findings are cross-culturally comparable, even if all the problems mentioned so far are avoided or kept under control. Answering this question in relation to values implies reaching the conclusion that the latent constructs (factors, dimensions, or types) are comparable. This is the most important issue, and all too often neglected in many international comparative projects; and such a question is even more difficult to answer in cases of values that have been defined as not directly observable (*i.e.* latent variables). Comparisons between countries are valuable if, and only if, latent variables are in fact comparable.

A minimum condition for comparability of latent variables between countries or cultures is that the same manifest variables be related to the same latent variables. That is, the structure of the latent variables model needs to be equivalent across countries.

If this condition is not met, the values will be too different to compare. In other words, the values will have varying meanings or conflicting interpretations in different countries or cultures. Values will then appear to be *nation-specific,* even though this may not be the case.

If the same manifest variables do refer to the same latent variables, one can put forward the argument that all correlations between latent and manifest variables are exactly the same in all countries; and, if that is the case, one may, following Przeworski and Teune (1973), speak of identical values and conclude that the scores on the latent variables are really comparable.

5.   Conclusion

The fact that a research project on democratic values has never been undertaken implies that many elements of research and analysis have to be invented, although, as is shown above, many elements are known and have been studied.

From what is already known, one may conclude that values may be defined as latent dispositions guiding a wide variety of behaviours. In analytical terms, and for the purposes of research, this implies a search for latent variables that may be detected by observing a variety of behaviours. It will become clear that a single indicator will not be sufficient to describe a value, as one indicator may represent only a single aspect of a value. Conversely, in order to be as close as possible to the very concept of values, as many indicators as possible, concerning as many aspects of a value orientation, must be investigated. Of course, in the practice of social research, this will not be feasible, and the number of indicators will need to be reduced. However, more than one indicator should be selected.

In recent years, attempts have been made to measure a variety of values, and some of those values may be regarded as democratic. The SOCON project (Felling et al., 1983; 1986; 1987; Eisinga et al., 1992), although limited to the Dutch situation, and the EVS project (Halman et al., 1987; Halman, 1991) demonstrate many indicators that may be used to trace a variety of value orientations that can be called democratic.

In the rich literature concerning political value orientations, a variety of available measures refer indirectly to democratic orientations, although it has to be said, once again, that in no study is reference made to democratic values per se. However, investigations such as Civic Culture by Almond and Verba (1965; 1980), Political Action (Barnes et al., 1979; Jennings and van Deth, 1990), and Inglehart's (1977; 1990) efforts to measure materialist and postmaterialist values may be similarly, if indirectly, valuable for the study of democratic values. The advantage of such projects is that comparative measures and more or less reliable scales have been developed that can be used in a variety of ways for international comparative research. In short, there already exists a variety of measures of what may be called democratic values; and these measures could be used to pioneer a direct study of democratic values.

Notes

1. Parts of this chapter have appeared in Ester, P., Halman, L., and de Moor, R. (eds.) (1993), *The Individualizing Society: Value Change in Europe and North America,* Tilburg University Press, Tilburg.

2. The survey also has to be conducted by means of a standardised questionnaire containing pre-coded answer categories. This method has its disadvantages. On the one hand, questions will be answered by those who have never thought about the issue. On the other hand, there will be people who have a more elaborate view than the pre-coded answer categories allow them to express. These restrictions have been noted by all involved.

3. This list is far from exhaustive, and serves mainly as a guide to possible topics of research.

4. Items include "protection of freedom of speech" and "get more say in government decisions". Statements such as these may be used to search for democratic values. Statements like "fighting rising prices" or "more emphasis on order and authority" do not clearly refer to democratic values.

5. SOCON's first study was in 1979, followed by surveys in 1985 and in 1990. The Catholic Universities of Nijmegen and Tilburg co-operated in the project. For more information about this longitudinal large-scale project please refer to Felling *et al.* (1986; 1987), and Eisinga *et al.* (1992). The European Values Study (EVS) is a comparative study of basic values in Europe and North America. A first survey took place in 1981. However, the same questionnaire was used in more than twenty countries all over the world. For more information about the European Values Study of 1981, please refer to Stoetzel (1983), Halman *et al.* (1987), Inglehart (1990), and Halman (1991).

References

AJZEN, I., and FISHBEIN, M. (1980), *Understanding Attitudes and Predicting Social Behavior,* Prentice Hall, Englewood Cliffs, NJ.

ALMOND, G.A., and VERBA, S. (1965), *The Civic Culture: Political Attitudes and Democracy in Five Nations,* Little, Brown and Company, Boston, MA.

ALMOND, G.A., and VERBA, S. (eds.) (1980), *The Civic Culture Revisited,* Little, Brown and Company, Boston, MA.

ARMER, M. (1973), "Methodological problems and possibilities in comparative research", in M. Armer and A.D. Grimshaw (eds.), *Comparative Social Research: Methodological Problems and Strategies,* John Wiley, New York, pp. 49-81.

BARNES, S., KAASE, M., *et al.,* (1979), *Political Action: Mass Participation in Five Western Democracies,* Sage, Beverly Hills, CA.

BECKER, J.W., and NAUTA, A.P.N. (1983), "Enkele gegevens over waarden in Nederland na 1945", in J.W. Becker *et al., Normen en waarden: Verandering of verschuiving?,* Vuga, the Hague, pp. 13-116.

BRANDSMA, P. (1977), *Het waardenpatroon van de Nederlandse bevolking,* Dissertation, Department of Sociology, University of Groningen, the Netherlands.

BRISLIN, R.W. (1986), "The wording and translation of research instruments", in W.J. Lonner and J.W. Berry (eds.), *Field Methods in Cross-Cultural Research,* Sage, Beverly Hills, CA, pp. 137-164.

BRISLIN, R.W., LONNER, W.J., and THORNDIKE, R.M. (1973), *Cross-Cultural Research Methods,* John Wiley, New York.

BULMER, M. (1984), "Facts, concepts, theories and problems", in M. Bulmer (ed.), *Sociological Research Methods,* Transaction Books, New Brunswick, pp. 37-50.

CASTEMILLER, P. (1988), *Participatie in beweging: Ontwikkelingen in politieke participatie in Nederland,* Sociaal Cultureel Planbureau, Rijswijk.

DETH, J.W. van (1984), *Politieke waarden,* CT Press, Amsterdam.

DOGAN, M. (ed.) (1988), *Comparing Pluralist Democracies: Strains on Legitimacy,* West View Press, Boulder, Colorado.

EISINGA, R., and SCHEEPERS, P. (1989), *Etnocentrisme in Nederland,* ITS, University of Nijmegen, Nijmegen.

EISINGA, R., FELLING, A., PETERS, J., and SCHEEPERS, P. (1992), *Religion in Dutch Society 90: (Preliminary) Documentation of a National Survey on Religious and Secular Values in 1990,* Steinmetz Archive, Amsterdam.

ELSINGA, E. (1985), *Politieke participatie in Nederland,* CT Press, Amsterdam.

FELLING, A., PETERS, J., and SCHREUDER, O. (1983), *Burgerlijk en onburgerlijk Nederland*, Van Loghum Slaterus, Deventer.

FELLING, A., PETERS, J., and SCHREUDER, O. (1986), *Religion in Dutch Society: Documentation of a National Survey on Religious and Secular Values in 1979*, Steinmetz Archive, Amsterdam.

FELLING, A., PETERS, J., and SCHREUDER, O. (1987), *Religion in Dutch Society 85: Documentation of a National Survey on Religious and Secular Values in 1985*, Steinmetz Archive, Amsterdam.

FREY, F.W. (1970), "Cross-cultural survey research in political science", in R.T. Holt and J.E. Turner (eds.), *The Methodology of Comparative Research*, The Free Press, New York, pp. 173-294.

FRIEDRICHS, J. (1968), *Werte und soziales Handeln: Ein Beitrag zur soziologischen Theorie*, J.B.C. Mohr (Paul Siebeck), Tübingen.

HAGENDOORN, L. and JANSSEN, P. (1983), *Rechts Omkeer*, Ambo Boeken, Baarn.

HALMAN, L. (1991), *Waarden in de westerse wereld*, Tilburg University Press, Tilburg.

HALMAN, L. and de MOOR, R. (1991), *Information Bulletin EVSSG 1991*, Tilburg University, and IVA, Tilburg.

HALMAN, L., HEUNKS, F., DE MOOR, R., and ZANDERS, H. (1987), *Traditie, secularisatie en individualisering*, Tilburg University Press, Tilburg.

INGLEHART, R. (1977), *The Silent Revolution*, Princeton University Press, Princeton, NJ.

INGLEHART, R. (1990), *Culture Shift in Advanced Industrial Society*, Princeton University Press, Princeton, NJ.

JENNINGS, M.K., and van DETH, J.W. (eds.) (1990), *Continuities in Political Action*, De Gruyter, Berlin and New York.

KAASE, M. and MARSH, A. (1979), "Political action reporting: changes over time and a new typology", in S. Barnes, M. Kaase *et al., Political Action*, Sage, Beverly Hills, CA, pp. 137-166.

KLINGEMANN, H.D. (1979), "Measuring ideological conceptualizations", in S. Barnes, M. Kaase *et al., Political Action*, Sage, Beverly Hills, CA, pp. 215-254.

KLINGEMANN, H.D. (1984), "Perspektiven der inhaltsanalytischen Erforschung des gesamtgesellschaftlichen Wertwandels", in H. Klages and P. Kmieciak (eds.), *Wertwandel und gesellschaftlicher Wandel*, Campus Verlag, Frankfurt and New York, pp. 453-462.

KLUCKHOHN, C. (1959), "Values and value-orientations in the theory of action: an exploration in definition and classification", in T. Parsons and E.A. Shils (eds.), *Toward a General Theory of Action*, Harvard University Press, Cambridge, MA, pp. 388-433.

KMIECIAK, P. (1976), *Wertstruktur und Wertwandel in der Bundesrepublik Deutschland*, Verlag Otto Schwartz and Co, Göttingen.

LAUTMANN, R. (1971), *Wert und Norm: Begriffsanalysen für die Soziologie*, Westdeutscher Verlag, Opladen.

MALPASS, R.S., and POORTINGA, Y. (1986), "Strategies for design and analysis", in W.J. Lonner and J.W. Berry (eds.), *Field Methods in Cross-Cultural Research*, Sage, Beverly Hills, CA, pp. 47-83.

MCLAUGHLIN, B. (1965), "Values in behavioural science", *Journal of Religion and Health*, Vol. 4, pp. 258-279.

MIDDENDORP, C. (1979), *Ontzuiling, politisering en restauratie in Nederland. Progressiviteit en conservatisme in de jaren 60 en 70,* Boom, Meppel.

PRZEWORSKI, A., and TEUNE, H. (1973), "Equivalence in cross-national research", in D.P. Warwick and S. Osherson (eds.), *Comparative Research Methods,* Prentice Hall, Englewood Cliffs, NJ, pp. 119-173.

REICH, B., and ADCOCK, C. (1976), *Values, Attitudes and Behaviour Change,* Methuen, London.

ROKEACH, M. (1968), *Beliefs, Attitudes and Values,* Jossey-Bass, San Francisco, CA.

ROKEACH, M. (1973), *The Nature of Human Values,* Free Press, New York.

SCHEEPERS, P., and EISINGA, R. (eds.) (1991), *Onderdanig en intolerant. Lacunes en controverses in autoritarisme studies,* ITS, University of Nijmegen, Nijmegen.

SCHEEPERS, P., FELLING, A., and PETERS, J. (1986), *Theoretische modellen ter verklaring van etnocentrisme,* ITS, University of Nijmegen, Nijmegen.

SCHOLL-SCHAAF, M. (1975), *Werthaltung und Wertsystem,* Bouvier Verlag Herbert Grundmann, Bonn.

SEGERS, J.H.G. (1988), "Economische waarden in politieke teksten", in J.J.J. van Dijck and J.A.M. van Wezel (eds.), *Beweging en blokkering in het sociaal en economiqch beleid,* Kluwer Academic Publishers, Deventer, pp. 57-80.

STOETZEL, J. (1983), *Les valeurs du temps présent: une enquête européenne,* Presses Universitaires de France, Paris.

VERBA, S. (1969), "The uses of survey research in the study of comparative politics: issues and strategies", in S. Rokkan, S. Verba, J. Viet, and E. Almasey, *Comparative Survey Analysis,* Mouton, The Hague, pp. 56-106.

VERBA, S. (1971), "Cross-national survey research. The problem of credibility", in I. Vallier (ed.), *Comparative Methods in Sociology,* University of California Press, Berkeley, CA, pp. 309-356.

WARWICK, D.P. and OSHERSON, S. (1973), "Comparative analysis in the social sciences", in D.P. Warwick and S. Osherson (eds.), *Comparative Research Methods,* Prentice Hall, Englewood Cliffs, NJ, pp. 3-41.

WHITE, R.K. (1951), *Value Analysis,* Libertarian Press, Glen Gardner.

WILLIAMS, R.M., Jr. (1968), "The concept of values", in D.L. Sills (ed.), *International Encyclopedia for the Social Sciences,* MacMillan, New York, pp. 283-287.

Personality Theories and Developmental Processes:
Their Implications for Indicators of the Quality of Schooling
Les théories de la personnalité et les processus dynamiques: incidences pour les indicateurs qualitatifs de l'enseignement

by

Helmut Fend
University of Zurich, Switzerland

Evaluating an education system solely on the basis of scholastic goals neglects other legitimate perspectives related to the total development of students. Five largely independent theoretical traditions provide ways of measuring how well an education system performs with regard to the social functioning of students. These traditions are found in: religious or secular ethical virtues and values; structural-functional approaches to cross-curricular competencies; compatibility between institutional demands and personality; clinical concepts of "healthy" personality; and coping with school in a developmental perspective. The traditions vary in their ability to be measured. Nevertheless, an array of new goals for educational policies has been formed on the basis of psychology, developmental psychology and functionalism. Those competencies and values used by students to cope successfully which are associated with areas of personality that can be measured include work attitudes, mentally healthy functioning, pro-social attitudes and "political" education, general competencies used in shaping one's life, and indicators of developmentally specific risks.

*

* *

Note de synthèse

Dès lors que l'on évalue un système d'enseignement en se fondant uniquement sur la réussite scolaire, on laisse de côté d'autres points de vue légitimes qui peuvent apporter une contribution tout aussi importante aux travaux du réseau. Les évaluations qui reposent sur la réussite scolaire sont certes importantes, mais elles ne permettent pas de donner une description complète d'un système d'enseignement. Cette optique peut cependant être élargie en y incorporant d'autres points de vue qui peuvent contribuer à l'évaluation de l'évolution globale des élèves dans un système éducatif donné.

Trois traditions théoriques distinctes peuvent être appliquées à l'analyse des effets de l'enseignement qui couvrent l'ensemble du programme, et fournir un moyen de mesurer à quel point un système éducatif réussit à développer le fonctionnement social de ses élèves. Ces traditions concernent :

- *les vertus et les valeurs qui découlent des traditions religieuses ou éthiques et laïques ;*
- *l'adoption d'une approche structurelle/fonctionnelle pour définir les compétences transdisciplinaires ;*
- *la compatibilité des exigences institutionnelles et du fonctionnement de la personnalité ;*
- *le concept clinique de la personnalité « saine » des élèves ; et*
- *l'école envisagée dans une perspective évolutive.*

Il existe entre ces traditions des différences sensibles quant à la possibilité de les mesurer. Alors que les traditions psychologiques et cliniques et l'étude de la personnalité contiennent des instruments et des techniques de mesure divers, les complexités présentées par des notions telles que les vertus et les valeurs et l'approche structurelle/fonctionnelle soulèvent des difficultés considérables. Néanmoins, on a récemment élaboré un ensemble de nouveaux objectifs des politiques scolaires qui reposent directement sur la psychologie de la personnalité, la psychologie évolutive et le fonctionnalisme. La méthode adoptée pour atteindre ces objectifs consiste à demander quelles sont les compétences dont les élèves doivent disposer à la fin de leurs études pour être des citoyens productifs. Au cours des cinq dernières années, des recherches ont été menées sur cette question par la Fondation Carnegie, la Fondation Johann Jacobs et le bulletin d'information intitulé Skills for Life. *S'il existe entre ces sources quelques variations dans la façon de poser la question, toutes ont produit des listes de compétences analogues. Les compétences et les valeurs dont les élèves se servent pour réussir et qui correspondent aux domaines de la personnalité que l'on peut mesurer comprennent 1) les attitudes au travail, 2) un bon fonctionnement mental, 3) des attitudes sociales positives et une éducation « politique », 4) des compétences générales servant à prendre sa vie en main, et 5) les indicateurs des risques propres à l'évolution. La mesure de ces critères d'évaluation constitue la première phase de cette étude qui a pour objet d'évaluer les compétences transdisciplinaires.*

*

*   *

1. Overview

Although any evaluation of an education system must focus upon scholastic achievement, an alternative point of view suggests that this should not be concentrated upon exclusively. The following must also be taken into account:

- High achievement at all costs must not be the goal. If high achievement is reached to the detriment of health, in the form of great psychosomatic strain for example, then a critical point has been reached. Here the psychological costs of achievement must receive serious attention.
- A country making great efforts to set up education systems hopes to foster more than subject knowledge in the coming generation. The fostering of "whole" persons, their ability to cope well with life in general and the ensuring of a nation's value infrastructure all more or less explicitly underlie the efforts of the education system. If success in these areas is to be measured, however, problems arise mainly in regard to making such general goals precise and specific in measuring instruments.

The ways in which this can be done, taking the entire personality of the young person into consideration, will be outlined in this chapter. In the evaluation perspective it is thus necessary to include the more general effects of scholastic achievement.

- A third evaluation focus receives its impulse from the current trend to use the education system as a basis for comprehensive preventive efforts such as the prevention of health problems, the prevention of delinquency and violence or the prevention of risk behaviour. Because of these new tasks assigned to the public school, evaluation in the field of risk behaviours becomes significant.

2. The Perspectives

The above perspectives constitute an argument for evaluating the education system in a comprehensive fashion, rather than evaluating a system by concentrating exclusively upon subject-area achievement. Fostering the total development of young people, and their ability to be productive in managing their lives is emphasised here.

This general issue will be treated in the context of those conceptual frameworks that have helped to formulate perspectives more precisely and, in part, to make them measurable.

Several largely independent lines of thinking help to clarify the general question of how well-prepared for life a young generation is after nine or ten years of schooling. At present, mandatory school attendance ends between the ages of 15 and 17. This is therefore an appropriate point at which to evaluate the achievements of a school system.

Theoretical Traditions

Five theoretical traditions will be considered in the following review. Each provides different viewpoints on cross-curricular effects of schooling and draws attention to different areas of possible effects. They throw light upon the evaluation of an education system and on how well it does in terms of various aspects of human functioning.

- The *oldest tradition* is firmly rooted in *religious or secular ethical conceptions* of the ideal forms of human existence, and is expressed in terms of virtues and values.
- *Socially inspired derivations* of the competencies and virtues required by the functioning of a modern society increase awareness of people's psychic infrastructures, which are in turn transmitted by the school in order to help them to function effectively.
- *Comparison between differential experience* in the education system and the prerequisites of a functioning personality, examining that which is either detrimental to or fosters growth, allows new, possible effects of the education system to come into view. Therefore, from various psychological perspectives within *personality theory,* the effects of schooling transcending subject-matter knowledge have been formulated in partly negative and partly positive terms.
- *Clinical psychological views* on the education system emerge from these personality theory perspectives. They emphasize the person's adaptation to school in the framework of mental health, of internalising or externalising behaviour.
- The school's *cross-curricular* effects on abilities to cope with future demands raise the issue of the value of behaviours emerging during the school years for *predicting* behaviours later on in adulthood. Usually, this topic is dealt with in the context of developmental psychology.

These approaches will be described briefly in the following section. In a second step, perspectives of evaluation resulting from the approaches will be discussed. Here, the main emphasis will be placed upon possibilities to measure the resulting evaluative criteria.

Values and Virtues

In every culture which has established formal systems of long-term schooling, there are normative guidelines. These generate a blueprint of the goals to be reached in education and everyday school life. Without such working blueprints, education would consist of largely arbitrary reactions to stimuli provided solely by children and adolescents.

Principles of desired behaviour and attitudes are reflected in constitutional laws and reappear as guidelines in curricula. As they generally represent a minimum consensus among various societal powers, they often take on a very general form. At the top of the list stand education in the spirit of humanity, tolerance, respect for human dignity, and willingness to behave in socially acceptable ways. Respect for moral norms, self-discipline, and a willingness to achieve are mostly considered as top-priority ethical principles. In justifying these normative models, religious and "transcendental" commitments are often referred to.

In addition to such formulations, which focus on the concept of virtue, there exist new approaches based on *cross-curricular* competence, such as self-competence, social competence, and achievement motivation, which are further differentiated into various abilities involved in *successful coping.*

Ideals laid down in constitutions also relate to needs of societies, and to prerequisites for peaceful coexistence and for democracy and freedom, which are all postulated as being indispensable for the coexistence of diverse individuals and groups in a society.

Possibilities of Measurement and Potential for Evaluation

The attractiveness of the ideals formulated above is based upon the fact that those ideals correspond to the cultural knowledge base of desirable forms of human existence and human behaviour and thus are understood *intuitively* by supporters of a particular culture. However, or perhaps for this very reason, translating these ideals into measurable characteristics of people poses considerable difficulties. Nonetheless, disagreement manifests itself only at the stage of operationalisation.

Indicators for actual achievement of the virtues striven for can hardly be constructed through tests or questionnaires. Whether or not citizens have been educated to be clean and orderly may perhaps be derived from the state of public toilets or the degree of vandalism to school buildings and other public facilities in the inner city.

Here, however, one quickly becomes aware of possible explanations of cause other than educational programmes (*e.g.* the problems of poverty). It may be that we can find indicators for a school's fostering of friendliness, openness, and tolerance of foreigners, hospitality towards people of other nations, and races. Attainment, however (or lack of attainment), of education goals of "international understanding" and democratic virtues may well only become visible in times of economic difficulty.

The fact that an individual life or the life of a community contains the proof of whether having lived for years within an education system has been *a)* beneficial, *b)* useless, or even *c)* detrimental must be taken into consideration in the following attempts to measure attainment of general goals by an education system. After all, an education system does not produce a product that is finished once and for all. Nonetheless, the following attempts to measure the educational effects of school can be seen as attempts to describe a bit more exactly the general normative framework. And possibly, this can result in a new view of those human qualities essential to successful personal and social survival and interaction.

Structural-Functional Approaches to Defining Cross-Curricular Competencies

The normative view of the educational tasks of school assumes that an education system consciously sets general goals that it plans and attempts to fulfil through conscious, common efforts. In contrast to this is the sociologically inspired opinion that the significance of intentional effort is overestimated, and that the real effects of the actual, institutionalised school experience are underestimated.

The intuitive insight that institutions as such *educate*, that their *rules of functioning* make a deep impression upon personality, is found early in the history of sociological thought on societal conditions and education systems. The concept was present in the work of Max Weber (see particularly the formulation of Hennis, 1987) as well as in the work of Karl Mannheim (1930). Siegfried Bernfeld (1925) likewise was one of the first to point out the possible contradiction between the institutional educational programme of schools and formal pedagogical goals; and during the 1950s and 1960s, this perspective was developed systematically by Parsons (1968) and Dreeben (1968).

The basic idea of this particular view remains as follows: from the *malleable matter* of the infant soul, institutions pick out certain traits and reinforce them by means of their institutional system of sanctions.

In school, this occurs with behaviours which may lead to a generalised achievement orientation. In classrooms, the same demands are made of all students in a homogeneous age group. It is expected that each member of a school class will make the maximum effort to achieve his or her best.

Achievement is then evaluated in comparison with classmates and thus subject to an objective measure of quality. The institution confines itself to these objective evaluations of performance and fosters the formation of a *character* that automatically *a)* concentrates attention upon certain goals, *b)* strives to achieve the best possible results through investing effort, and *c)* subjects the results to critical evaluative standards. Idleness, indifference, "laissez-faire" attitudes, corrupt and devious means of gaining favour are diametrically opposed to this mental orientation.[1] In this way, from the *malleable matter* of human possibilities, the *modern soul* becomes formed, goal-oriented for *perfection,* together with an orientation towards planning and a sense of responsibility, attention to the plans of others and their possible interference with one's own, latent competitiveness and the rejection of all that is irrational or frightening (see here especially Mannheim, 1930).

This line of thinking has in recent years found additional social and historical support insofar as psychological dispositions learned through practice in the institutions of the education system have been placed in the context of the requirements of modern society, in particular of a market-oriented economy.

The central point of this argument incorporates the following considerations: in contrast even to the beginning of this century, school attendance of at least nine full school years and many further part-time school years, or a volume of time of at least 20 000 hours of instruction, leaves its mark on children and young people. The school career *prestructures* life's avenues and the goals of development, and it anticipates one's job opportunities, which are decisive in terms of later life. Moreover, there have been shifts away from the workplace and towards school as the field of experience in adolescence. While in 1953, 70 per cent of young people between 15 and 17 years of age worked, in 1984, working youth comprised only 20 per cent of the "student population" (Zinnecker, 1987, p. 313).

In the light of this development, the question becomes meaningful how the experiences of 20 000 hours in school affect development.

The answer reached by philosophers and sociologists comes down to this: the main thrust of socialisation in institutions lies in the formation of habits which have to do with disciplined completion of tasks, with work and achievement. In the framework of the school as a *social* organisation, prototypes of social relationships, of superordinates and subordinates, and of relationships between equals are experienced and internalised as *self-evident*. Related to this is the paradigmatic experience and familiarity with the typical functioning of a social organisation, which can be crucial for the stability of a particular political system.

In addition to these important and socially reproductive functions, the functionalist view points to those functions that are central in terms of the individual's coping with his or her own life. The most important is without doubt that the education system, over a period of many years, gives the student the opportunity to find out where his or her abilities lie and what his or her interests are, so that he or she has a basis upon which to choose and plan his or her future working career.

However, as comparative studies in Asia (China and Japan), Europe and the United States show (Stevenson, 1991), the formal functions of modern education systems take on a different significance according to whether they are embedded within cultures where community is greatly stressed (China and Japan) or in individualistic cultures (Europe and the United States).

Possibilities of Measurement and Potential for Evaluation

The functionalist perspectives discussed above draw our attention to central effects of the education system, but they do not do more than give intuitive indications of how these effects might be measured. The main focus is upon forms of coming to terms with and internalising achievement demands. Further, attention is drawn to the scholastic selection process, or the self-canalisation of pupils into various academic or job-oriented careers.

A second area that becomes apparent involves the *mental infrastructure* required by a society. Here, questions become relevant as to the effectiveness of the education system in strengthening democratic (or, conversely, autocratic) attitudes in the coming generation.

Without doubt, areas of significance are pointed out here that must give direction to discussions of the quality of an education system. The success of an education system in transmitting disciplined achievement attitudes will be just as relevant as its effectiveness in political education.

Difficulties show up when one attempts to measure the effects. Understandably, structural-functional theories, due to their *focus at the level of social systems,* offer no well-developed conceptions of the way in which system-functional features become represented in the psychological make-up of individuals. If mere intuitive measurements do not serve the purpose, theoretical concepts of the psychological structures of young people, in which the institutional effects must be localised, can be used.

The Compatibility of Institutional Demands and Personality Functioning

While structural-functional theories concentrated mainly upon issues of the socially desirable personality, psychological personality theory, from the turn of the century onwards, focused on efforts to specify the criteria of psychological health. The basic idea is that a person requires certain particular experiences in order to function in an optimal way. The human system has laws which, if violated, will lead to negative consequences. It could happen that an education system for many young people has only unfavourable experiences in store. For example, an accumulation of repeated failures is thought to be detrimental to their mental health.

Holistic Theories of Personality

In the meantime, several lines of personality research have developed that deal with the optimal functioning of the person and the necessary prerequisites thereof. At the beginning, rather general concepts of personality were formulated. Through further development, these concepts became more and more differentiated.

Psycho-analytical Research

The field of psychoanalysis offers a wide range of thinking on the topic of the well-functioning personality. Starting with Freud's famous definition of personal integrity as consisting in the ability to work and love, we encounter detailed elaborations of the abilities of people to deal with their own emotions, to relate to other people, and to develop ego-strength.

Adler's (1973) theories have become particularly important with regard to the education system, as he was the first to express useful formulas for normal and deviant development affected by school experience. According to Adler, the person strives for greatness and integrity, for the productive unfolding of wishes, and for superiority. Deficits are overcompensated for by means of disproportionate efforts. If a person does not find satisfaction in striving for superiority or striving to belong (whether due to authoritarian denial of his needs or overprotection) that person will not learn to develop his or her potential productively or to contribute to community life.

In the education system, such problems in the family can be continued, if children are not able to unite their self-interest with the interests of the community. Productive development of the self within the community is the mark of successful individual development. Forms of aggression (externalising conflict solutions) and forms of withdrawal (internalising conflict solutions) are characteristic of negative pathways. The way in which school deals with these needs will to a large extent determine its educational success in producing socially capable individuals.

Humanistic Personality Theories

In the humanistic research tradition, the person is conceptualised as an active, meaning-generating and self-developing entity. A productive person is thus able to generate meaning in his or her life, to develop personal projects with regard to what he or she wants to be or aspires to. That person seeks self-fulfilment and is able to adjust this basic motivational force to situational constraints. That person is also the object of thought about himself or herself. The welcome result of this self-reflective effort is considered to be a state of inner harmony and congruency (Rogers, 1984) between what one feels one is and what one wishes to be.

Problems arise when the education system, with its own demands, offerings, and sometimes unreasonable expectations, becomes significant in a person's life. Instead, the education system must become a part of the student's own tendencies towards self-realisation. If the school remains "foreign" and "external", it becomes a burden to the student and a hindrance to the search for meaning and significance.

Socio-Cognitive Personality Research

Action regulation and action control figure at the centre of socio-cognitive personality theories. Bandura (1986) has especially influenced thinking on optimal adaptation with his concept of self-efficacy. The generalisation of control and planning abilities constitutes the *effective* personality; and the concept of *locus of control* (Rotter and Hochreich, 1979) expresses a similar view. Being one's own master and mastering one's worldly affairs is seen in contrast to a situation in which a person feels that he or she is the victim of circumstance. Not feeling oneself to be the helpless victim of situational forces is considered to be a central indicator of successful personality development and mental health.

Within this pragmatic approach, the education system represents a part of the growing person's problem-solving capacity. School becomes, for example, the means of building a professional career; and it strengthens the person if this plan succeeds, and makes him or her feel powerless when the plan fails. Such *strength* or *weakness* can generalise and affect one's orientation to various areas of life and thus promote the growth of a personality that feels either strong or weak.

Construct-Specific Personality Research

As in other scientific areas, increasing differentiation has taken place within personality research, in that rather than focusing upon the holistic structure of the personality, research has concentrated upon specific functional systems. In the following, some of these areas, which prove especially productive in the analysis of the effects of school, will be briefly discussed.

The fulfilling of tasks and one's relation to demands for achievement are strategic aspects of adaptive personal functioning under the conditions of modern life. For this reason, the *anatomy of achievement motivation* (Heckhausen, 1984) has been considered an important field of research. In a long-standing tradition, these and similar issues have been examined:

- how children and adolescents develop pleasure in their activities, develop interests, relate to school and later job demands;
- how they learn to accept standards of excellence;
- how they learn to interpret their achievement results;

- how they learn to handle emotions within the contexts of success and failure; and
- how they learn to persist and maintain effort over long periods of time (Kuhl and Beckmann, 1994).

All these aspects converge in habits of *mastery orientation* or attitudes of *helplessness* (Henderson and Dweck, 1990).

Self-discipline and planning abilities and the ability to tolerate delay of gratification receive main emphasis in a similar research tradition (Mischel *et al.,* 1988). With these concepts, the broad field of *work virtues,* which played a large role in both the virtue catalogues and in structural-functional theories, becomes more ascertainable.

In recent decades, research on the development of the self has become one of the main foci of interest (see Damon, 1983; Harter, 1990). Self-related thinking was considered to be a central part of human functioning. On the assumption that there is an inherent tendency to prefer a positive image of the self (narcissistic homeostasis), deviation from the pathway to favourable self-related cognitions became a key indicator of unfavourable development. Furthermore, maladaptive functioning was seen in a low sense of self-efficacy, in unrealistic self-evaluations, in defensive self-cognitions, and so on.

The basic assumption underlying these concepts maintains that a *strong* and *efficient* person has a positive relationship to himself or herself, an optimistic and critical attitude towards the self and the world outside, and a sense of agency which prevents him or her from becoming a victim of circumstance.

These concepts of the self allow people to focus upon the effects of school on the core of the personality. Success and/or failure in the education system are represented in the self of the person, are a part of one's understanding of one's self, self-acceptance, and a sense of self-competence.

Possibilities of Measurement and Potential for Evaluation

Personality theories are a rich source for the development and application of appropriate instruments in the context of educational evaluation. A great number of instruments are available to measure various aspects of attitudes towards work and towards the self. In the following discussion, some of these aspects will be outlined in such a way that opportunities of reformulating education goals in terms of personality functioning become obvious.

Research on the structure and development of achievement motivation yields the following list of competencies that constitute part of a *clear intentional structure and a strong will to achieve:*

- the ability to create and maintain high levels of aspiration, to adapt and differentiate standards with regard to personal and social constraints;
- the ability to persist when facing obstacles and drawbacks;
- the ability to maintain a high level of effort and endurance;
- the flexibility of coping strategies;
- the ability to delay immediate reward and to fend off the temptation to engage in alternative activities, for the sake of reward in the future;

- the ability to follow through on plans and projects; and
- the ability to hold fast to plans even in the light of temptations to engage in more pleasant matters.

These competencies all contribute to the formation of a coherent approach to life, to work, and to leisure, to the past and the future, to oneself, to others, and to tasks. Hence, they are not curriculum-specific.

The various aspects of the self that become constituted through, or at least are affected by, experience within the education system could, if formulated in a normative way, be outlined.

Under the general heading of *self-concept,* the following competencies can be formulated:

- adequate and realistic self-perception that is open to new information and leads to a coherent concept of the self; the opposite here is confusion about oneself (*e.g.* about one's own abilities). Adequate perception of the self implies interest in one's self and the ability to resist stereotyping on the part of others; a strongly established reality principle ensures such an approach to the self;
- adequate handling of one's own emotions; keeping anxiety under control in task and achievement situations (anxiety, pride, shame); productive handling of success and failure;
- a high level of self-efficacy in personally relevant domains; being in control with regard to important demands in life;
- maintaining a high level of positive self-evaluation, self-esteem, and self-worth; avoiding self-derogation;
- the ability to choose domains of possible success and the ability to differentiate between personally more or less relevant kinds of involvement; and
- ability to develop personal projects, to approach the future with a planned format; having an ego-ideal, having a *sense of purpose.*

Examples of measurements of these characteristics can be found in both Wylie (1989) and Robinson *et al.* (1991).

Clinical Concepts of the "Healthy" Personality in Children of School Age

School experience can reinforce psychological disturbance which has its roots out-side school, or school can be the actual cause of malfunctioning. This hypothesis is not disputed, although evaluation of how *good* a school system is seldom takes place accor-ding to the yardstick of how well the school succeeds in causing the fewest possible clinically relevant disturbances in its students. In larger *epidemiological* studies, the degree of the distribution of psychological disorders is assessed in total, without refe-rence to the effects of school.

Research in the German-speaking realm has paid attention to this perspective of the pathogenic aspects of school. In the *Constance Studies* (see for example, Fend *et al.,* 1976; Fend and Knörzer, 1977; Helmke, 1983) this aspect played an important role, as it did in the *Bielefeld Studies* (Hurrelmann *et al.,* 1984; Mansel and Hurrelmann, 1991). In these investigations, the following school-related areas of psychological disturbance were central:

- psychosomatic disturbances, such as headaches, disturbed patterns of sleep, stomach aches;
- test anxiety in the sense of obsessive tension and an impaired ability to concentrate during tests; and
- general impaired state of health requiring the use of medication.

These patterns of disturbance can develop into more severe general symptoms. For example, symptoms of the spectrum of depressive symptomatology may manifest themselves. Here, we find distinct impairment of psychological functioning that, among other things, can lead to a loss or decrease in activity and ability to complete tasks because of feelings of fatigue, meaninglessness, and a sense of one's own worthlessness.

Possibilities of Measurement and Potential for Evaluation

Without doubt, the efficacy of an education system in the achievement area should in the long run not be reached at the cost of impairment to mental health. For this reason, evaluation in this area, as a safeguard to evaluation of achievement, is of crucial significance.

As psychopathology has reached a considerable degree of standardisation with regard to such impairments, possibilities of accurate measurement are continually improving. A number of instruments are already available (see Fend *et al.,* 1976; Helmke, 1983; Mansel and Hurrelmann, 1991; Achenbach and Edelbrock, 1978) and have been implemented in larger research surveys.

Coping with School from a Developmental Perspective

In addition to the clinical elaboration of personality theory's considerations in the areas in which the education system affects psychological growth, differentiations made by developmental psychologists have in recent years played an important role. Developmental psychology has contributed the insight that the education system affects *people in certain phases of development,* which each have their own structure, so that in different phases the very same objective experiences can cause very different effects. Phrased positively, this means that school should respond differently to children and adolescents in different phases of their development. Children can tolerate certain kinds of experience that adults would reasonably reject, and adolescents can enjoy certain types of experience that would put a strain on adults and children.

During adolescence, compulsory schooling comes to an end, so that in this phase of life a first balance sheet of the developmentally related effects of school can be drawn up. The concept of *age-specific developmental tasks* makes it possible to make an appraisal of what it is that the child must learn and master in the various phases of development, including adolescence. In this phase of life, as pointed out as early as in the work of Havinghurst (1972), it is important that adolescents learn the following:

- to reorganise their social relationships in such a way that they are able to form relationships with the opposite sex, to cultivate friendships, and to become emotionally less dependent upon parents;
- to have knowledge about their own bodies, to accept their physical selves, and to treat their bodies responsibly;
- to articulate their interests, to have an understanding of their own abilities, and, on this basis, to develop career interests; and
- to orient themselves in the world, to be able to describe the most important features of the political systems in which they live, and thus to function well within their own societies and cultures.

Possibilities of Measurement: Indicators of Risk

It is obvious that of the above developmental tasks, two are particularly relevant to the evaluation of an education system: 1) the task of choosing a career, with all of the psychological processes involved and 2) the task of finding one's orientation within the world. The number of students who succeed, on the basis of school information, in gaining a realistic view of their abilities and in forming appropriate, clear goals is just as relevant in evaluation as the question of how many students develop commitments relevant for long-term career perspectives.

At the core of the issue of *world orientation* is the evaluative topic of political education. It also, however, includes aspects of general competence in dealing with life. In other words, a comprehensive orientation must include the necessary abilities, if one is to cope within a particular culture. Knowledge and abilities taught in specific subject areas form the core of what the school especially concerns itself with. Here, developmental and psychological perspectives point out areas for evaluation that will be discussed in later chapters.

Modern developmental psychology has not only concerned itself with age-specific potentials and the foci of learning, but has, in recent years, increasingly investigated the factors of risk within each of the phases of development. This is particularly important for the period of life during which compulsory schooling ends. At that time, the following areas of risk become significant:

- use of legal (alcohol, nicotine) and illegal (marijuana, heroin) drugs;
- risk behaviour in traffic;
- aggressive and delinquent behaviour;
- irresponsible sexual behaviour resulting in pregnancy and disease; and
- eating disorders.

US research, in particular, has been concerned extensively with age-specific risk behaviours and has involved schools through intervention programmes. As large bodies of research evidence show that these problem behaviours are closely connected with school achievement behaviour, the question arises whether evaluation of education systems should not include this aspect. After all, the education system will soon be required to take more of the task of *prevention* of risk behaviours. Related surveys, which assess the *achievements* of whole communities in terms of care for the young, are now widely available in the United States (Benson, 1993).

Character and Competence: New Concepts of Coping

We have discussed research traditions that in our culture have led to the formulation of new goals in educational policies for the entire younger generation. As the examples below illustrate, these goals reflect conceptual frameworks stemming from personality psychology, developmental psychology, and functionalism. A last approach can be summed up in this general question: "What do young adults at the end of education need in terms of skills, in order to be able to play a constructive role as a citizen in society?"

The Carnegie report *Turning Points* (Carnegie Foundation, 1989) posed this issue in a slightly different form: "What qualities do we envision in the 15-year-olds who have been well served in the middle years of schooling? What do we want every adolescent to know, to feel, to be able to do upon emerging from the educational and school-related experience?" (p. 15). The answer suggests that an educated person must become:

- an intellectually reflective person;
- a person "en route" to a lifetime of meaningful work;
- a good citizen;
- a caring and ethical individual; and
- a physically and mentally healthy person (Carnegie Foundation, 1989, p. 15).

As a starting point for the Johann Jacobs Foundation, which is engaged in supporting the development of adolescents, a similar perspective has been formulated. A positive attitude towards one's future and one's self, the ability to take initiatives and make good decisions, positive values, tolerance, and acceptance of cultural diversity are considered to be strategic aspects of a strong and happy future generation.

This yields a catalogue of competencies and value-orientations that can be representative of many others, such as the following:

- social competence;
- problem-solving skills;
- autonomy, the ability to act independently, and to exert some control over one's environment; and
- a sense of purpose and future.

In a similar approach, psychosocial competencies required for achieving the above goals are specified. They are called *skills for life,* and are listed under the concept of successful coping. An illustrative list includes the following:

- communication skills;
- decision-making skills;
- problem-solving skills;
- critical thinking;
- interpersonal skills;
- assertiveness;

- peer pressure resistance skills;
- skills for coping with emotions;
- stress and anxiety management;
- social adjustment skills; and
- self-awareness (WHO, 1992).

It is apparent that these summary lists also include abilities in the social area that did not stand at the heart of this chapter's discussion. Characteristics of strong and mentally healthy personalities capable of showing initiative and acting appropriately, must, of course, play an important role. However, in the above approaches, work attitudes and modern forms of discipline seem under-represented.

3. Summary: Evaluation Topics and Instruments of Measurement

Against the background of the above functionalist, personalistic, theoretical, clinical, and developmental concepts, it is important to take into account the following areas of personality in the evaluation of education systems:
- concepts of work attitudes and career orientation;
- concepts of mentally healthy functioning (*i.e.* a positive self-concept);
- pro-social attitudes and "political" education;
- indicators of general competencies in shaping one's life; and
- indicators of developmentally specific risks.

Decisions concerning the possibilities of measuring these various evaluative criteria determine the first phase of our studies on assessing cross-curricular competencies.

Note

1. Another aspect of this tradition of thought is found in Jackson's (1968) *Life in the Classroom*, since he investigated the concrete expression of scholastic achievement expectations in school classes from an interpretative-interactionist perspective. The ways in which institutional expectations take on everyday forms become apparent, as well as the strategies teachers and pupils use in their attempt to survive. Here social strategies are practised, and social virtues and vices become established which not infrequently consist of attitudes of avoidance, waiting, fitting in, etc. Learning as a "social game" comes to the fore.

References

ACHENBACH, T.M., and EDELBROCK, C.S. (1978), "The classification of child psychopatho-logy: a review and analysis of empirical efforts", *Psychological Bulletin*, No. 85, pp. 1275-1301.

ADLER, A. (1973), *Individualpsychologie in der Schule*, Fischer Taschenbuch Verlag, Frankfurt.

BANDURA, A. (1986), *Social Foundations of Thought and Action*, Prentice Hall, Englewood Cliffs, NJ.

BECK, A.T., and CLARK, D.A. (1988), "Anxiety and depression: an information processing perspective", *Anxiety Research*, Vol. 1, pp. 23-36.

BENSON, P.L. (1993), *The Troubled Journey. A Portrait of 6th-12th Grade Youth*, Search Institute, Minneapolis, MI.

BERNFELD, S. (1925), *Sisyphos oder die Grenzen der Erziehung*, Frankfurt.

Carnegie Foundation, (ed.) (1989), *Turning Points. Preparing American Youth for the 21st Century*, Carnegie Corporation, Carnegie Council on Adolescent Development, NewYork.

DAMON, W. (1983), *Social Personality Development. Infancy through Adolescence*, Norton, New York.

DREEBEN, R. (1968), *On what is Learned in School*, Addison-Wesley Publishing Company, Massachusetts.

EISENBERG, N., and STRAYER, J. (1987), *Empathy and its Development*, Harvard University Press, Cambridge, MA.

FEND, H. (1982), *Gesamtschule im Vergleich*, Beltz, Weinheim.

FEND, H. (1990*a*), *Vom Kind zum Jugendlichen: Der Übergang und seine Risiken. Entwicklungspsychologie der Adoleszenz in der Moderne, Bd. 1*, Huber, Bern.

FEND, H. (1990*b*), "Ego-strength development and pattern of social relationships", in H. Bosma and S. Jackson, *Coping and Self-Concept in Adolescence*, Springer Verlag, Berlin, pp. 92-111.

FEND, H. (1991), *Identitätsentwicklung in der Adoleszenz. Lebensentwürfe, Selbstfindung und Weltaneignung in beruflichen, familiären und politisch-weltanschaulichen Bereichen*, Huber, Bern.

FEND, H., and KNÖRZER, W. (1977), *Beanspruchung von Schülern. Aspekte der schulischen Sozialisation*, Bundesminister für Bildung und Wissenschaft, Bonn.

FEND, H., KNÖRZER, W., NAGL, W., SPECHT, W. AND VATH-SZUSDZIARA, R. (1976), *Sozialisationseffekte der Schule. Soziologie der Schule II*, Beltz, Weinheim.

HARTER, S. (1990), "Self and identity development", in S.S. Feldman and G.R. Elliott (eds.), *At the Threshold,* Harvard University Press, Cambridge, MA, pp. 352-387.

HAVINGHURST, R.J. (1972), *Developmental Tasks and Education,* 3rd edn, McKay, New York.

HECKHAUSEN, H. (1980), *Motivation und Handeln,* Springer Verlag, Berlin.

HECKHAUSEN, H. (1984), "Emergent achievement behavior: some early developments", in J. Nicholls, *The Development of Achievement Motivation,* JAI Press, Greenwich, pp. 1-32.

HELMKE, A. (1983), *Schulische Leistungsangst: Erscheinungsformen und Entstehungsbedingungen,* Lang, Königstein im Taurus.

HENDERSON, V.L., and DWECK, C.S. (1990), "Motivation and achievement", in S.S. Feldman and G.R. Elliott (eds.), *At the Threshold. The Developing Adolescent,* Harvard University Press, Cambridge, MA, pp. 308-329.

HENNIS, W. (1987), *Max Webers Fragestellung: Studien zur Biographie des Werkes,* JCB Mohr (Siebeck), Tübingen.

HURRELMANN, K., ROSEWITZ, B., and WOLF, H. (1984), "Untersuchungsberichte: Die Belastung von Jugendlichen durch die Schule. Bieten gegenwärtige Bildungs-, Ausbildungs-, und Arbeits marktbedingungen verbesserte Chancen der Persönlichkeitsentwicklung?", *Die Deutsche Schule,* Vol. 76, pp. 381-391.

JACKSON, P.W. (1968), *Life in Classrooms,* Holt, Rinehart and Winston, New York.

KOHLBERG, L. (1981), *The Philosophy of Moral Development (Vol. 1),* Harper and Row, San Francisco, CA.

KUHL, J., and BECKMANN, J. (1994), *Volition and Personality,* Hogrefe and Huber Publishers, Seattle.

LOEVINGER, J. (1976), *Ego Development: Conceptions and Theories,* Jossey-Bass, San Francisco, CA.

MANNHEIM, K. (1930), "Über das Wesen und die Bedeutung des wirtschaftlichen Erfolgstrebens. Ein Beitrag zur Wirtschaftssoziologie", in *Archiv für Sozialwissenschaften und Sozialpolitik,* pp. 449-512.

MANSEL, J., and HURRELMANN, K. (1991), *Alltagsstre' bei Jugendlichen,* Juventa Verlag, Weinheim.

MISCHEL, W. (1983), "Delay of gratification as process and as person variable in development", in D. Magnusson and V. Allen, *Human Development,* Academic Press, New York, pp. 149-166.

MISCHEL, W., SHODA, Y., and PEAKE, P.K. (1988), "The nature of adolescent competencies predicted by preschool delay of gratification", *Personality and Social Psychology,* No. 574 (4), pp. 687-696.

OFFER, D., OSTROV, E., HOWARD, K.I., and ATKINSON, R. (1988), *The Teenage World. Adolescents' Self-Image in Ten Countries,* Plenum, New York.

OPPENHEIM, A.N., and TORNEY, J. (1974), *The Measurement of Children's Civic Attitudes in Different Nations,* Almquist and Wiksell International, Stockholm.

PARSONS, T. (1968), "Die Schulklasse als soziales System. Einige ihrer Funktionen in der amerikanischen Gesellschaft", in T. Parsons, *Sozialstruktur und Persönlichkeit,* Europäische Verlagsanstalt, Frankfurt.

ROBINS, L.N., and RUTTER, M. (1990), *Straight and Devious Pathways from Childhood to Adulthood,* Cambridge University Press, New York.

ROBINSON, J.P., SHAVER, P.R., and WRIGHTSMAN, L.S. (eds.) (1991), *Measurement of Personality and Social Psychological Attitudes,* Academic Press, New York.

ROGERS, C.R. (1984), "Die Grundlagen des personenzentrierten Ansatzes", in AG Personzentrierte Gesprächsführung, *Persönlichkeitsentwicklung durch Begegnung,* Österreichischer Bundesverlag, Wien, pp. 10-26.

ROTTER, J.B., and HOCHREICH, D. (1979), *Persönlichkeit, Theorien, Messung, Forschung,* Springer Verlag, Berlin.

SCHMIDT, G., KLUSMANN, D., and ZEITZSCHEL, U. (1992), "Veränderungen der Jugendsexualität zwischen 1970 und 1990", *Zeitschrift für Sexualforschung,* Vol. 5 (3), pp. 191-218.

SCHULZE, G. (1977), *Politisches Lernen in der Alltagserfahrung. Eine empirische Analyse.* Juventa Verlag, München.

SELMAN, R.L. (1971), "Taking another's perspective. Role-taking development in early childhood", *Child Development,* Vol. 42, pp. 1721-1734.

SELMAN, R.L. (1980), *The Growth of Interpersonal Understanding: Clinical and Developmental Analysis,* Academic Press, New York.

STEVENSON, H.W. (1991), "The development of prosocial behavior in large-scale collective societies: China and Japan", in R.A. Hinde and J. Groebel (eds.), *Cooperation and Prosocial Behavior,* Cambridge University Press, New York.

WHO Newsletter (1992), *Skills for Life,* A network co-ordinated by the WHO Division of Mental Health, No. 1, August, World Health Organization, Geneva.

WYLIE, R.C. (1989), *Measures of Self-concept,* University of Nebraska, Lincoln.

ZINNECKER, J. (1987), *Jugendkultur 1940-1985 (Herausgegeben vom Jugendwerk der Deutschen Shell),* Leske and Budrich, Opladen.

Problem-Solving and Communication Skills as Part of Preparation for Real Life

Les techniques de résolution des problèmes de communication dans la préparation à la vie réelle

by

G. Douglas Hodgkinson and **Michelle Crawford**
Ministry of Education, British Columbia, Vancouver, Canada

Problem-solving and communication skills are recognised as an integral part of the curriculum in many Canadian jurisdictions. These cross-curricular competencies were examined by Network A in autumn 1993 at a meeting devoted to the development of relevant instruments. There was, however, some doubt whether the assessment of transferability of skills from school to real life would give a true indication of success in post-school activities, and of the quality of education received. Solutions put forward included the requirements that individual items should use both problem-solving and communication skills, and should not be too time-consuming, vulnerable to cultural bias or expensive to administer. Another difficulty was that the domains of problem-solving and communication are so broad that they cannot be fully measured by a limited number of items. Fortunately, a number of international studies had already addressed certain aspects of these domains, so that the testing carried out in British Columbia in June 1994 was able to focus on just five items. The purpose was to determine whether these items were appropriate for the 16-year-old age group. The results demonstrate that students thought that the items did have real-life applications and were cross-curricular in orientation. The indicators show considerable potential for further application and development.

*

*   *

Note de synthèse

Associées dans le monde entier à la prospérité économique, les techniques de résolution des problèmes et de communication sont considérées comme faisant intégralement partie du programme d'études dans nombre d'instances canadiennes. Ces compétences transdiciplinaires ont été examinées par le Réseau A du projet INES de l'OCDE à l'automne 1993, lorsque le réseau a commencé de mettre au point des outils permettant de décrire les résultats scolaires dans ces domaines. En juin 1994, ces outils ont été testés en situation à Victoria, en Colombie britannique.

On s'est inquiété à plusieurs titres de l'exactitude de l'outil de mesure des compétences transdisciplinaires au cours de sa mise au point. On se demandait, par exemple, si l'évaluation de la possibilité de transférer les compétences du contexte scolaire à celui de la vie réelle donnerait une véritable indication de la réussite des élèves dans l'enseignement post-secondaire et dans la vie active, tout en reflétant la qualité de l'enseignement qui leur était dispensé.

Pour répondre aux questions posées tout au long de l'élaboration de ces questionnaires, on a demandé que chaque question posée concerne à la fois les compétences de résolution des problèmes et les compétences de communication. Il fallait en outre que les questions ne demandent pas trop de temps aux élèves, ne soient pas trop sensibles aux préjugés culturels, et ne coûtent pas trop cher à poser et à exploiter.

La mise au point des questionnaires s'est heurtée à une autre difficulté qui tient au fait que les domaines de la résolution des problèmes et de la communication sont si vastes et si complexes qu'ils ne peuvent être entièrement mesurés ou décrits par le petit nombre d'éléments qui composent le panier. (Le terme de panier décrit l'instrument de mesure dans son ensemble, qui associe plusieurs domaines, avec un nombre limité de questions pour chacun d'eux.) Toutefois, pour utiliser cette méthode, il faut que l'on reconnaisse dans tous les pays que les éléments choisis pour être inclus dans le panier représentent bien la gamme des connaissances théoriques et pratiques que les élèves doivent maîtriser pour réussir dans le monde réel.

Heureusement, plusieurs études internationales ont traité de certains aspects de ces domaines, ce qui facilite le déroulement de cette étude. Les cinq questions retenues ont été testées en situation à Victoria sur quinze élèves âgés de seize ans qui représentaient des degrés d'aptitude scolaire divers. Ce test avait pour objet de déterminer que ces questions convenaient bien à cette tranche d'âge, autrement dit, de s'assurer que les questions mesuraient l'aptitude à résoudre les problèmes et de chercher à savoir si les élèves pensaient qu'elles pouvaient s'appliquer à la vie réelle. Il ressort des résultats de cette étude que les élèves estiment que ces questions peuvent s'appliquer à la vie réelle et qu'elles couvrent l'ensemble du programme scolaire. Bien que les travaux du sous-groupe des compétences transdisciplinaires aient été en grande partie exploratoires, ces indicateurs semblent présenter d'intéressantes possibilités d'utilisation pratique et les travaux entrepris pour les mettre au point vont se poursuivre.

*

* *

1. Focus on Outcomes

In 1989, the OECD released *Education and the Economy in a Changing Society,* which outlined the changes taking place in the global economy. The document states that national education systems "(...) hold the key to possible progress and (...) determine each country's medium-and long-term prospects in world competition" (p. 5). Indeed, during the past few decades many nations have observed a link between education and economic prosperity and have concluded (sometimes without much empirical evidence) that their educational institutions are not providing students with the skills that they will need if they (and their country) are to be competitive in a modern global economy. Business communities are already demanding that educational institutions turn out individuals who have good communication and problem-solving skills; and employers lament the fact that the job market is full of people who do not "(...) have the ability to write and speak effectively, the ability to learn easily on the job, the ability to use quantitative skills needed to apply various tools of production and management, the ability to read complex material, and the ability to build and evaluate arguments" (Resnick, 1987, pp. 6-7).

Various jurisdictions have responded to the alarm noted above by focusing instruction and assessment more closely on the outcomes of education. Griffith and Medrich write that in the United States international achievement comparisons are now directly associated with the nation's education goals and that "(...) interest in international policies, practices and outcomes has increased dramatically, and [policy-makers] now seek information on state performance in an international context" (Griffith and Medrich, 1992, p. 477).

In general, problem-solving and communication skills are an integral part of the curriculum in many jurisdictions. Such skills are frequently identified as elements or dimensions within particular disciplines, or are buried inside the curriculum guides of specific subject areas – in some cases they are overtly presented as key cross-curricular competencies. For example, the document, *Improving the Quality of Education* (Province of British Columbia, 1993, p. 2), explicitly states that the ability to solve problems is an essential basic skill that students need. Problem-solving and communication skills are also implicit in the province's mission statement, which contains the following:

- Educated citizens are:
  - thoughtful, able to learn and to think critically, and to communicate information from a broad knowledge base;
  - creative, flexible, self-motivated, and possessing a positive self-image;
  - capable of making independent decisions;
  - skilled and able to contribute to society generally, including the world of work;
  - productive, able to gain satisfaction through achievement, and to strive for physical well-being;
  - co-operative, principled, and respectful of others, regardless of differences; and
  - aware of the rights and prepared to exercise the responsibilities of an individual within the family, the community, Canada, and the world (Province of British Columbia, 1989, p. 4).

Similarly, as outlined by Broadfoot (1994) in *Making Education Count*, the National Curriculum Council of England and Wales refers to the following types of competencies:

- Fundamental core skills underpinning almost all employment functions and formal programmes of instruction:
  - problem-solving;
  - communication; and
  - personal skills.
- Equally important but less generic, the following core skills may be selectively present in learning and occupational performance:
  - numeracy;
  - information technology; and
  - modern language competence.
- Cross-curricular themes that ought to constitute a part of the learning goals for senior secondary and general vocational education:
  - social and economic understanding;
  - scientific and technological understanding; and
  - aesthetic and creative understanding (Broadfoot, 1994, p. 241).

It is not surprising, therefore, that early in the discussions about the development of Cross-Curricular Competencies (CCC) as part of the OECD INES Network A activities, the topics of communication skills and problem-solving were suggested as potential areas for indicator development. It was equally clear that the development of such indicators would require substantial conceptual and technical work if instruments were to be constructed that would perform successfully in an international setting.

2. CCC Background

As part of the overall structure for a pilot study on Cross-Curricular Competencies, it was decided in the autumn of 1993 that work should be undertaken to develop frameworks and look for potential instruments to describe student performance in these key areas. The instrument, it was decided, should be developed on the basis of a criterion-referenced or standards-referenced approach, since the Cross-Curricular Competencies indicator framework is structured around levels of competence, which has implications for the types of item that can be extracted from other sources. There was a recognition that although the task had many obvious difficulties, it was worth attempting, because Cross-Curricular Competencies add significantly to the face validity of the INES indicators.

A First Step

As a first step, a review was undertaken of the literature pertaining to the assessment and evaluation of student performance in communication skills and problem-solving. Not surprisingly, despite the large volume of material written on these topics, there was little that directly addressed the issues that were faced by the CCC sub-group, in developing an assessment framework that would be international and intercultural in nature, and have a focus on real life. With regard to problem-solving, the literature focuses on this competency within particular disciplines, most often mathematics, or on the intellectual question of what constitutes problem-solving. During the search for items that could be used in an international problem-solving assessment instrument, Wells' definitions of a problem and the problem-solving process were loosely followed:

- A *problem* is a situation for which no routine solution process applies and for which alternative solutions exist.
- The *problem-solving process* is the series of stages an individual would progress through to efficiently address and solve some aspect of a problem. The stages can be labelled as follows:

Stage 1: Understanding the problem.
    Step a: Identify components of the problem.
    Step b: State the problem clearly.
    Step c: Obtain information to better understand the problem.
Stage 2: Planning a Solution.
    Step a: Identify alternatives.
    Step b: Choose *best* solution.
Stage 3: Checking the Solution.
    Step a: Develop a plan for checking the solution.
    Step b: Carry out the plan.
Stage 4: Evaluating Results.
    Step a: Draw conclusions.
    Step b: Relate results to general understanding (Wells, 1983, p. 5).

In almost all cases, the items that fell into line with these criteria were real-life problems that were given to students as research projects, not test items. It also was clear that the work that would have gone into these research projects was not necessarily critical for real life.

Problem-solving and communication skills were chosen as competencies to be assessed because they are viewed as important for success in real life; however, the real-life aspect adds significant difficulty to the task of developing an assessment tool in the context of Cross-Curricular Competencies. The degree to which there is transferability of skills from the school context to the real-life context will determine to a great extent whether or not such assessment results give a true indication of students' success in post-secondary activities and the workplace, and of the quality of the education that the student is receiving.

Investigating the social construction of questions and answers in the primary classroom, Schubauer-Leoni *et al.* (1989, p. 674) observed that "(...) pupils will have the tendency to simply follow the teacher's instructions without concerning themselves with the aim of the exercise or what follows". Case (1992, p. 16) came to a similar conclusion when he observed that his students were unable to solve a problem on a field trip, despite the fact that they had already successfully solved the same problem in the classroom. In addition, Schubauer-Leoni *et al.* (1989) observed that when questions are asked within the classroom, responses conform to the concepts or operations learned at school; yet when the same questions are given to students in a one-to-one relationship with the experimenter outside the classroom, "(...) written solutions are more heterogeneous in nature, using natural language, illustrative drawings, etc." (p. 675).

Communication Skills

In an attempt to gain insight into how well students' writing skills transfer from one context to another, the province of British Columbia, Canada administered an assessment of writing for specific, or non-school, audiences as part of their 1994 assessment of *communication skills*. The study was undertaken to determine whether students are prepared to do the types of writing that will be required of them after they graduate or leave school, as well as to assess students' abilities to change their writing for different audiences and purposes. The study addresses the need for an increased emphasis on public accountability and on student career preparation. In addition to a traditional rubric, students will be scored on their use of appropriate tone and diction in relation to different audiences. On the basis of preliminary results available at the time of writing, it appears that many students' writing is of a high calibre and that they are in fact able to write for non-school, real-life purposes, such items as letters of application for employment or letters of resignation.

Although we often use the terms *communication skills* and *problem-solving* as if they were discrete concepts, separate from knowledge, attitudes and other skills, it is not clear that it is possible to assess them *meaningfully* without regard to their context. Resnick (1987, p. 18) states that "cognitive research yields repeated demonstrations that specific content area knowledge plays a central role in reasoning, thinking, and learning of all kinds". She goes on to say:

> "Each discipline has characteristic ways of reasoning, and a complete higher-order education would seek to expose students to all of these. Reasoning and problem-solving in the physical sciences, for example, are shaped by particular combinations of inductive and deductive reasoning, by appeal to mathematical tests, and by an extensive body of agreed upon fact for which new theories must account. In the social sciences, good reasoning and problem-solving are much more heavily influenced by traditions of rhetorical argument, of weighing alternatives, and of 'building a case' for a proposed solution. Mathematics insists on formal proofs – a criterion absent in most other disciplines (p. 36)."

When institutions in the United Kingdom attempted the assessment and reporting of the skills about which Resnick speaks as communication and problem-solving issues, separate from any particular curriculum, experts simply could not distinguish levels of achievement. Furthermore, the skill levels reported appeared to be meaningless without subject-area context. The result of the Certificate of Pre-Vocational Education's (CPVE's) separate assessment of core skills in 1981-82, was an "unbroken mass of detailed core statements which end-users found difficult to interpret and hence value" (Bell, 1990, quoted in Wolf, 1991, p. 192).

Not all authorities agree with that position. Ennis (1985a, p. 29) argues that: "Although I am firmly convinced that a thorough knowledge of the subject about which one is thinking is essential for critical thinking, *I am also convinced that there are general principles that bridge subjects, that have application to many subjects*'' (emphasis in the original). However, while there may in fact be *general principles* that apply to many subjects, it must be stressed that a thorough literature search turned up no items that successfully tapped a given skill in isolation from other skills or other knowledge.

In the early stages of the development of CCC instruments, attempts to produce high-level items in problem-solving were found to contain significant elements of communication skills. Similarly, independently developed items in communication skills were seen to require students to solve problems. As a result, at the time of writing, the five potential items that were generated or found to assess problem-solving skills also measure communication skills in that a significant amount of reading and writing is required. The nature of these items is discussed later in this chapter.

3. Idealism and Pragmatism

As with all instrument development, there needs to be a balance between idealism and pragmatism. There is little point in developing an instrument that will reflect the latest in thinking about problem-solving and communication skills, one that includes performance tasks, for example, if the result is that it is too time-consuming to be administered or too vulnerable to cultural bias to be effective in an international setting. For example, the IEA International Study of Written Composition undertook the challenge of developing ''(...) a procedure that would make it possible to rate compositions written by students in several countries and in several different languages in as comparable a manner as possible'' (Takala and Vähäpassi, 1987, p. 92). Problems related to the construction of the tasks, the allocation of the tasks, and the rating of student scripts were addressed in developing writing tasks and their scoring, and nine different writing tasks were developed. When it came to developing a scoring system, an elaborate multi-stage procedure was instituted to establish internationally acceptable scores for compositions written in several languages. After this procedure was first undertaken in 1984, it was concluded that ''the scoring metric is too elastic to allow robust cross-national comparisons of scores on any one task or group of tasks (...) further work is needed'' (Takala and Vähäpassi, 1987, p. 101). Of the nine writing tasks, only Numbers 1, 2, and 3, all of which are predominantly informative in purpose, were identified as prospective cross-national tasks.

From a purely pragmatic viewpoint, it would be desirable to draw on existing international instruments. Unfortunately, although there are several instruments specifically designed to measure problem-solving and communication skills, those instruments do not explicitly measure *real-life* skills. An exception is the National Centre for Education Statistics's *Adult Literacy in America*. However, in this study, the tasks were specifically designed for adults; they did note use any multiple-choice formats.

Measuring a Broad Domain

Another significant difficulty in developing an instrument to measure problem-solving and communication skills in the context of Cross-Curricular Competencies is that the domains are so broad and complex that they cannot be fully measured or described by the small number of items in the *basket*. (The term *basket* refers to the analogy that is being used to describe the overall CCC instrument, which will be a combination of various domains, with a limited number of items in each domain.) Any sub-category of the cross-curricular instrument can only describe the performance of students on some limited criteria, and not on an entire domain such as problem-solving. Therefore, the content validity at the domain level will probably be insufficient. If one accepts the limitation that the content validity will only be determined for the basket as a whole, then one problem is avoided only to be replaced by another; the selection of items for the basket as a whole needs to be accepted by the international community of educational stakeholders as being representative of the range of knowledge and skills important for students to learn in order to succeed in the world.

Fortunately, there have been a number of international studies that have addressed certain *aspects* of these domains, and which form a part of the INES project as a whole. In particular, the IEA Reading Literacy Study and the IEA Third International Mathematics and Science Study (TIMSS) cover certain aspects of communication skills and problem-solving as part of their design. Although these studies were not specifically designed to focus on a real-life perspective, the *IEA Adult Literacy Study* and Population Three in TIMSS, are arguably sufficiently valid, rendering it unnecessary to include as Cross-Curricular Competencies those concepts which were, or will be, covered in these IEA studies. If this approach were to be used, it would allow narrower and more manageable domains to be described and would therefore reduce the cost of developing and administering the instrument. Specifically, it would be possible to take an approach to measure problem-solving that did not need to look at mathematics and science, thereby freeing resources to develop areas such as social studies. It also would allow for a reduction in effort, if writing could be assessed without reading.

Furthermore, it was hoped that it may not be necessary to develop *entirely new* items for an instrument of this sort. It would simplify the task somewhat if problem-solving items were drawn from international studies that had a performance assessment component, or which assessed disciplines other than mathematics, science, or reading. In particular, there are some items in the performance assessment and the geography assessment components of the IAEP that have a real-life focus and, with modifications, hold some promise as items for the basket (see Figure 8.1). In addition, three others were deemed to be acceptable for field testing as part of a CCC instrument to measure problem-solving. Subsequently, these items were modified based on feedback. An example is presented here in its latest version (see Figure 8.2).

These items were *focus-tested* along with some other items in Victoria, BC, Canada, in June of 1994. For the testing, fifteen 16-year-old students representing a range of abilities were selected from mathematics classes in two secondary schools in the Saanich area. The students spent approximately two hours solving problems that were developed by the British Columbia Ministry of Education, taken directly from Shell Centre for

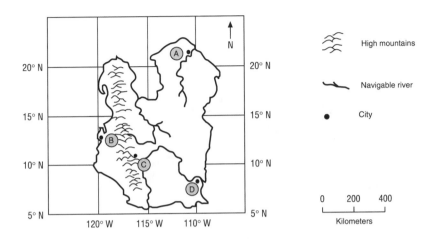

Figure/*Graphique* 8.1. **Island – Geography item**
L'île – Géographie

The island shown above is in an early stage of economic development.

Which of the following would most likely bring about the greatest change in the way of life of the people living in Village C?

Discuss each of the four options and indicate which option is the best answer, and why:
1. An increase in the birth rate.
2. Construction of a road from City B to City D through Village C.
3. Construction of airports in Cities A and D.
4. Occurrence of a flood in the village.

Source: IAEP and CAEP (1992).

Mathematical Education (1983), or, as stated earlier, taken from IAEP and modified. The focus testing was meant to provide insight into whether the items piqued the interest of 16-year-olds and whether the items were appropriate for this age group with respect to level of difficulty. In addition, it was hoped that the focus testing would indicate whether the items were in fact measuring aspects of problem-solving ability and whether the students thought that the problems had real-life applications.

These latter two issues were explored through discussion with students after they had attempted to solve the problems. Teachers asked the students *how* they went about solving problems and had a list of problem-solving strategies that they could refer to when questioning the students. The students thought that the problems were indeed real-life; they also classified the problems as mathematics, physics, social studies, biology and even art, which indicates that the items were at least *perceived* to be cross-curricular in nature.

Figure/*Graphique* 8.2. **The race – Sample item**
La course – Problème-type

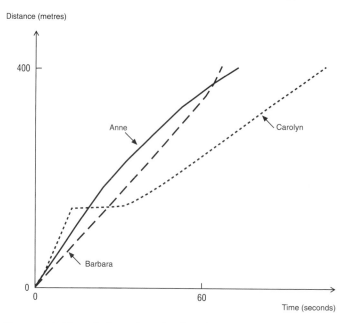

Distance (metres)

400

Anne

Carolyn

Barbara

0

0

60

Time (seconds)

The rough sketch graph shown above describes what happens when three athletes A, B, and C enter a 400 metres race.

Imagine that you are the race commentator. Describe what is happening as carefully as you can. You do not need to measure anything accurately.

Source: IAEP and CAEP (1992).

Real-Life Problems

When questioned about real-life problems, the students stated that problems having to do with people, time, travel, sports, money and food have real-life applications. The students were asked whether they could think of some real-life problems and more than one student suggested financial and budgeting problems. Some tried to come up with mathematical word problems that had to do with time, distance, and speed, gasoline consumption and the amount of radiation in the sun's rays. (It must be remembered, of course, that real-life to a 16-year-old student may not fit our adult view of real-life problems.) This poses an interesting dilemma: *Is it more valid for the basket to contain items that reflect the skills that adults consider critical for success in real life, or should the basket contain items that measure the skills that students identify as important in real life?* The five potential items assume the latter. However, there is a belief within the CCC sub-group that the basket should reflect skills critical for success in real life and unbounded by the curriculum.

The students' work was marked holistically with a rubric that was developed by the British Columbia Ministry of Education (see Figure 8.3). The rubric worked well for the items; the scores on all of the items ranged from 1 (Minimal Achievement) to 5 (Exceptional Achievement); this range of score suggests that the items are appropriate for 16-year-olds. Although inter-rater reliability is not an issue in such a limited pilot, in most cases the markers were in agreement or came within one mark of one another.

Cost and Format

There will have to be some decisions taken about the degree to which jurisdictions are prepared to pay for sophisticated approaches such as performance-type items and group rather than individual assessment. There are compelling reasons for assessing group rather than individual problem-solving, since in real life, *teams* are more commonly used to solve major problems. At the same focus-testing session discussed above, two groups of five students were given the group problem-solving task *Plan a Trip*. The task was developed for the British Columbia Ministry of Education and was designed with the following parameters in mind:

- a problem-solving activity requiring a group of five 16-year-old students to work together to develop solutions to a given problem;
- an integrated problem-solving task that requires students to use information from a variety of sources (print, map, timetables), make simple calculations about time and money, and reach a consensus;
- an open-ended problem with a number of variable factors to be identified and evaluated, and with no single, clear, or correct solution; and
- as the prompt for the problem-solving process, a hypothetical situation that the intended sample of students would find realistic, challenging, and engaging.

The hypothetical situation presented to the students required them to take on the roles of a committee responsible for planning a one-day outing or social activity for a group of thirty teenagers from 14 to 17 years old who belonged to the teen club at the city's Community Recreation Centre. The planning committee's task involved working within guidelines that included fixed budget, timeline, and information about potential activities. The hypothetical teen club's membership included a 17-year-old boy in a wheelchair and two 16-year-old girls who were exchange students from Japan and Finland. The complete package of materials given to students included the following:

- a description of the hypothetical situation, setting up the context, the planning committee's role and responsibilities, the task, and outlining seven potential options;
- a map of the city;
- a map of the geographical district;
- a bus schedule for the city's public transport system;

Figure/*Graphique* 8.3.   **General description of achievement levels**
Description générale des niveaux de compétence

LEVEL 1

– demonstrates little understanding and limited comprehension of the problem
– uses only the most basic parts of the information provided
– mixes facts and opinion
– states conclusions hastily after considering only a few pieces of information
– does not consider consequences

LEVEL 2

– demonstrates only very general understanding of scope of problem
– focuses on single aspect of the problem
– uses only the information provided
– may include opinion as well as information provided
– conclusions stated after quite limited examination of information
– limited consideration of consequences

LEVEL 3

– demonstrates general understanding of the scope of the problem
– uses information provided PLUS at least one idea from personal knowledge
– conclusions built on examination of information AND some consideration of consequences

---

LEVEL 4

– demonstrates clear understanding of the problem
– focuses on at least two aspects of the problem
– uses main points of the information PLUS relevant and consistent personal knowledge
– conclusions are built on the examination of major evidence
– considers at least one alternative and the possible consequences

---

LEVEL 5

– demonstrates a clear, accurate understanding of both scope and ramifications
– uses all information provided PLUS extensive personal knowledge that is factual, relevant and consistent
– conclusions based on thorough examination of the evidence
– explores reasonable alternatives
– evaluates consequences

Source: British Columbia Ministry of Education.

- rental rates for buses and minivans by the hour or day;
- a promotional letter about Woodlands Wildlife and Bird Sanctuary;
- an advertisement and a brochure about a Shakespeare theatre company;
- two fliers promoting displays at the city's museum;
- a flier advertising the city's amusement park and fun fair; and
- a promotional letter for a day trip on a cruise boat.

The hypothetical situation was constructed to include a number of variable factors that might affect the outcome as well as the problem-solving process, such as the following:
- the feasibility of each option (for example, cost, time, accessibility by available transportation, and random factors, such as weather);
- the level of interest and appeal inherent in each option;
- the interests and characteristics of the thirty teenagers as a group;
- special considerations related to individuals within the group;
- the social context within which the outing was sponsored and funded; and
- the extent to which the available information enabled students to make an informed choice about the viability of a particular option.

The draft scoring criteria for an assessment of problem-solving skills and strategies employed by the groups in the focus testing were intended to be consistent with those used to assess the individual items. The general framework used for the criteria and rubrics involves the following three stages:
- understanding the scope of the problem (Gathering information);
- using information to develop a position (Processing information); and
- reaching solutions and considering consequences (Applying information).

The two groups completed the activity in about one hour and approached their tasks with positive attitudes, displayed a high level of engagement with the hypothetical situation they had been presented with, and appeared to maintain their interest and willingness to work together co-operatively throughout the activity.

On the basis of feedback received from the students, teachers and CCC subgroup members, the task has been modified to reduce its complexity and therefore the amount of time that would be taken up administering it, and scoring the student responses.
- it is now presented as an individual task rather than a group task;
- the number of options has been reduced to four and the bus schedule simplified;
- several detail changes have also been made to the material provided to make it less susceptible to cultural bias;
- the communications component has now been expanded and includes a few multiple choice questions on reading comprehension, to establish whether or not the student has understood the material presented; and
- in addition to a scoring rubric for problem solving, there is now a simple rubric for scoring communication skills (see Figure 8.4).

Figure/*Graphique* 8.4. **Rubrics for effective communication standards**
Rubriques concernant les compétences en matière de communication

Expresses ideas clearly

4   Clearly and effectively communicates the main idea or theme and provides support that contains rich, vivid and powerful detail.

3   Clearly communicates the main idea or theme and provides suitable support and detail.

2   Communicates important information but not a clear theme or overall structure.

1   Communicates information as isolated pieces in a random fashion.

Creates quality products

4   Creates a product that exceeds conventional standards.

3   Creates a product that clearly meets conventional standards.

2   Creates a product that does not meet one or a few important standards.

1   Creates a product that does not address the majority of the conventional standards.

Source: British Columbia Ministry of Education.

4. Conclusion

Clearly, the *Plan a Trip* task requires a significant amount of communication. Students must read through the materials that they are provided with and communicate orally with one another in order to make decisions and reach a consensus. It is proposed to code the task to measure cross-curricular listening and speaking skills. The costs and complexity associated with this approach may make it unsuitable for the major data-gathering exercise. It may be possible to administer this task to a sub-sample of students, that is, a number of students could attempt this item specifically, instead of the other items.

Much of the work of the CCC sub-group has been exploratory in nature, and whether or not valid and reliable indicators of cross-curricular outcomes can be developed is not clear at this time. In the areas of problem-solving and communication skills the challenges are many and the answers, as yet, few. Nevertheless, as these indicators show considerable potential, development work will continue.

References

BAILIN, S. (1987), "Critical and creative thinking", *Informal Logic,* Vol. 9 (1), pp. 23-30.

BAKER, E.L., O'NEIL, HAROLD F., and LINN, R.L. (1993), "Policy and validity prospects for performance-based assessment", *American Psychologist,* Vol. 48 (12), pp. 1210-1218.

BRIDGES, D. (1993), "Transferable skills: a philosophical perspective", *Studies in Higher Education,* Vol. 18 (1), pp. 43-51.

BROADFOOT, P. (1994), "Achievements of learning", in OECD, *Making Education Count: Developing and Using International Indicators,* OECD, Paris, pp. 237-263.

CASE, R. (1992), "On the need to assess authentically", *Holistic Education Review,* Winter, pp. 14-23.

CASSIDY, W.E. and BOGNAR, C.J. (1992, April), *Critical Thinking in Social Studies: Methods and Findings of a Wide-scale Assessment,* Paper presented at the annual meeting of the American Educational Research Association, San Francisco, CA.

CIZEK, G.J. (1993), "Some thoughts on educational testing: measurement policy issues into the next millennium", *Educational Measurement: Issues and Practice,* Vol. 12 (3), pp. 10-16.

COOMBS, J.R. (1986), *Practical Reasoning: What is it? How do we Enhance it?,* Paper presented at the international conference on thinking and problem-solving, Ohio State University, June.

Critical thinking tests (1985), Compiled by Robert H. Ennis for the eighth annual and sixth international conference on critical thinking and educational reform, June.

ENNIS, R.H. (1985a), "Critical thinking and the curriculum", *Phi Kappa Phi Journal,* No. 65 (1), pp. 28-31.

ENNIS, R.H. (1985b), *A Taxonomy of Critical Thinking and Abilities,* Paper presented at the annual meeting of the American Federation of Teachers, Washington, DC, July.

ENNIS, R.H. (1989), "Critical thinking and subject specificity: clarification and needed research", *Educational Researcher,* Vol. 18 (3), pp. 4-10.

ENNIS, R.H. (1990), "The extent to which critical thinking is subject specific: further clarification", *Educational Researcher,* Vol. 19 (4), pp. 13-16.

ETS (1990), *Annotated Bibliography of Tests: Reasoning, Logical Thinking, Problem-solving,* Educational Testing Service, Princeton, NJ, February.

FACIONE, P.A. (1991), *Using the California Critical Thinking Skills test in Research, Evaluation, and Assessment,* California Academic Press, Millbrae, CA.

GORMAN, T.P., PURVES, A.C. and DEGENHART, R.E. (eds.) (1988), *The IEA Study of Written Composition I: The International Writing Tasks and Scoring Scales,* Pergamon Press, Oxford.

GRIFFITH, J. and MEDRICH, E.A. (1992), "What does the United States want to learn from international comparative studies in education?", *Prospects,* Vol. 22 (4), pp. 476-485.

HALLS, W.D. (1988), "The French secondary school today", in Robert F. Lawson (ed.), *Changing Patterns of Secondary Education: An International Comparison,* University of Calgary Press, Calgary, Canada, pp. 47-71.

HANNA, G., LADOUCEUR, A., and POSTI, B. (1986), *Bias in the Translation of Achievement Tests from English to French in the Second International Mathematics Study,* Paper presented at the annual meeting of the Educational Research Association, San Francisco, CA.

HECKLEY K.J. and MARTIN-KNIEP, G. (1992), "Students' geographic knowledge and skills in different kinds of tests: multiple choice versus performance assessment", *Social Education,* No. 56 (2), pp. 95-98.

HOFFMAN, J.K. and HOFFMAN, C.C. (1990), *Training Assessors to Produce High Interrater Reliability in Evaluating Complex Writing Samples,* Paper presented at the IPMAAC conference on personnel assessment, San Diego, CA, June.

HOLENESS, M. (1990), "Well-rounded attainment", *Education,* No. 175 (17), pp. 414-415.

HUOT, B. (1990), "Reliability, validity, and holistic scoring: what we know and what we need to know", *College Composition and Communication,* No. 41 (2), pp. 201-213.

HUOT, B. (1990), "The literature of direct writing assessment: major concerns and prevailing trends", *Review of Educational Research,* No. 60 (2), pp. 237-263.

International Assessment of Educational Progress and Centre for the Assessment of Educational Progress (1992*a*), *Learning about the World,* Report No. 22-CAEP-05, IAEP/CAEP, Princeton New Jersey, June.

International Assessment of Educational Progress and Centre for the Assessment of Educational Progress (1992*b*), *Performance Assessment: An International Experiment,* Report No. 22-CAEP-06, IAEP/CAEP, Princeton, New Jersey, July.

JESSUP, G. (1991), *Outcomes: NVQs and the Emerging Model of Education and Training,* Falmer Press, London.

KNEEDLER, P.E. (1993), "Assessment of the critical thinking skills in history-social science", *Social Studies Review,* No. 27 (3), pp. 2-93.

KNOLT, E.A. (1984), *The Aims Approach: More Effective Writing for the Real World,* Paper presented at the annual meeting of the conference on college composition and communication, New York.

KOBAYASHI, T. and OTA, H. (1988), "Secondary education in Japan", in Robert F. Lawson (ed.), *Changing Patterns of Secondary Education: An International Comparison,* University of Calgary Press, Calgary, Canada, pp. 143-163.

LAWSON, R.F. (ed.) (1988), *Changing Patterns of Secondary Education: An International Comparison,* University of Calgary Press, Calgary, Canada.

LINK, F. (1991), "Thinking to write: assessing higher-order cognitive skills and abilities", in Arthur L. Costa (ed.), *Developing Minds: Programs for Teaching Thinking, revised edition,* Association for Supervision and Curriculum Development, Alexandria, VA, Vol. 2.

MAYBERRY, P. (1984), *Analysis of Cross-cultural Attitudinal Scale Translation Using Maximum Likelihood Factor Analysis,* Paper presented at the annual meeting of the American Educational Research Association, New Orleans, April.

MITTER, W. (1988), "Secondary education in the Federal Republic of Germany", in Robert F. Lawson (ed.), *Changing Patterns of Secondary Education: An International Comparison,* University of Calgary Press, Calgary, Canada, pp. 89-108.

MODJESKI, R.B. and WILLIAM, M.B. (1983), "An evaluation by a panel of psychologists of the reliability and validity of two tests of critical thinking", *Educational and Psychological Measurement,* Vol. 43, pp. 1187-1196.

MUTHÉN, B.O. (1989), "Using item-specific instructional information in achievement modeling", *Psychometricka,* Vol. 54 (3), pp. 385-396.

NORRIS, S.P. (1985), "Synthesis of research on critical thinking", *Educational Leadership,* May, pp. 40-45.

OECD (1989), *Education and the Economy in a Changing Society,* OECD, Paris.

PAUL, R.W. and NOSICH, G.M. (1991), *A Proposal for the National Assessment of Higher-order Thinking at the Community College, College, and University Levels,* Paper commissioned by the United States Department of Education, Washington, DC.

POPHAM, J.W. (1981), *Modern Educational Measurement,* Prentice Hall, Englewood Cliffs, NJ.

Province of British Columbia, Ministry of Education (1989), *Mandate for the School System,* Queen's Printer, Victoria, British Columbia, Canada.

Province of British Columbia, Ministry of Education (1993), *Improving the Quality of Education in British Columbia: Changes to British Columbia's Education Policy,* Queen's Printer, Victoria, British Columbia, Canada.

QUELLMALZ, E. (1986), *Recommendations for the Design of NAEP Writing Tasks,* Paper commissioned by the Study Group of the National Assessment of Student Achievement and cited in Appendix B to their final report "The Nation's Report Card", NCES, US Department of Education, Washington, DC.

RESNICK, L.B. (1987), *Education and Learning to Think,* National Academy Press, Washington, DC.

SCHROEDER, T.L. (1992), *Qualities of Problem-solving,* Report of a project conducted in conjunction with the 1990 British Columbia Mathematics Assessment.

SCHUBAUER-LEONI, M.L., BELL, N., GROSSEN, M. and PERRET-CLERMONT, A.N. (1989), "Problems in assessment of learning: the social construction of questions and answers in the scholastic context", *International Journal of Education Research,* No. 13 (6), pp. 671-684.

Shell Centre for Mathematical Education (1983), *The Language of Functions and Graphs: An Examination Module for Secondary Schools,* Joint Matriculation Board, Manchester.

STACEY, K. and SOUTHWELL, B. (1991), *Teacher Tactics for Problem Solving,* Curriculum Corporation, Melbourne.

TAKALA, S. (1988), "Origins of the international study of writing", in T.P. Gorman, A.C. Purves, and R.E. Degenhart (eds.), *The IEA Study of Written Composition I: The International Writing Tasks and Scoring Scales,* Pergamon Press, Oxford.

TAKALA, S. and VÄHÄPASSI, A. (1987), "Written communication as an object of comparative research", *Comparative Education Review,* No. 31 (1), pp. 88-105.

TALBOT, J. (1986), "The assessment of critical thinking in history/social science through writing", *Social Studies Review,* No. 25 (2), pp. 33-41.

WELLS, K.M. (1983), *The Development of a Critical Thinking Skills Performance Assessment: An Interdisciplinary Approach to Validating Achievement of School Goals,* Paper presented at the annual meeting of the American Education Research Association, Montreal, Quebec, April.

WERNER, P.H. (1991), "The Ennis-Weir critical thinking essay test: an instrument for testing and teaching", *Journal of Reading,* No. 34 (6), pp. 494-495.

WESTAT, Inc. (1993), *Establishing Proficiency Levels and Descriptions for the 1992 Maryland School Performance Assessment Program (MSAP),* Background paper submitted to the Maryland State Department of Education by Westat, Inc., Rockville, Maryland.

WOLF, A. (1991), "Assessing core skills: wisdom or wild goose chase?", *Cambridge Journal of Education,* No. 21 (2), pp. 189-201.

WRIGHT, I. (1992), "Critical thinking: curriculum and instructional policy implications", *Journal of Education Policy,* No. 7 (1), pp. 37-43.

Developing an Indicator of National Education Goals
Mise au point d'un indicateur d'objectifs nationaux de l'enseignement

Introduction

by

Marit Granheim
Ministry of Education, Research and Church Affairs, Oslo, Norway

The Goals Orientation and Attainment in Learning Systems (GOALS) project is described in Chapters 9, 10, and 11. The network's interest in this project centres on linking measures of student outcomes to national goals and policies. Chapter 9, by Marit Granheim and Sten Pettersson, begins this part by presenting an overview of the processes which countries use to formulate, implement, assess and monitor the goals of their education systems. In determining whether a country has reached its goals, the authors assess its intended, implemented, and achieved curriculum. Concepts surrounding this achieved curriculum are explored in Chapter 9, in which the authors create a framework in which these goals are grouped, and conclude by outlining a pilot study that examines goals in a range of countries. The results of this pilot study, which involved eight countries, are contained in Chapter 10.

In Chapter 10, Astrid Eggen Knutsen, who co-ordinated the pilot study, describes some of the problems faced by the network in developing an instrument that could capture the education goals of a country. This study examines the ways in which educational objectives are determined, and the overall policy orientations that guided their establishment within eight OECD Member countries. Because the issue of data collection, and the way in which the aims of the study were communicated, were as important as the results themselves, the task of completing the survey was assigned to at least two panels of representatives drawn from various sectors of each country's educational system. The survey included questions allowing participants to comment on the implementation instrument itself. This chapter presents the preliminary findings from this pilot study as well as suggestions for its improvement.

As noted earlier, the study of achieved curricula plays an integral role in evaluating a country's education goals. In Chapter 11, Kevin Piper furthers the research of this project by creating a typology of curricula to determine the viability of using curriculum style as a process variable. His study of teachers in twenty schools finds a relationship between their curriculum styles and the education goals of their programmes. While this finding is valuable to the GOALS project, his typology cannot be incorporated into the work of the network until further studies are conducted to determine its relevance to the education systems of other OECD countries.

The GOALS project intends to advance the understanding of national education system comparisons by studying the relationship between the goals of a country's system and the manner in which it strives to achieve those goals. To this end, these chapters present the latest empirical and theoretical work of the network.

Introduction

par

Marit Granheim
Ministère de l'Éducation, de la Recherche et des Cultes, Oslo, Norvège

Le projet sur le choix des objectifs et leur réalisation dans les systèmes d'enseignement (GOALS) est décrit aux chapitres 9, 10 et 11. Avec ce projet, le réseau s'intéresse surtout à la possibilité de lier les mesures de résultats scolaires aux politiques et objectifs nationaux. Rédigé par Marit Granheim et Sten Pettersson, le chapitre 9 présente un aperçu des procédés utilisés par les pays pour formuler, mettre en œuvre, évaluer et suivre les objectifs de leurs systèmes d'enseignement respectifs. Pour déterminer si un pays a atteint ses objectifs, les auteurs évaluent son programme éducatif tel qu'il a été prévu, mis en œuvre puis réalisé, et analysent les concepts entourant le programme réalisé. Ils établissent ensuite un cadre dans lequel ils regroupent les objectifs et, en conclusion, décrivent brièvement une étude pilote qui examine les objectifs de divers pays. Les résultats de cette étude, à laquelle ont participé huit pays, sont présentés au chapitre 10.

Au chapitre 10, Astrid Eggen Knutsen, coordonnatrice de l'étude pilote, expose certains des problèmes qu'affronte le réseau dans l'élaboration d'un outil susceptible de définir les objectifs éducatifs d'un pays. L'étude examine la façon dont sont déterminés ces objectifs et les orientations politiques globales qui ont présidé à leur établissement dans huit pays de l'OCDE. Comme le problème de la collecte des données et la manière dont les buts de l'étude ont été communiqués étaient aussi importants que les résultats eux-mêmes, la réalisation de l'étude a été confiée à au moins deux panels de représentants appartenant à divers secteurs du système éducatif de chaque pays. L'étude comportait des questions permettant aux participants de commenter l'outil lui-même. Le chapitre présente les conclusions préliminaires de l'étude pilote ainsi que des propositions en vue de l'améliorer.

Comme nous l'avons remarqué plus haut, l'étude des programmes réalisés joue un rôle essentiel dans l'évaluation des objectifs d'un pays en matière d'enseignement. Dans le chapitre 11, Kevin Piper approfondit la recherche relative à ce projet en créant une typologie de programmes d'études afin de déterminer si l'utilisation d'un style de programme en tant que variable de processus est viable. Son étude sur les enseignants de vingt écoles permet de déduire qu'il existe un rapport entre les styles des programmes et les objectifs d'enseignement. Bien que cette observation soit utile au projet GOALS, la typologie ne peut être intégrée dans les travaux du réseau avant que ne soient effectuées des études complémentaires afin de déterminer sa pertinence pour les systèmes d'enseignement des autres pays de l'OCDE.

Le projet GOALS vise à améliorer les comparaisons des systèmes éducatifs nationaux grâce à l'étude de la relation entre les objectifs des systèmes et la manière dont les pays s'efforcent de les atteindre. A cette fin, les chapitres réunis ici décrivent les travaux empiriques et théoriques les plus récents du réseau.

Goals Orientation and Attainment in Learning Systems
Le choix des objectifs et leur réalisation
dans les systèmes d'enseignement

par

Marit Granheim
Ministry of Education, Research and Church Affairs, Oslo, Norway

and

Sten Pettersson
National Agency for Education, Stockholm, Sweden

The purpose of this chapter is to discuss the possibilities of identifying the goals set for education systems in different countries, and to reflect them in indicators, so that information about goal orientations can be taken into account when interpreting evidence on the outcomes of education. Of primary interest are not only the content specifications and various demands expressed, but in the first instance the *types* of goal which an education system may use; secondly, to establish where responsibility for setting goals is located in the education system; and thirdly, to indicate whether (and, if so, where) responsibility for evaluating the goals can be found in the system. This chapter proposes a structure of different types of education goals. This structure was used as the conceptual framework for a pilot survey of national goals undertaken in eight OECD countries.

*

* *

Note de synthèse

On étudie dans ce chapitre la façon dont les pays identifient leurs objectifs en matière de systèmes d'enseignement, et comment ils les formulent sous forme d'indicateurs. Bien que l'enseignement ait des objectifs dans tous les pays, il existe une grande diversité dans le choix de ces objectifs, l'importance relative qui leur est attribuée et les moyens utilisés pour en évaluer la réalisation.

On peut rapprocher les différents types de résultats des différents niveaux ou lieux qui existent dans un système éducatifn : le lieu où les objectifs sont formulés, le lieu où ils sont mis en contexte et le lieu de la réalisation. Pour piloter un système éducatif il existe trois instruments principaux : les objectifs, le programme d'études et l'évaluation.

Il est possible d'évaluer les résultats de chaque pays en fonction du programme prévu, mis en œuvre, évalué et mené à bien. Pour mesurer cette évolution, il existe des méthodes diverses (par exemple, l'analyse des déclarations d'intention officielles, ou l'analyse du contenu du programme d'études). Ce sont moins les objectifs eux-mêmes qui sont les plus intéressants ici que le fait qu'ils constituent le point de départ pour évaluer le fossé qui existe entre les résultats scolaires tels qu'ils sont actuellement mesurés et les intentions et attentes. Autrement dit, on s'attache à la façon dont les intentions s'expriment à travers la configuration des objectifs.

On peut examiner trois grandes catégories d'objectifs. La première comprend :

- *les valeurs et les principes fondamentaux – les principes éthiques ou moraux qui constituent les fondements de l'éducation ;*
- *les objectifs novateurs de l'école tout entière ;*
- *les objectifs qui ont un retentissement direct sur les élèves.*

La deuxième catégorie comprend les objectifs disciplinaires suivants :

- *les objectifs prévisionnels – les objectifs qui ne sont jamais entièrement atteints dans la pratique mais qui servent à centrer l'enseignement d'un contenu particulier ;*
- *les objectifs à atteindre – qui sont liés à certains domaines particuliers du savoir ;*
- *les compétences de base – certains objectifs à atteindre qui représentent le minimum de maîtrise de la lecture, de l'écriture et du calcul dont les élèves ont besoin pour fonctionner dans la vie de tous les jours.*

La troisième catégorie comprend les objectifs transdisciplinaires suivants :

- *les techniques de vie en société qui aident les élèves à devenir des citoyens indépendants ;*
- *les compétences essentielles telles que la communication, la résolution des problèmes et le raisonnement critique ;*
- *les techniques de communication qui font partie des compétences essentielles.*

Les catégories d'objectifs précédentes ont servi de cadre conceptuel pour l'étude pilote portant sur huit pays de l'OCDE. Les résultats montrent que les pays ne réagissent pas tous de la même façon à la présentation du questionnaire. La plus grande difficulté posée par l'élaboration de l'indicateur est la définition des objectifs et des catégories de réponses, ce qui montre bien la nécessité d'autres recherches préliminaires. Il faut garder à l'esprit que l'identification d'une méthode qui permet de mesurer les objectifs, pour importante qu'elle soit, n'est qu'une première étape, l'objectif ultime restant de développer des indicateurs de résultats dans l'enseignement qui permettent d'évaluer les progrès réalisés pour atteindre les buts.

*

*   *

1. Introduction

Growing interest in many countries in the quality of education and the outcomes of education has led to school reform that has focused on revising the work of teachers and teacher training through a changing conception of pedagogy. Currently, there is concern to provide teachers with more autonomy, privilege, and status. Words such as *reflection*, *empowerment*, and *teacher control* are used to speak about the new roles and conditions which are to reform schools.

The traditional means of steering by rules, regulations, and allocations of funds from the national level to the local level are being supplemented by more emphasis on the formulation of goals, on monitoring, reporting, and on evaluation and professionalisation of teachers and school administrators.

There also is a growing interest in national curriculum plans and national goals. Some countries, in fact, have had curriculum plans for a long time; and in these countries, the focus is on how goals are followed up and how outcomes are evaluated. Another interest is whether the goals in these plans are formulated in such a way that they can be used as criteria for evaluation. Countries that have had no national curriculum plan seem to see the need to develop plans to influence the contents of education and its outcomes.

Many countries face the challenge of developing a functional distribution of responsibilities, roles, and accountability in the education sector, and of developing systems of evaluation and reporting of outcomes at the main levels in the system.

The purpose of this chapter is to discuss a number of issues that have arisen in connection with the work on indicators of *outcomes* of education, especially possibilities of constructing indicators that can reflect goals set for the education systems of different countries. It is interesting and relevant to compare how different countries choose to formulate their intentions in goals and curricula and how they assess and monitor those elements.

Examination of the outcomes of a country's education system in terms of student achievement is important of course, but can yield an incomplete picture of the functioning of the education system, particularly if it is not related to the whole complex of prerequisites. A fuller picture requires an understanding of what a country *wants* to achieve – that is, its education goals and its aims for education – and an understanding of how the curriculum is established, maintained and developed. From a system perspective, curriculum goals can also be seen as types of outcome produced somewhere in the system as a whole, but representing essential parts of intended student outcomes.

Countries stress the need for explicit goals differently. There also is a great variety between countries concerning the content of desirable outcomes, and the ways of formulating them. What is common among most countries is their intent (*i.e.* what countries want to achieve through their education system).

Starting from intent as a point of departure, the aim of this chapter is to investigate whether it is possible to develop a method to describe *what kind* of explicit goals different countries work with. The focus, as previously stated, is on understanding the types of goal which an education system uses and on establishing where responsibility for setting these goals is located in the education system, as well as on indicating whether – and if so where – responsibility for evaluating whether goals are achieved and how well goals are incorporated in the system. Reaching an understanding of what kinds of goal a country pursues is not an end in itself, but a prerequisite for assessing the gap between actually measured student outcomes and what was intended and expected.

2. A Frame of Reference

A frame of reference is needed in which goals for education can be examined in relation to different levels or «arenas» in school systems. In accordance with the models of frame factors for curriculum analysis proposed by Lundgren and others, we distinguish three arenas, as follows:

- *formulation arena* – a central level that may be at the national or state level;
- *contextualisation arena* – a system or institutional level that may be a municipality or a school district; and
- *realisation arena* – a level of realisation.

3. Outcomes Related to Different Levels or Arenas

The responsibility of a formulation arena is to formulate goals for the school and to design the framework within which the latter is supposed to operate. The outcome is curriculum, syllabus, and economic resources (*i.e.* demands and dimensions).

The contextualisation arena, which is framed by the formulation arena, is responsible for organisational and material matters and must contextualise what is prescribed by the different institutional settings. The outcome here is the extent to which the institution can *produce* different types of desired *products*, and includes the institution's resources, possibilities, and management. In many countries, such responsibilities are decentralised to peripheral areas, from state to municipalities or local authorities. Evaluation systems can be seen as a part of the contextualisation arena.

The realisation arena is the level of the individual student. Student outcomes can be seen as the kind of knowledge and experience the students gain from their education processes in the schools. This can be aggregated, as has been done within the INES project, through indicators of achievement.

If this is accepted, we can go a step further and observe that different outcome arenas may be connected with different levels. Put another way, the outcome in one arena is a prerequisite for the next. Goals formulated at a national or central level very often contain different types of goals and also general statements concerning the character of schooling.

A fundamental principle in the thinking we are using (Granheim and Lundgren, 1991) is that we can distinguish between the following:

- fundamental principles for work in school, which are incorporated in legislation;
- education goals, which are expressed in curriculum guidelines and which comprise the basis of the work of each school; and
- innovation goals which may be defined in national and local plans and form the basis for work on development and improvement in school.

The goals for the school are many and diversified. An evaluation of the results of schooling should, as far as possible, take account of this range of objectives.

That the school should promote intellectual freedom and tolerance is not a goal *per se*, but a fundamental principle that is valid for all work in the school. That the school should promote the student's development as a useful and independent individual is a socialisation goal, which cannot be related to a specific knowledge structure. Such a goal deals with one's competence as a citizen and as a learner. That the school should provide students with good general knowledge is a knowledge-based goal related to specific knowledge structures (*i.e.* what knowledge should be included and how this knowledge should be organised).

In the arena of realisation, these different principles and goals mean different types of activities, rules, and traditions. All of them have a relationship, given that the outcome is seen as a complex structure of elements of knowledge of facts and principles, attitudes towards knowledge and learning, social competencies, and so on.

From the perspective of the students and with results in focus, we can see the arena of realisation as follows:

- a social context framed by certain (ethical) principles;
- with certain rules and demands that are supposed to be followed; and
- a body of knowledge to be learned.

Outcomes Related to Arenas

Seen from an institutional perspective (the arena of contextualisation), the outcome is not so much a matter of considering what is "in the heads and bodies" of the students, but more to provide the necessary organisational framework and resources for the realisation arena to achieve the goals of the system.

Figure 9.1 gives an overview of what has been said so far and of the concept we are using.

To see the outcome in the perspective broadly sketched here, means, as we understand it, a possibility of seeing it in the context of intended, implemented, assessed and achieved curriculum; and what can be done is to work with the following:

- *Analysis of officially recognised goal statements* – in curriculum and other official educational documents of the various countries.
- *Analysis of the content of curriculum.* What can be found in the curriculum? The structure and content? This can make it possible to develop a method for describing "the student's journey through the curriculum", or what knowledge-base the school gives to a population. This is to be seen in turn as an outcome at an institutional or system level.
- *Analysis of official national tests of achievement* (including examinations) already being used by individual countries, to gain insight into the extent to which individual countries have found such national assessment necessary.
- *Identification of a set of "complex" goals* (*e.g.* equality, tolerance) and development of methods to survey:
  - how these goals are incorporated in the system,
  - what means are used to attain such goals, and
  - what methods are used to assess progress towards the goals.

Figure/*Graphique* 9.1. **Outcomes related to arenas**
Résultats par type d'opération

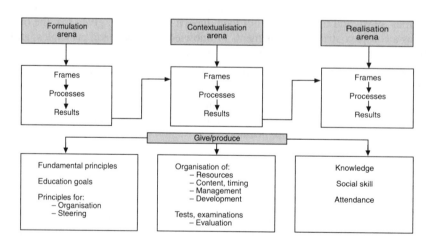

Source: Authors.

170

Goals

In the following discussion, we shall limit ourselves to the first element above (goal statements). Our purpose, to reiterate, is to investigate whether it is possible to find a method of describing with *what kinds* of explicit goals different countries work. The focus of interest is threefold: firstly, not the specific contents and demands expressed, but the types of goals an education system uses; secondly, to establish a picture of where responsibility for setting goals is located in the education system; and thirdly, to indicate whether (and, if so, where) responsibility for evaluating the goals can be found.

For the above purpose, a structure of different types of education goals has been developed, in which categories of goals are defined. The structure and definitions are given below, and are stimulated by an interest in what the system desires to give its students and an interest in the means of achieving what is desired. The categories of goals will be related to the following questions:

- To what extent are the different kinds of goals made explicit in a country's education system?
- Where in the system are the different kinds of goals formulated? Who (what level) is responsible for establishing the goals?
- To what degree are the different goals incorporated in a country's education system?
- Where is the responsibility for evaluation of goals located in a country's education system?

To help to answer these questions, a set of fixed response possibilities has been developed for each question. This, of course, means a reduction in information, but corresponds to our limited descriptive ambitions. The set of fixed responses is given towards the end of this chapter.

There is a wide range of possibilities for steering a country's education system. There are, besides funding, rules of organisation, and teacher training of different kinds, three main instruments for governing an education system: 1) goals, 2) curriculum, and 3) evaluation. Each of these implies a range of options for influencing educational development, which can be dealt with in different arenas and contexts of responsibility. However, in the remainder of this chapter the goals are in focus. The main interest is not the content of education as expressed by the goals themselves, but the way intentions are communicated through a certain *structure* of goals.

A possible classification of categories of education goals is proposed below. The first distinction is between systemic and individual goals.

A 1.   Fundamental principles and values
A 2.   Innovation goals

B 1.   Prospective goals
B 2.   Attainment goals
B 2.1 Basic skills

171

C 1.   Community life skills (prospective)
C 2.   Essential skills
C 2.1 Communication skills

These different types of goals are not explicitly formulated at different levels within a country's education system, and they imply different contents. However, what is of primary interest is that the categories represent a structure in which goals can be observed.

The elements do not refer to specific phenomena or have necessarily similar expressions within differing contexts. However, they do establish *frames* for different fields or main types of goals. The fields that are demarcated vary with respect to what kind of competence they focus upon, their referents, and their grade of embeddedness.

The reasoning behind the *taxonomy* used is as follows. Firstly, we make a distinction between goals related to student achievement and goals related to the activity or functioning of the entire system.

Achievement-related goals can either be orientated towards students' social proficiencies (cross-subject-related goals) or towards intended outcomes within specific areas of knowledge (subject-related goals).

Activity-related or system-related goals can be divided into fundamental principles and values that are supposed to be valid for the activity as a whole, and goals for innovation and development. It is also possible to add, here, goals related to student and parental influence.

Another step can then be taken by classifying knowledge-related goals into prospective goals, attainment goals, and goals for basic skills. Social proficiencies are in the same step divided into goals for community life skills (which can also be labelled socialisation goals), goals for essential skills, and, within these, the more specific goals for communication skills.

In this way, we are able to identify relevant categories. However, the classification is not all-inclusive; it only covers the main features of what a country's education system aims to achieve. The model can be expanded and adapted in all dimensions used, if so desired.

Figure 9.2 gives an overview of the concepts used. The arrows indicate different dimensions: hierarchy of areas of competence; specifics within areas of competence; and process quality, which includes allowance for change and influence.

Categories of Goals

The categories of defined goals are broad. However, the fact that goals of a certain kind are to be found in education does not mean that all aspects mentioned here have to be included.

A 1. Fundamental Principles and Values

Fundamental principles and values are not goals in the exact meaning of the word. They are ethical or moral principles and fundamental values that can be regarded as

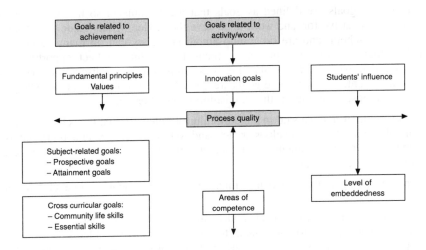

Source: Authors.

foundations of education or guidelines for education. They are, in fact, valid for all activities in education.

An example of this universality can be seen if a country's Schools Act stresses that all children and young people shall have equal access to education, and that education shall be equal (or that school, together with home, shall support the student's harmonious development into a person conscious of his or her individual responsibility within society).

A 2.   *Innovation Goals*

Innovation or development goals are of the same type as A 1. The referent here is the school as a whole, rather than the student. Principally, innovation goals can be defined as goals for organised units within the education system. Goals can be said to result from organisational development processes (*i.e.* OD goals). That is, goals leading to activities that will improve the school and gradually be incorporated into the school's daily work. Innovation goals form the basis of the work for development and innovation in schools and can be intended for the whole of compulsory schooling or for single schools, states, or other *units* within the system. What is characteristic of innovation goals is that they explicitly state that 1) certain areas are objects for development, that 2) goals are set for the work, and that 3) the results of the efforts will be followed up. The goals have a relation to what are conceived as *needs* identified by the organised unit itself.

B 1.   Prospective Goals

Prospective goals are defined as goals that are formulated so that the school can attempt to realise, strive for, and work to achieve them. Here, goals guide the orientation of the work in school, and are broad and ambitious. They can, in many cases, not be attained in their entirety, but provide a focus for teaching, reflect opportunities for development that exist in the school and provide support for local discussion on choosing educational content. As such, these goals are related to a specific base of knowledge, but they do not impose a ceiling on the acquisition of knowledge.

For example, it may be said in the curriculum framework that the school shall strive to ensure that the student develops a rich and subtle language, and understands the importance of cultivating language; or that the student shall learn to communicate in more than one foreign language.

A prospective goal in mathematics might be that the student shall develop his or her ability:

- to understand and use fundamental mathematical concepts and methods;
- to use mathematics to understand, formulate, and solve problems and to interpret and validate solutions in accordance with the problem situation given; and
- to create and use simple mathematical models and to examine critically the prerequisites, constraints, and uses of the models.

B 2.   Attainment Goals

In contrast to prospective goals, attainment goals specify precisely what students shall receive in school. These goals are related to specific areas of knowledge and are similar to those labelled *basic skills*. The difference is that basic skills only cover a few subject areas, whereas attainment goals cover a broader range. One criterion to determine whether this type of goal can be said to be part of a country's structure of goals is that there should be goals of this kind covering a broader content than what is covered by basic skills. Basic skills form, accordingly, a part of what is here defined as attainment goals or standards.

Every pupil leaving compulsory school shall:

- have a mastery of fundamental mathematical thinking in order to be able to solve everyday problems;
- know and understand fundamental concepts and contexts within natural sciences, technical, social, and humanistic areas; and
- be able to communicate in speech and writing in English.

In mathematics, every pupil shall be able to understand and use basic statistical concepts, be able to put together, interpret, and assess data in tables and diagrams, and be able to understand and use the concept of probability in random situations.

B 2.1. Goals for Basic Skills within Certain Subject Areas

Goals for basic skills can be a part of what are defined above as *attainment goals*. This kind of goal deals with what is considered a minimum level of knowledge within reading, writing, and arithmetic. Such goals state, then, what every student should achieve as a minimum to be able to function in everyday life.

C 1. Goals for Community Life Skills

These goals, sometimes labelled *socialisation goals*, deal with the task of schooling to promote the student's development towards becoming an independent human being within a community. These are goals related to upbringing and to what sort of competence education should give students as citizens (and not to a specific knowledge structure). The goal here is to focus on understanding and accepting the customs, standards, traditions, and overall culture of the society of which the pupil is a member, and active co-operation and communication within that society.

Community life skill goals cannot be achieved in isolation from essential learning areas, but they are here defined as *specific skills, proficiencies, and attitudes expressed as aims and objectives for a country's education system*. Principally, these goals have two dimensions, both related to certain groups of competencies – one refers to skills and the other to attitudes. (One example of a group of competencies might be co-operation, in which the education goal is not only to develop the student's co-operative skills, but also to develop a positive attitude towards co-operation in general.)

C 2. Essential Skills

Another group of competencies relates to the teaching of communication, problem-solving, self-management, self-confidence, learning, studying, critical reasoning, and to creativity and practical life experiences, and sees all of these as *essential skills*. In contrast to C 1 goals, which have a "collective" and process focus, these goals use the student as referent.

C 2.1. Goals for Communication Skills

Goals for communication skills are a basic part of what has been defined here as essential skills goals. Communication goals are objects of a special study within Network A of the INES project, and are therefore given a category of their own.

Goals for communication skills involve the skills that are essential for real life. They mostly aim to promote communication for the purpose of learning, of developing thinking, of sharing information, of demonstrating understanding, of influencing others, of making connections with others, and for social ritual and the enrichment of a student's life through culture. Goals for communication skills are generally considered to contain the following six elements or dimensions: reading, writing, speaking, listening, viewing and representing.

Goals of this kind may be expressed as follows:

- *Business education*: students will have opportunities to develop and to apply appropriate communication skills in various business and personal contexts.
- *Art education*: students will have opportunities to demonstrate an ability to communicate through the visual image.
- *Mathematics education*: students will have opportunities to develop mathematical power by learning to communicate mathematically.

A Pilot Study

In 1994, the categories of goals defined above were, in a slightly different form, the subject of a pilot study conducted in eight countries. The purpose of the study was to test the validity of the model and of a survey instrument developed to elicit information on the education goals with which different countries work.

The following four questions with fixed responses were used, and each of the different types of goals above was supposed to be labelled according to them. Each type of goal was by that procedure related to the four questions:

Question I. To what extent are the following kinds of goals explicit in the country's education system?

Responses to be used:

1 = Full extent; represents goals that are valid for the whole country.
2 = Medium extent; represents goals that are valid for a majority of the different parts of the country with responsibility for education.
3 = Low extent; only some parts of the education system of the country have goals of this kind.
4 = No extent; this kind of goal cannot be explicitly found in the country.

Question II. Where in the system are the following goals formulated? Who (what level) is responsible for setting the aims and objectives?

Responses to be used:

NA = National level
ST = State/*Länder*/Canton level
MU = Municipality level
SC = School level
CR = Classroom/Teacher level
0 = not relevant question according to earlier answer

Question III. To what degree are the following goals, aims, and objectives incorporated in the country's education system?

Responses to be used:

1 = Fully incorporated; the goal is fully mandated and defined operationally. There is also an evaluation system in place.
2 = Medium incorporated; incorporated in the system through specific documents

such as curricula and syllabuses, operating memoranda, statutes or legislation that define organisational objectives to be achieved. Some evaluations are made.

3 = Low incorporated; appears in documents on the general purpose of schooling, but there are no specific relevant organisational objectives defined. No evaluation of outcome.

4 = Unincorporated; even if it is important, it is undocumented or only sparsely documented. No clear organisational objectives are defined. No evaluation of outcome is made.

Question IV. Where is the responsibility for evaluation of the following aims and objectives located in the country's education system?

Responses to be used:
NA = National level
ST = State/*Länder*/Canton level
MU = Municipality level
SC = School level
CR = Classroom/Teacher level
0 = not relevant question according to earlier answer

The responses and comments from the participants indicated that although there were differences between countries regarding response procedures (and cases where the layout and presentation of the survey instrument hindered responses), the most significant obstacles standing in the way of indicator development lie in the definitions of goals and response categories. Overall, the study yielded information that could be put in the form of indicators that would be useful and informative. However, the categorisation of goals presented in this chapter differs from that used in the pilot study. Changes have been made according to experiences gained. The next step is to initiate a new pilot study with the categories of goals presented here, as well as a new instrumentation. It is important to bear in mind that the effort to identify a method for measuring education goals is only a first step, albeit an important one. Ultimately, the objective is to develop indicators of outcomes of education that allow the assessment of *progress* towards goal attainment. Information about goals – about what is expected – is a necessary prerequisite for interpreting data on student achievement, whether in subject or cross-curricular areas.

Reference

GRANHEIM, M. and LUNDGREN, U.P. (1991), *Losnotat No. 7*, Noras.

The GOALS Study: Analysis and Implications
L'étude GOALS: analyse et incidences

par

Astrid Eggen Knutsen
University of Oslo, Norway

The writing of a report based on the GOALS study conducted for Network A must contend with the problem of where to put the primary focus. As opposed to single-issue pilot projects within international educational research, the aim of this Network A pilot has been to cover several issues. Therefore, it was first necessary to evaluate the data-collection procedure, including the distribution of instruments, as well as the sources of information, and the different participants' contributions. Secondly, it was important to obtain a feedback on whether the terminology, questions and scales corresponded to the aims of the survey. The third, and perhaps the main issue, was to gain an indication of the instrument's capacity to capture a single country's aims, objectives, policy orientations, and degree of incorporation. This chapter will cover mainly the first two issues. The conclusions will take into account the three main areas that need to be discussed further; these areas involve conceptual, procedural, and instrumental issues, including reliability and validity aspects.

*

* *

Note de synthèse

Les données de l'enquête pilote GOALS (Goals Orientation and Attainment in Learning Systems ou Le choix des objectifs et leur réalisation dans les systèmes d'ensei-

gnement) ont été recueillies dans chaque pays par des panels composés de trois à cinq personnes. L'enquête comprend deux sections principales : a) objectifs et b) choix des pouvoirs publics. Les réponses exactes de chaque pays sont présentées sous forme de tableaux.

L'exactitude des données, c'est-à-dire l'accord entre les deux panels de chaque pays, est prise en compte pour chaque item. L'exactitude est généralement plus grande pour les questions relatives aux objectifs que pour celles qui concernent les choix des pouvoirs publics.

Les commentaires des coordinateurs nationaux, des membres du Réseau A et des pays participants comprennent les questions qui devront être posées à l'occasion des futures études pilotes ainsi que les suggestions en vue d'une amélioration de l'enquête. En ce qui concerne les questions de méthode, les pays ne procèdent pas tous de même pour constituer les panels, en choisir les participants, et concilier les différences entre panels. Par ailleurs, trois pays ont traduit le questionnaire d'enquête. Il serait bon que les pays reçoivent des informations précises quant à la traduction et à la composition des panels, ainsi que des instructions sur la méthode à suivre par les panels et les coordinateurs.

Pour ce qui est du questionnaire d'enquête, il est proposé qu'il soit raccourci en éliminant les questions redondantes, que l'on y ajoute des instructions et des explications supplémentaires et que deux versions du questionnaire soient rédigées et distribuées, l'une destinée aux coordinateurs nationaux et aux coordinateurs des panels et l'autre aux membres des panels.

Quant au contenu de l'enquête, plusieurs pays ont trouvé que les termes buts, objectifs, finalités et normes engendraient la confusion ; il est proposé que seul le mot « objectifs » soit utilisé. Il faudra établir un système de classification des objectifs englobant toutes les dimensions dont le réseau doit tenir compte. Les pays ont trouvé que la notion de degré d'incorporation était peu claire ; ce barème devra être révisé. Les pays dans lesquels les responsabilités sont partagées entre divers niveaux ont trouvé difficile de répondre à l'enquête. Les niveaux doivent correspondre à ceux que l'on utilise dans d'autres projets INES (c'est-à-dire niveau de l'école, niveaux intermédiaires 1 et 2, et niveau national). Les choix des pouvoirs publics sont interprétés différemment d'un pays à l'autre ; ces définitions devront être revues.

1. Procedure for Data Collection

It was decided at the network's meetings in Stockholm and Berlin in the autumn of 1993 to use the same procedure for data collection as was employed by Network C for the development of the indicators concerned with the locus of decision-making. The key idea behind this procedure is the belief that a cost-effective way of capturing a country's incorporation of goals is to establish discussion groups of people with experience at different levels of the education system. It was decided to collect the data in panels consisting of three to five persons. To ensure a certain degree of reliability, it also was decided to establish two parallel panels in each country and to give the national co-ordinators the task of reconciling the panels' responses, if necessary.

2. Survey of Aims and Objectives

The results from this part of the survey are presented as written by the countries.[1] Some countries have not made a final decision on some of the questions. In such cases, the results from both panels are presented. In order to arrive at an overall view of the results, each question is written as it appeared in the instrument that was sent out. The response categories are listed in Table 10.1 (Questions A to D), which also presents the answers supplied by the countries.

3. Policy Orientations Survey

This part of the questionnaire included two questions. All the countries answered the first question (Question E) and most provided additional documentation. Not all of the countries responded to the second question (Question F), but responses are included to give an impression of the variety of ways in which it was interpreted.

4. Response Reconciliation Table

Questions G and H show which questions have the highest inter-panel reliability. The ''X'' means that there was agreement in the country about the question. It was decided to give the degree of agreement between the two panels in the country for each question, as a main factor of the question's reliability. The validity of the questions is discussed towards the end of the chapter.

5. Remarks Concerning Procedure, Content and the Instrument

Countries' remarks concerning procedures and instrumentation are based on two questionnaires issued to the national co-ordinators and Network A members, and on other comments made by the participating countries. First-hand experience of the meeting held in Oslo, and of following the process in Norway, has also had an impact on the overall impression given here of how the questionnaires were completed. Included are remarks about the procedure of data collection, comments about the instrument in general, and details about the terminology, the questions, and the scales used in the two sections of the instrument. The main purpose is to indicate the different issues that need to be addressed in the continuation of the survey. Some suggestions for improving the instrument and the procedure for data collection are also offered.

Table/Tableau 10.1.

GOALS pilot study results

Résultats de l'étude pilote GOALS

Question A: Please indicate the extent to which the different categories of aims and objectives represent goals that are applicable to the entire country by circling one number from the following four-point scale:

Question A : Indiquer dans quelle mesure les différents objectifs ci-après sont adoptés dans l'ensemble du pays en entourant d'un cercle le chiffre correspondant à l'une des catégories suivantes :

Responses to be used:

1 = Category represents goals that are valid for the entire country.
2 = Category represents goals that are valid for a majority of the different parts of the country with responsibility for education.
3 = Category represents goals that are valid for only some parts of the education system of the country.
4 = Goals in this category cannot be found explicit anywhere in the country.

Aims and Objectives	Belgium (Flemish Community)	Finland	Denmark	Norway	Portugal	Spain	Sweden	USA
A. Fundamental principles and values	1	1	1	1	1	1	1	1
B. Goals for development of social skills	1	1	1	1	1	1	1	2
B1. Attainment of cross-curricular competencies	1	1	1	1	1	1	1	2
C. Goals for acquisition of knowledge and skills	1	1	1	1	1	1	1	3
C1. Attainment goals or standards	1	1	1	1	1	1	4	3
C2. Goals for basic skills within certain subject areas	1	1	1	1	1	1	1/4	1
D. Development goals	1	1	1	1	1	1	1/4	1

Table/Tableau 10.1. (cont'd/suite)

GOALS pilot study results

Résultats de l'étude pilote GOALS

Question B: Please indicate what level of the education system is primarily responsible for establishing aims and objectives in the different categories by circling a response from the following list:

Question B : Indiquer quel niveau du système d'enseignement est responsable au premier chef de la définition des objectifs dans les différentes catégories ci-après en entourant d'un cercle l'une des réponses proposées dans la liste suivante :

Responses to be used:

NA = National level.
ST = State/Länder/Canton level.
CO = Municipality level.
SC = School level.
CR = Classroom/teacher level.
O = Not relevant.

Aims and Objectives	Belgium (Flemish Community)	Finland	Denmark	Norway	Portugal	Spain	Sweden	USA
A. Fundamental principles and values	NA	NA	NA	NA	NA	NA	NA	ST
B. Goals for development of social skills	NA	NA	NA	NA	NA	NA	NA/CO/SC/CR	CO
B1. Attainment of cross-curricular competencies	NA(SC)	SC	NA	NA	NA	NA	NA/CO/SC/CR	CO
C. Goals for acquisition of knowledge and skills	NA(SC)	NA	NA	NA	NA	NA	NA/CO/SC/CR	CO
C1. Attainment goals and standards	NA(SC)	NA	NA	NA/SC	NA	NA	NA/CO/SC/CR	CO
C2. Goals for basic skills within certain subject areas	NA(SC)	NA	NA	NA/SC	NA	NA	NA/CO/SC/CR	ST
D. Development goals	NA(SC)	NA	NA	NA	NA	NA	NA/CO/SC/CR	ST

Table/Tableau 10.1. (cont'd/suite)

GOALS pilot study results

Résultats de l'étude pilote GOALS

Question C: Please indicate the extent to which the different categories of aims and objectives are formally incorporated in your country's education system by circling one number from the following four-point scale:

Question C : Indiquer dans quelle mesure les différentes catégories d'objectifs sont officiellement prises en compte dans le système d'enseignement de votre pays en entourant d'un cercle l'un des quatre chiffres ci-après :

Responses to be used :

1 = *Unincorporated*. Aims and objectives in this category either do not exist in an education system or are considered important but are undocumented or only sparsely documented. They may be held as national ideals and may be specified in a national constitution or other documents, but are not explicitly linked to education.

2 = *Low incorporated*. Aims and objectives in this category appear in documents on the general purpose of schooling such as articles of a constitution, an education ministry mission statement, or a set of national education goals. However, there are no specific organisational objectives or educational initiatives related to aims and objectives in this category and no mechanisms to monitor progress.

3 = *Medium incorporated*. Aims and objectives in this category are incorporated into the system through specific documents such as national curricula and syllabuses, operating memoranda, or statutes or legislation that define organisational objectives or establish initiatives related to this category, but there are no mechanisms to monitor progress in this area.

4 = *Fully incorporated*. Aims and objectives in this category are incorporated into the system in the same way as medium incorporated aims and objectives, but there is a method of monitoring progress in this area with the expectation that remediation will occur.

Aims and Objectives	Belgium (Flemish Community)	Finland	Denmark	Norway	Portugal	Spain	Sweden	USA
A. Fundamental principles and values	3/4	4	4	3	3	3	3	3
B. Goals for development of social skills	3	3	4	3	3	3	3/4	3
B1. Attainment of cross-curricular competencies	3/2	3	4	3	3	3	3/4	2
C. Goals for acquisition of knowledge and skills	3/4	4	4	4	3	4	3/4	2
C1. Attainment goals and standards	3/4	3	4	4	3	4	2/3	2
C2. Goals for basic skills within reading, writing, and arithmetic	3/4	4	4	4	3	4	2/3	2
D. Development goals	3	4	4	3	2	3	1/3	3

Table/Tableau 10.1. (cont'd/suite)

GOALS pilot study results

Résultats de l'étude pilote GOALS

Question D: Please indicate where the primary responsibility for the evaluation of the following aims and objectives in the different categories is located in your country's education system by circling a response from the following list:

Question D : Indiquer quel niveau du système d'enseignement de votre pays est responsable au premier chef de l'évaluation des objectifs relevant des catégories ci-après en entourant d'un cercle l'une des réponses proposées dans la liste suivante :

Responses to be used:

NA = National level.
ST = State/Länder/Canton level.
CO = Municipality level.
SC = School level.
CR = Classroom/teacher level.
O = Not relevant.

Aims and Objectives	Belgium (Flemish Community)	Finland	Denmark	Norway	Portugal	Spain	Sweden	USA
A. Fundamental principles and values	NA	CO	CO	NA/CO	NA	NA	NA	ST
B. Goals for development of social skills	NA/sc	SC	CO	NA/SC	NA	SC	NA/CO/SC/CR	CR
B1. Attainment of cross-curricular competencies	SC/CO	SC	CO	NA/SC	NA	SC	NA/CO/SC/CR	CR
C. Goals for acquisition of knowledge and skills	NA/SC/CO	CR	CO	NA/SC	NA	CR	NA/CO/SC/CR	CO
C1. Attainment goals and standards	NA/CR	CR	CO	NA/SC	NA	CR	NA/CO/SC/CR	CO
C2. Goals for basic skills within reading, writing, and arithmetic	NA/SC	CR	CO	NA	NA	CR	NA/CO/SC/CR	ST
D. Development goals	NA(SC)	NA	CO	NA	NA	NA	NA/CO/SC/CR	ST

Table/Tableau 10.1. *(cont'd/suite)*

GOALS pilot study results

Résultats de l'étude pilote GOALS

Question E: Indicate the degree of incorporation of each of the following policy orientations using the scale 1 to 4.
Question E : Indiquer dans quelle mesure les objectifs généraux ci-après influent sur l'action menée par le système d'enseignement en utilisant une échelle allant de 1 à 4.

Policy Orientations	Belgium (Flemish Community)	Finland	Denmark	Norway	Portugal	Spain	Sweden	USA
Promotion of lifelong learning	4/3	3	4	3	2	4	4	3
Equal access to educational opportunity	3/4	4	4	2	3	4	4	4
Ambition of the education system to achieve excellence	4	3	2	4/2	2	4	1/2	2
Achieving basic levels of literacy	4	4	4	2	2	4	3	3

Table/Tableau 10.1. (cont'd/suite)

GOALS pilot study results

Résultats de l'étude pilote GOALS

Question F: In addition to the four policy orientations examined here, list any other major systemic goals of your education system. Please provide references for any documents on how these goals are incorporated into the system.
Question F : Outre les quatre grands objectifs retenus, citer d'autres objectifs importants du système d'enseignement de votre pays. Donner les références de documents indiquant comment ces objectifs sont pris en compte dans l'ensemble du système.

Country	Policy Orientation				
Belgium (Flemish Community)	Primary and elementary education	Provision for individual educational needs; and the same chances for boys and girls	Decentralisation; budget quality; and teacher training	Special education; psycho-social centres	Comprehensive structure of secondary schools
Denmark	Schools should function as local community centres				
Spain	Full development of student's personality	Education concerning the linguistic and cultural plurality of Spain	Peace, co-operation and solidarity between different parts of the country	Development of creative abilities and the ability to make critical evaluations	Relationship with the social, economic and cultural environment; and education for respect towards and preservation of the environment
Sweden	Democratic values	Equality: • Socio-economic backgrounds • Geography • Boys/girls	Pupils influence and responsibility	Internationalisation	Environment
Finland	Environmental education	Technology education	Individuality and differentiation	The position of minorities	Social support
USA	Safe, disciplined and drug-free schools				

Table/Tableau 10.1. (cont'd/suite)

GOALS pilot study results

Résultats de l'étude pilote GOALS

Question G: Part 1: Survey of Aims and Objectives.
Question G : Partie 1 : Vue d'ensemble des buts et objectifs adoptés selon les pays.

Question	Belgium (Flemish Community)	Finland	Denmark	Norway	Portugal	Spain	Sweden	USA
1A	X	X	X	X	X	X	X	X
1B	X	X	X	X	X	X	X	
1B1	X	X	X		X	X	X	
1C	X		X	X	X	X	X	
1C1	X		X		X	X	X	X
1C2	X	X	X		X	X		
1D					X	X		
2A	X	X	X	X	X	X		X
2B	X	X	X	X	X	X	X	X
2B1			X	X	X	X		
2C			X	X	X	X		X
2C1		X	X		X	X		X
2C2		X	X		X	X		X
2D		X	X		X	X		
3A		X		X	X		X	
3B	X			X	X			X
3B1				X	X			
3C			X	X	X	X		
3C1		X	X	X	X	X		
3C2			X	X	X	X		
3D	X	X		X	X			
4A	X	X	X		X	X		X
4B		X			X			X
4B1					X			X
4C					X			
4C1				X				X
4C2				X				X
4D	X	X	X			X		

Table/Tableau 10.1. *(cont'd/suite)*
GOALS pilot study results
Résultats de l'étude pilote GOALS

Question H: Part 2: Policy Orientations Survey.
Question H : Partie 2 : Vue d'ensemble des grands objectifs adoptés selon les pays.

Question	Belgium (Flemish Community)	Finland	Denmark	Norway	Portugal	Spain	Sweden	USA
Promotion of lifelong learning		X	X	X		X	X	
Equal access to educational opportunity		X	X	X		X	X	X
Ambition of the educational system to achieve excellence	X					X		X
Achieving basic levels of literacy	X	X	X	X		X	X	X

Procedural Comments

Different countries have implemented the pilot in disparate ways. Some countries translated the instrument before the panel discussions took place. There also was a difference in the way the countries arranged the panel discussions, decided who participated, and determined how the reconciliation was done. The national co-ordinators were not required to give information of this kind, hence there are only a few examples of how the pilot was implemented in the countries:

- Finland sent the Finnish version to the panel members in advance. The Finnish process was described as involving discussions and negotiations. The second panel discussed the instrument, was given the result from the first panel, and was then instructed to reach a final answer.
- Norway had the two panels meet at the same time, and called upon the national co-ordinator to reach a final answer. The instrument was sent in advance to the panel members.
- The United States had the two panels meet at different times, and called a conference to conciliate and summarise the responses.

The instrument was translated by Belgium (Flemish Community), Finland and Portugal. The translation procedure differed among these countries, but they all found it convenient to carry out the pilot in their own language. However, they also considered it necessary to examine the English version during the panel discussion, in order to settle questions about the interpretation of the instrument.

Layout and Comments on the Instrument

- *The instrument was considered to be too long,* and could be shortened by including only once the scales, questions, and categories of aims and objectives. This would result in an instrument that might be easier to handle.
- *The instrument should be written and distributed in two versions.* One version should contain specific instructions for the national co-ordinator, including the instrumentation and a form for the co-ordinator to fill out. There should also be instructions on when the panel members would need to receive a copy of the instrument. The second version should be intended primarily for panel leaders and other panel members. This version should consist only of the information needed for filling out the questionnaires.
- *The part about centralised/decentralised countries should be omitted, as it was seen as redundant.* This part was considered irrelevant to the countries and therefore confusing for the participants in the panels.
- *There were difficulties in using 1992 as the reference year.* Several countries stressed the problem of responding according to the situation that prevailed in 1992. This argument seems to be linked to the implementation of school reforms both before and after that year. Participants tended to use documentation distributed recently, but not necessarily corresponding to the year 1992.

- *The premises for filling out the questionnaire* needed to be explained more fully. Emphasis needs to be given to the application of ISCED levels, and it has to be stated more explicitly what part of the education system is in focus.
- *Documentation for the national co-ordinators was inadequate.* The letter of invitation did not state clearly in either text or heading what the national co-ordinators should do and when.

Content, Terminology and Scales

The intention here is not to draw conclusions about the results of this pilot or to make any suggestions for the main study, which still is to be conducted, but to point to the problems that several countries faced in carrying out the pilot. There was general consensus on the following aspects of Part 1 and Part 2 of the survey.

Part 1

- Aims and Objectives

Several countries mentioned a problem in defining "development goals". The term seems difficult to use because of an earlier use of the term in connection with individual goals. Some countries found it difficult to separate C1 and C2. It also seemed redundant to ask questions about both a group of goals (*e.g.* C) and, at the same time, sub-groups (*e.g.* C1 and C2). The use of terms such as "aims", "objectives", "goals", and "standards" is confusing.

- Scale of Degree of Incorporation

It should be stressed that it is *not* the degree of implementation that is of concern, but the extent to which a certain aim or objective has been written down and is considered to be important as one of the intentions of a country's education system. The expression "monitoring progress" is confusing to some of the countries because of the possibility of several interpretations of the term. (The term seems to indicate the possibility of a form of evaluation, a possibility of evaluation in progress, and a demand for counselling or control and inspection.)

- The Use of "Levels" in Questions 2 and 4

Several countries had difficulty because, in most cases, the levels share the responsibility. The questions have to be split up. Question 4: the question has to be rewritten to include some evaluation of the extent to which the system is achieving its goals.

Part 2

- ISCED Levels 1 and 2

Some of the questions do not apply particularly to ISCED levels 1 and 2. The *premises for answering these questions have to be reviewed*. That is also the case with the definitions of the "four policy orientations". The significance of these policy orientations for comparison is raised as a consequence of the literature which is cited. Their importance seems very obvious to the participating countries but, at the same time, it is difficult to "pin it down".

6. Implications for a Conceptual Framework, Data-Collection Procedure and Revision of the Instrument

Conceptual Framework

The general impression, based on replies from the countries, is that the instrument managed to capture interesting aspects of the education systems, but, in order to improve the validity of the results, a few changes will have to be made. The categories of aims, objectives and goals in Part 2 of the survey are confusing to the countries. Therefore, only the term "goals" should be used, and the framework of different goals should be further developed. This framework is necessary as a basis for designing the main data collection. At present, we do not have a classification system that includes all the dimensions of goals that the network has to take into consideration, and it may be necessary to improve the categories included in questions 1 to 4 in Part 1 of the instrument. It is therefore considered important to develop a classification system for goals that includes the following dimensions:

- *Short-term goals and long-term goals.* Some goals are expressed as standards that are to be achieved within a certain time limit. Hence, short-term goals and long-term goals must be stated as objectives that systems or individuals should aim for in their teaching, learning, or administrative activity, within the education system.
- *Goals to prescribe the activities and priorities at the different levels of the education system (national, regional, district, school, teacher, and student).* It is considered important for most countries to establish aims for the educational activities and the development of the system, at all levels.
- *Valid goals.* Goals could be valid for the entire education system, or they could be made explicit in only parts of the country's school system.
- *It is necessary to group goals with regard to what they express, or the aspect of the education system or individual progress they describe or prescribe.* The classification of goals into the three categories of skills, attitudes, and knowledge is limited to the teaching of certain subjects and hence has to be incorporated into the framework. It is also necessary to develop similar categories at a system level.

Procedure for Data Collection

The procedure for collecting data in the next phase should be further discussed, once the revision of the instrument is completed. The process of interpreting results from the first pilot should also be discussed. It was generally agreed that the procedure carried out in the pilot served its purpose. The role of the national co-ordinators is questionable, but it was also agreed that Network A members could play an important role, and that the panels and the reconciliation process both added valuable information to the answering of the instrument. It is necessary to take into consideration that, in order to interpret the results, the procedure used in the different countries needs to be standardised. It is therefore necessary to give more detailed information on the following aspects of implementation:

- translation of instrument;
- levels of education system which should be represented in the panels;
- distribution of instruments ahead of panel meetings;
- what kind of literature to include in the reference list;
- role of national co-ordinators versus Network A members (maybe include training for Network A members); and
- premises for answering questions: ISCED levels to be included; part of school system to be included; and the reference period to which questions relate.

Revision of the Instrument

A further revision of the instrument has to include the following:

- Layout of the instrument. The preface and introduction should contain an explanation of the concepts used in a conceptual framework as well as directions for filling out the questionnaire. The instrument could also be shortened.
- The categories of aims and objectives have to be revised and a framework for categories of goals needs to be developed.
- The scale of the degree of incorporation should be split up, to capture better the systems' emphases on the different goal areas.
- The levels that are used should be consistent with the levels used in other surveys sponsored or conducted by the INES project.
- Explanations and examples of the policy orientations should be given, and the heading of this part of the instrument should be changed.

Note

1. Belgium (French Community) undertook the pilot too late for the results to be included in the report or in the discussion at the Network A meeting held in Copenhagen from 21 to 23 February 1994.

Curriculum Style as a Process Variable
Le style du programme d'études en tant que variable de processus

by

Kevin Piper
Council for Education Research, Camberwell, Victoria, Australia

The curriculum is central to schooling and a principal determinant of student learning outcomes. Such an obvious truism would hardly warrant re-assertion if it were not for the widespread neglect of curriculum variability in large-scale studies of student learning outcomes. Some studies do look superficially at content coverage or textbook usage – the IEA studies, for example, use an analysis of topic coverage and time allocation as an indicator of "opportunity to learn" – but such topical analysis is simply that, topical, and tends to ignore the underlying, and more fundamental, sources of curriculum variability. It was, in fact, the practical need for a more meaningful procedure for classifying and categorising curriculum variability that gave rise to the development of a typology of curriculum style (Piper, 1979).

*

*   *

Note de synthèse

Le style du programme d'études est une notion analytique qui sert à classer la viabilité des programmes. En étudiant le style des programmes, on distingue trois styles principaux : a) le type I (centré sur le contenu); b) le type II (centré sur le processus); et c) le type III (centré sur le contexte). Deux études ont confirmé d'une façon générale l'adéquation et l'utilité de cette typologie de base et ont mis à jour trois dimensions supplémentaires des programmes à l'intérieur de chaque style principal : il s'agit du programme a) centré sur la discipline enseignée, b) centré sur la société ou sur le milieu ambiant, et c) centré sur l'apprenant. Les trois styles principaux (ou dimensions fonction-nelles) et les trois sous-styles (ou dimensions dérivées) forment la base de la typologie et aboutissent à neuf styles particuliers. Comme dans toute typologie, celle des styles de programmes représente un idéal. Dans la pratique, un programme quel qu'il soit repré-sente tous les styles dans des proportions variables, l'accent étant généralement mis sur un style donné. On donne une explication détaillée et des exemples de chaque style et sous-style.

On peut déduire des données limitées dont on dispose qu'il existe un rapport manifeste entre le style du programme d'études et les objectifs de l'enseignement. Piper a effectué une étude de cas sur vingt écoles et a demandé aux enseignants d'évaluer les objectifs du programme qu'ils enseignaient. Il a constaté que l'on admettait très généra-lement l'existence d'une conformité entre le style du programme et ses objectifs, bien que l'on n'ait pas étudié les sous-styles. Il ressort aussi de l'étude que les enseignants des programmes de types II et III sont plus satisfaits de leurs programmes dans la pratique que ceux qui enseignent les programmes de type I.

Aucune étude n'a été consacrée aux rapports entre le style du programme d'études et les résultats scolaires, mais il est peu probable qu'une relation de ce genre existe, étant donné le caractère non évaluateur de la typologie. Cependant, les quelques indices dont on dispose amènent à penser que les différences entre les styles de programme sont liées (sans doute pas de façon déterminante) aux différences des convictions des ensei-gnants quant à la nature du savoir et l'acquisition des connaissances.

Les techniques utilisées pour mettre au point la typologie comprennent a) l'observa-tion des classes, b) l'analyse du contenu des documents et programmes de travail, c) les questionnaires, et d) les cartes portant un choix de questions. On s'est servi des notes moyennes attribuées à l'orientation principale des programmes pour mettre au point un profil du programme d'études de chaque école étudiée.

La typologie est solidement ancrée sur la recherche bien que celle-ci se limite aux écoles australiennes et aux matières particulières que sont l'éducation sociale et l'anglais. Cependant, il n'est pas possible d'inclure directement la typologie des styles de programmes dans les travaux du réseau avant que des études pilotes de portée limitée aient été conduites dans chaque pays Membre pour en vérifier les possibilités d'applica-tion et définir les modifications nécessaires.

*

*   *

1.   The Concept of Curriculum Style

The concept of curriculum style, and the typology it gave rise to, was developed and elaborated empirically from a study of curriculum practice in social education in twenty case-study schools in two Australian state systems (Piper, 1983), and employed to good effect by Sturman (1989) in a study of curriculum decision-making in three Australian state systems.

Style itself derives from criticism in literature and the arts, where it occupies a key position roughly analogous to that occupied by a *model* in the sciences. Style is a seminal and highly flexible concept, functioning as an analytical construct for the classification of the work, the artist, or the period. Thus, while style is essentially idiosyncratic (*le style est l'homme même,* in Buffon's much-quoted phrase), its idiosyncratic nature does not preclude broad classifications encompassing a high degree of generalisation (*e.g.* Classical, Romantic, Baroque).

Style in this broader sense is defined by its *focus,* not by the breadth of its vision or the range of its concerns. Style so defined suggests the general construct of a work without any necessary implications concerning the absolute quality of that work; it suggests focus without implying a narrowness of focus. In adopting the concept from criticism in literature and the arts, the typology of curriculum also adopts the principle of definition by *focus.*

2. A Typology of Curriculum Style

Studies in the area identify three basic curriculum styles: a *Type I,* or expository, style, with its focus on *content;* a *Type II,* or functional, style, with its focus on *process;* and a *Type III,* or situational, style, with its focus on the *context* within which the learning takes place (see Table 11.1). Normally, a curriculum will contain all three elements of content, process, and context, and will almost certainly pay some attention to all three. What distinguishes one style from another is its selection of one of those elements to provide the *principal focus* around which the curriculum is defined, structured, and organised. It is stressed again that classification by style carries with it no implication of breadth or narrowness of focus, or of programme quality, but is concerned strictly with focus as a broad classification.

Table/Tableau 11.1.

A typology of curriculum style

Typologie des différents styles de programme d'études

	Type a (discipline-focused)	Type b (society/environment-focused)	Type b (learner-focused)
Type I (content-focused)	*	*	*
Type II (process-focused)	*	*	*
Type III (context-focused)	*	*	*

Source: Adapted from Piper (1979, p. 92).

Piper's two studies generally confirmed the feasibility and usefulness of the basic typology as a means of classifying school programmes in social education and English language education. However, it also was clear from the evidence of the studies that there remained marked differences between programmes classified together under the same broad stylistic type. The typology, therefore, if it was to be useful beyond the immediate needs of the studies themselves, had to take at least some account of within-style differences.

Through Piper's earlier study of school programmes in social education, it became clear that within-style differences did not arise from inadequacies in the definition of the basic style types, but rather from the fact that curriculum varied along a number of different dimensions. The basic typology had been essentially concerned with only one dimension, albeit an important one, namely the structural or *organisational* dimension.

Another important dimension of difference evident in the case-study schools' programmes in social education was what could be termed the curriculum's *derivational* dimension: a concern with sources outside itself which provide it, even if only implicitly, with its justification, substance, and purpose. Thus, it was common to find curricula or programmes focused on traditional school "subjects", themselves typically associated with an academic "discipline", and taking their justification, substance, and purpose from the body of knowledge associated with that subject or discipline. Alternatively, a curriculum or programme could focus on the "real" world, deriving its justification, substance, and purpose from elements of that world (*e.g.* the society, the environment, or the workforce). Yet again, a curriculum or programme could take as its focus the learner, deriving its justification, substance, and purpose from the needs, abilities, and interests of an individual student or group of students. The focus in the aforementioned cases is not on organisation, but on whatever force *determines* the subjects to be taught.

From the analyses, it also became clear that this derivational focus cut across the structural or organisational focus represented by the basic style types, providing another independent dimension within which curriculum could be differentiated. These observations led from the original study to the development of an extended typology that postulated three further style types – a *Type a,* or definitive style, with its focus on the *subject* or the *discipline*; a *Type b,* or interactive style, with its focus on the *society* or the *environment;* and a *Type c,* or responsive style, with its focus on the *learner* – occurring *within* each of the basic style types. The extended typology thus identified nine specific style types classified according to both organisational and derivational focus (Table 11.1).

It should be noted that since the above are not the only dimensions along which curriculum can vary, they are not the only means of classifying within-style differences. For example, within *Type I* (content-focused) styles there is a clear distinction between programmes that define their content in terms of topics (*e.g.* French Revolution; Bushmen of the Kalahari; constitutional monarchy) and those that define their content in terms of *themes* or *issues* (*e.g.* continuity and change; population; sustainable development), a distinction which is likely to have important implications for expected student learning outcomes. Although this distinction is likely to be accounted for within the distinction between a *Type Ia* style and a *Type Ib* style – for instance, the organisation of content is more likely to be characteristic of *Type b* (society-focused) styles – it is clear that this relationship is not deterministic, and there may be occasions when it is necessary in the interests of a particular study to extend or modify the typology. Such modification is quite within the spirit of typology itself, since typology is first of all a practical construct and only secondly a theoretical construct. Its virtue lies in its simplicity, its flexibility, and its grounding in the actual practice of schools. With that in mind, we can explore the typology of curriculum style, first by examining each broad type individually, and then by looking at what is an inevitable style *mix*.

3. Characteristics of Style Types

The allocation of curricula to style type is not always an unequivocal process. As has been shown in studies of teacher epistemologies, the practice of teachers and schools is not always logically consistent, nor is it always consistent with espoused beliefs and intentions (Young, 1981). In this sense, typology represents "ideal types", more likely to be approximated than demonstrated unequivocally. That said, however, it is possible to allocate programmes to style type with reasonable certainty, provided one is prepared to tolerate an element of inconsistency in practice.

Type I Styles

A *Type I* style is characterised by its primary focus on content knowledge, and will typically be defined and sequentially organised in terms of content areas. Skills and values are not necessarily ignored, but are likely to be treated *as if* they were content (*e.g.* skills treated as a set of routine procedures or rules, or values as contrasting points of view to be clarified). Three sub-styles are identified within the *Type I* style.

A *Type Ia* style, in addition to its organisational focus on content knowledge, is characterised by a derivational focus on traditional school subjects or academic disciplines. *Type Ia* programmes in social education, for example, are likely to be characterised by traditional courses in history and geography, sometimes within a token strand of civics or citizenship, especially when combined together as "social studies". *Type Ia* English programmes are typically characterised by a substantial literature component, particularly with a focus on literature as cultural transmission. The language component is likely to have a heavy structural emphasis, and to focus on structural elements such as grammar (not necessarily formal) and spelling. Both cases demonstrate what are typical *Type Ia* characteristics: a focus derived from a traditional body of knowledge.

A *Type Ib* style, in addition to its organisational focus on content knowledge, is characterised by a derivational focus on the society, the environment, or the labour force. *Type Ib* programmes in social education are likely to draw their content from a wide range of social science disciplines and to focus on relevant social or environmental issues. *Type Ib* English programmes are likely to emphasise practical or vocational content (*e.g.* business English) and to focus more on language than on literature. For *Type Ib*, the focus is, so to speak, "the world around us", and its courses are driven by practicality.

A *Type Ic* style, in addition to its organisational focus on content, is characterised by a derivational focus on the learner. Its primary concern, then, is with content relevant to the needs and interests of an individual student or group of students. A *Type Ic* programme is not simply a matter of selecting content of appropriate difficulty (*i.e. Type Ia* or *Ib* styles), but of selecting content that originates in and is justified by the perceived or expressed needs of the learner. Topics or themes in social education which are selected by students, or the use of the lyrics of popular songs as objects of study in English language programmes, are indicative of a *Type Ic* style. It is the student's experience in the world, rather than either traditional canons or social forces, that determines course content.

Type II Styles

A *Type II* style is characterised by its primary focus on the *process* of learning, and will typically be defined and organised, at least in part, in terms of generic processes, such as communication, enquiry and investigation, participation and interaction, critical thinking, problem-solving, and the like. Skills and values are likely to be emphasised and characterised in developmental terms. An important aspect of *Type II* styles, not always explicitly articulated, involves a view of process not only as something to be learned, but as a means of generating knowledge. Content knowledge becomes a product of the curriculum process, rather than its organisational force or focus. Three sub-styles are identified within this *Type II* style.

A *Type IIa* style, in addition to its organisational focus on process, is characterised by a derivational focus on school subjects or academic disciplines. Thus, a *Type II* programme in social education is likely to place a strong emphasis on methodology, and to view methodology as a uniquely discipline-specific instrument of process (*e.g.* the historical method, scientific method, philosophical enquiry). Content knowledge is likely to be viewed as problematic, open to interpretation, and generated through disciplined enquiry. English language programmes are likely to place a strong emphasis on literary criticism and text analysis, and to be more concerned with meaning than structure in the production of text, although the structure of scientific enquiry *is* the method through which one can know meaning.

A *Type IIb* style, in addition to its organisational focus on process, is characterised by a "real world" focus on the society, the environment, or the labour force. *Type IIb* programmes in social education are likely to place a strong emphasis on the investigation of "real world" phenomena through a process of rational enquiry, and to view enquiry as a generalised process drawing on a wide range of academic disciplines for its methods and techniques. In its purest form, a *Type IIb* programme based on enquiry will be concerned not only with learning to enquire, but also with learning *through* enquiry and learning *about* enquiry. The process of enquiry is not only an end in itself, but also a means of generating content knowledge, and an object of study in its own right. A *Type IIb* programme in English language education, for example, is likely to focus on language as communication, and to place a strong emphasis on language as the creation or carrier of meaning. Oral language is likely to be more strongly emphasised than in *Type I* or *Type IIa* programmes.

A *Type IIc* programme, in addition to its organisational focus on process, is characterised by a derivational focus on the learner. *Type IIc* programmes in social education are likely to place a strong emphasis on participation in the life of the community and to emphasise skills relevant to the individual student or group of students, (*e.g.* survival skills, social competence, personal growth and development, and discovery learning). Programmes in functional literacy and individualised language programmes that emphasise skill development are typical of *Type IIc* programmes in English language education.

Type III Styles

A *Type III* style is characterised by its primary focus on the context in which the learning takes place. Because of the wide range of possible contexts, and the often idiosyncratic nature of particular contexts, *Type III* styles are more difficult to define in general terms than *Type I* or *Type II* styles, although not necessarily more difficult to recognise in practice.

In situations where the context provides the *primary* consideration in curriculum decision-making, we are likely to see the emergence of a distinctive *Type III* style. We might, for example, find rural schools in areas with sharply defined local needs, multicultural inner-city schools, Aboriginal schools, particularly in exclusively Aboriginal communities, or religious schools concerned with informing their total curriculum with a particular religious or cultural ethos. Such schools respond to their particular environment with a distinctively contextualised curriculum, appropriately classified as exhibiting a *Type III* style; although it should be emphasised that not all such contexts will automatically result in the development of an identifiable *Type III* style. As with the other two basic style types, three sub-styles are identified within the *Type III* style.

A *Type IIIa* style, in addition to its primary organisational focus on the context within which the learning takes place, is characterised by a derivational focus on the school subject or academic discipline. As might be expected, *Type IIIa* styles are relatively rare, since they stem from somewhat contradictory tendencies. The study of curriculum practice in social education (Piper, 1979) identified two schools – one a Christian school exploring the implications of teaching the traditional subjects in a Christian context, and the other an international school seeking to inject its total curriculum with an internationalist and humanitarian focus – that could be described as moving towards the development of a *Type IIIa* style, but probably not at the stage of actually exemplifying one.

A *Type IIIb* style, in addition to its primary organisational focus on the context in which the learning takes place, is characterised by a derivational focus on the society or the environment. Social education programmes aimed at reflecting the multicultural context of Australian society and community language programmes aimed at improved cultural understanding exemplify a *Type IIIb* style. Language immersion programmes, aimed at the development of contextualised bilingualism, also can be classified as *Type IIIb* styles.

A *Type IIIc* style, in addition to its primary organisational focus on the context within which the learning takes place, is characterised by a focus on an individual learner or group of learners. *Type IIIc* styles are typically encountered in Australia in small alternative or community schools in which students are encouraged to explore their own particular interests and talents in largely individualised programmes or small group projects. Social education programmes aimed at meeting the specific cultural needs of ethnic minority groups, as well as specialised ethnic minority language programmes, typically display a *Type IIIc* style.

Mixed Styles

As might be expected, it is not uncommon to find some mixture of styles, especially where the unit of classification is the school's total curriculum as distinct from a particular subject or learning area, although even within subjects and learning areas it is not unusual for schools to offer alternative programmes (*e.g.* interest-based courses for the ''non-academic'' students), which may exemplify different style type characteristics. Some mixtures occur *within* one of the basic style types, others occur *across* the basic style types, while still others involve mixtures along *both dimensions* of the extended typology. One way of handling mixtures of styles is simply to classify programmes separately as mixed *(Type X)* or, within styles, as composites *(e.g. Type IIx)*. Another method is to classify them in terms of the specific style types contributing to the mixture. While the latter is more cumbersome, it may prove more useful for research purposes, as it tends to be more inclusive.

4. Curriculum Style and Education Goals

Data available to explore the relationship between curriculum style and education goals are limited, but suggest a clear, if not always straightforward, relationship between style and goals (Piper, 1979, pp. 73-82). It is clear, for instance, that differences in education goals are one of the factors contributing to observed differences in curriculum style, but it is also clear that other factors – among them individual school characteristics, staffing and resources, student characteristics, perceived parent and community expectations, examination and certification requirements, and teacher career structures – can intervene to produce a perceived dysfunction between espoused goals and the curriculum in practice (Piper, 1979, pp. 82-88).

As part of the data collection for the study of curriculum practice in social education (Piper, 1979), teachers of social education programmes in the twenty case-study schools (N = 91) were asked to select from a list of seven broad goals *the* goal they saw as indicating the main function of the programme(s) they taught, or to provide their own goal, if no existing goal was suitable. Two goals (*i.e.* to provide a sound basis for academic studies; and to introduce young people to their cultural heritage) were postulated as likely goals for *Type I* programmes; two (*i.e.* to develop young people who can think rationally and independently; and to equip young people to function effectively in society) were postulated as likely goals for *Type II* programmes; two (*i.e.* to help each student achieve his or her full potential as a human being; and to produce more students who can act as change agents in building a better society and a better world) were postulated as likely goals for *Type III* programmes; and one (*i.e.* to keep young people usefully occupied until they leave school) was included as a refuge for the cynics.

About three-quarters of the teachers of *Type II* and *Type III* programmes selected goals postulated for their style type. Phi coefficients were 0.30 ($p < 0.01$) for *Type II* goal-style relationships, and 0.50 ($p < 0.001$) for *Type III* relationships, with probabilities adjusted for sample design effects (Piper, 1979, p. 77). Unfortunately, the goals postulated for a *Type I* style attracted less than 10 per cent of teachers of *Type I* programmes, almost two-thirds of them selecting goals postulated for a *Type II* style.

With the benefit of hindsight, it is reasonably easy to see our failure to appreciate the importance of within-style differences as contributing to this result. In developing the questionnaire for the study, we tended to hypothesise as prototypical what we would now classify as specific *Types Ia, IIb,* and *IIIc,* and whereas it is true that they proved to be the most common within-style variants, the relatively frequent occurrence of *Type Ib* and *Type IIa* styles seems a possible, even probable, explanation of the limited relationships observed within *Type I* styles. Nevertheless, what was of necessity an exploratory and speculative item does appear to have uncovered a genuine relationship between curriculum style and underlying programme goals, certainly enough to encourage further investigation and development.

Another aspect of the relationship between curriculum style and education goals on which the data from the studies shed some light is the area of goal satisfaction. The studies investigated teacher and student perceptions of *a)* the *ideal* curriculum, or what ought to be taught, *b)* the *intended* curriculum, or what was planned to be taught, and *c)* the *operative* curriculum, or what was perceived to be taught in practice. It thus becomes possible, by comparing perceptions of the ideal and the operative curriculum, to obtain what could be considered a measure of satisfaction with the operative curriculum (*i.e.* the degree to which education goals and aspirations are realised in practice).

The most immediately obvious feature of any comparison is that whereas teachers in *Type I* programmes perceived a marked gap between their ideal curriculum and the curriculum in practice, both in the level and the pattern of emphasis, their colleagues in *Type II* and *Type III* programmes appeared to be much more satisfied with their curriculum in practice, with teachers in *Type II* programmes perceiving the greatest degree of concurrence between their ideal curriculum and the curriculum they were actually engaged in teaching. Although the degree of satisfaction perceived by students is somewhat less than that perceived by teachers, especially in the case of *Type II* programmes, there are clear style differences that suggest somewhat similar patterns to those observed among teachers.

As with teachers, it is the students in *Type I* programmes who perceived the greatest discrepancy between their ideal and their experienced curriculum. Students in *Type II* programmes, although not sharing with their teachers the euphoric view of the operative curriculum, were nevertheless happier with their experience than were their peers in *Type I* programmes. Students in *Type III* programmes, on the other hand, were much more in accord with their teachers on the degree of goal satisfaction provided by the operative curriculum, with a relatively close match between their ideal curriculum and the curriculum they experienced in practice (Piper, 1979, pp. 127-33). Insofar as teacher and student satisfaction can be considered as indicators of curriculum effectiveness, these findings suggest additional possibilities for the use of the typology in the network's research programme.

5. Curriculum Style and Learning Outcomes

To consider the relationship between curriculum style and student learning outcomes is to arrive at more speculative ground, although ground that is not entirely data-free. None of the studies in which the typology was developed and applied was evaluative in nature. It seems unlikely that there would be any direct relationship between curriculum style and the *quality* of student learning – there are no evaluative implications in the style type classification. Since curriculum style is identified by its focus, and focus is reflected in, and indeed identifiable by, the pattern of curriculum emphases – a point that will become clearer in the next section of this chapter – we would nonetheless expect distinctively different patterns of curricular emphasis to be reflected in distinctively different patterns of student learning outcomes, and probably also in distinctively different assessment procedures.

There is some evidence to suggest, too, that differences in curriculum style are associated, although probably not deterministically, with differences in teacher beliefs about the nature of knowledge and the nature of human learning (Piper, 1983; Sturman, 1989). Thus, if we view knowledge as objective, given, and largely unproblematic, and learning as a cumulative process quantitatively built up by the acquisition of more and more bits of knowledge, we are likely to adopt a content-oriented view of the curriculum and to develop a *Type I* style. If, on the other hand, we view knowledge as socially and culturally mediated and essentially problematic, and learning as an organic process qualitatively developed through doing and growing, we are likely to adopt a process-oriented view of the curriculum and to develop a *Type II* style.

Alternatively, if we view knowledge as personally constructed and idiosyncratically organised, and learning as an adaptive process, experientially acquired in response to changing situations and circumstances, we are likely to adopt a context-oriented view of the curriculum and to develop a *Type III* style; and if we have an eclectic view of knowledge and learning, or are ambivalent, confused, or uncommitted in our views, we are likely to adopt a less uniform view of the curriculum and to develop a mixed or composite style. Again, of course, this is an idealised exposition, and one that grossly oversimplifies the complex relationships between curriculum style and the epistemological and pedagogical beliefs of teachers – relationships that require a great deal more research before we can begin to feel confident in understanding them. Simple exposition does, however, serve to further underline the general point that differences in perception will almost certainly be reflected in differences in the nature and pattern of learning outcomes, and probably also in the procedures adopted to assess those outcomes.

The implications of this admittedly speculative discussion of the relationship between curriculum style and student learning outcomes are twofold – one relating to the development of appropriate procedures for the assessment of student learning outcomes, the other to the interpretation of the results of any such assessment. Both implications arise from that perennial problem of all large-scale assessment programmes, *differential validity*. Any assessment procedure will be more closely related to the actual curriculum experience of some schools, some programmes, and some students, than to the experience of others, and hence will be differentially valid as *an assessment device* for different schools, programmes, or students.

The problem can never be completely resolved, but it can be minimised by careful attention to the range of curriculum variability in the target population. This not only enables the development of more sensitive assessment instruments and procedures, but also provides a basis for a more sophisticated interpretation of variability in achievement, particularly where attention is paid to the *pattern* of learning outcomes rather than simply to the *level* of outcomes. The typology of curriculum style outlined in this chapter provides one approach to this more sensitive and sophisticated appraisal of learning outcomes.

6. The Measurement of Curriculum Style

A variety of techniques for gathering data was employed in the research studies that developed the typology of curriculum style, including 1) classroom observation, 2) content analysis of curriculum documents and work programmes, 3) flexibly structured interviews with teachers and students, and 4) measurement instruments designed to provide comparative data on curriculum emphases. The instruments devised for the measurement of teacher and student perceptions of curriculum emphases consisted of a questionnaire for teachers and a set of Q-sort cards for students.

The items on each instrument were parallel but, to facilitate communication across a range of age and ability levels, the language of the Q-sort cards was simplified and examples were provided to illustrate each item. The items were selected on the basis of the analysis of data from exploratory case studies in the sample schools, in particular teacher interview data and the content analysis of curriculum documents. In addition, items were designed to provide a broad overview of the relative emphases placed on different facets of learning in the schools' programmes and to explore the relationship between relative emphases and curriculum style.

Teachers were asked to rate each item on a three-point scale, according to the emphasis it received in their programme (*i.e.* a lot of emphasis; some emphasis; little or no emphasis). Provision was made for each item to be rated three times, once to represent the ideal programme, once to represent the programme as planned, and once to represent the programme in practice. Students were asked to arrange the Q-sort cards into three piles on the same scale of emphasis, rating each item twice, once to represent their

Figure/*Graphique* 11.1. **Profile of teachers' perceptions of the operative curriculum in three English-language programmes identified as exemplifying a Type I, Type II and Type III style**
Façon dont les enseignants conçoivent le programme d'études enseigné dans trois programmes de langue anglaise pouvant servir d'exemples pour les styles Type I, Type II et Type III

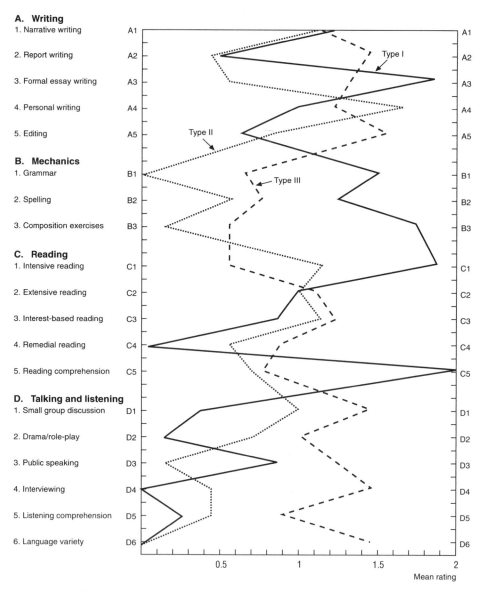

A. Writing
1. Narrative writing
2. Report writing
3. Formal essay writing
4. Personal writing
5. Editing

B. Mechanics
1. Grammar
2. Spelling
3. Composition exercises

C. Reading
1. Intensive reading
2. Extensive reading
3. Interest-based reading
4. Remedial reading
5. Reading comprehension

D. Talking and listening
1. Small group discussion
2. Drama/role-play
3. Public speaking
4. Interviewing
5. Listening comprehension
6. Language variety

Mean rating

Source: Kevin Piper (1983, p. 68).

perception of the ideal programme, and once to represent their perception of the programme in practice. Ratings were scored 2-1-0 to represent a lot of emphasis, some emphasis, and little or no emphasis.

Mean ratings of curriculum emphases were used as the basis for generating a curriculum profile for the programmes in each of the case-study schools. Separate profiles were generated for teacher and student perceptions, and for perceptions of the ideal, the planned, and the operative curriculum. Style type differences were evident in all profiles, but tended to be most sharply focused in teacher perceptions of the operative curriculum. Figure 11.1 shows a profile comparison of three school programmes in English language education representative of the basic style types, based on teacher perceptions of the operative curriculum in the respective programmes. As can be seen from the table, the basic style types produce quite distinctively different patterns of curricular emphasis, and these patterns are consistent with style type allocation on the basis of document analysis and interview data. In the research studies, data were used only to confirm the identification of basic types, since the extended typology and the identification of sub-styles was a later development. In principle, however, one might expect to find similar patterns of difference in programme emphases across the sub-styles, although this hypothesis has not been tested.

To compare profiles, the product moment correlation (r) and the distance measure (D) were used. The product moment correlation is useful, because it provides a measure of the degree of similarity between the *shape* of the two profiles – in other words, of the *relative emphasis* placed by the programmes being compared on the various facets of learning represented by the items in the profile. What the correlation coefficient does not tell us, however, is the degree of similarity in the *level of emphasis* accorded to the various facets of learning. This is where the distance measure (D) provides us with valuable additional information, since it takes into account *level* and *dispersion* as well as *shape* (Nunnally, 1967). By making use of both measures (*i.e.* the correlation coefficient and the distance measure), we have a simple but effective method of comparing profiles quickly and economically. The comparison data for the profiles are shown in Table 11.2.

Although correlation coefficients are readily interpretable, distance measures are less so, as they are dependent on the measurement scale being used and the number of items in the profiles being compared. For the curriculum profiles being compared in Figure 11.1, distance measures could range, theoretically, between 0, if the profiles

Table/Tableau 11.2.

Summary of profile comparison data

Synthèse des données comparatives sur les profils

	I/II	I/III	II/III
Product moment correlation (r)	0.13	–0.54	0.12
Distance measure (D)	3.41	3.74	2.84

were identical, and 8.72, if the profiles were completely polarised. In the actual study of curriculum practice in English language education, distance measures ranged between 0.48 and 3.75, with a mean of D = 2.06 and a median of D = 2.06 (Piper, 1983, p. 40).

7. Curriculum Style and the Network A Programme

Clearly, the typology of curriculum style as it has been outlined in this chapter cannot be adopted ready-made in the network's work programme. Although typology development has been substantially grounded in research, that research has been limited to the practice of Australian schools and to specific curriculum areas; and the application of the typology has to date been confined to relatively small-scale research studies. Moreover, the research studies on which the development of the typology was based were conducted over a decade ago, and while one can be reasonably confident that the typology is still relevant to current curriculum practice in Australian schools, that confidence has not been empirically tested. From the perspective of Network A's programme of work, the immediate questions which need to be answered, before any decision to use the typology can be made, are:

- How transferable is the typology between cultures and between countries?
- How transferable is the typology to areas of the curriculum other than those in which it has been investigated and applied?
- How transferable is the typology over time (*i.e.* is it still relevant to current curriculum practice)?

To answer these questions, small targeted pilot studies need to be conducted in each of the Member countries. Initially, the pilot studies might focus on one or two curriculum areas, to determine the applicability of the typology and what modifications, if any, might be required to meet particular contexts, as well as to identify the most appropriate items for inclusion in teacher and student questionnaires. This initial work could probably be done, at least at the level of the intended curriculum, largely through the analysis of curriculum documents. Ideally, however, studies would require some follow-up work in schools, given the observed discrepancies between the intended and the operative curriculum in Australian schools. Whether such pilot studies are feasible within the timetable, workplan, and resources of the network is for network members to decide, but such studies appear to be a prerequisite for any substantial use of the typology in the network's wider programme.

That said, there are exciting, but highly challenging, possibilities for strengthening both the descriptive and explanatory links between education goals and student learning outcomes through the use of the typology in the network's wider programme of work.

References

NUNNALLY, J. (1967), *Psychometric Theory,* McGraw-Hill, New York.

PIPER, K. (1979), *Curriculum Style and Social Learning* (ACER Research Monograph No. 4), Australian Council for Educational Research, Hawthorn, Victoria.

PIPER, K. (1983), *Curriculum Style and English Language* (ACER Research Monograph No. 19), Australian Council for Educational Research, Hawthorn, Victoria.

STURMAN, A. (1989), *Decentralisation and the Curriculum* (ACER Research Monograph No. 35), Australian Council for Educational Research, Hawthorn, Victoria.

YOUNG, R. (1981), ''A study of teacher epistemologies'', *Australian Journal of Education,* No. 25 (2), pp. 194-208.

Chapter 12

Towards a Strategic Approach for Developing International Indicators of Student Achievement*

by

Eugene Owen
National Center for Education Statistics,
US Department of Education, Washington DC, United States

and

G. Douglas Hodgkinson
Ministry of Education, Vancouver, British Columbia, Canada

and

Albert Tuijnman
OECD Secretariat, Paris, France

Since 1992, Network A has balanced the need to produce student outcome indicators quickly, using available data, with the need to outline a longer-term development strategy. Part 1 of this volume discussed some of the methodological issues that emerged during the development of student outcome indicators for *Education at a Glance* (OECD, 1992 and 1993), and represents the short-term approach used to date. Parts 2 and 3 provided information on the issues and processes developed to produce indicators in two new areas: National Goals (GOALS) and Cross-Curricular Competencies (CCC). These represent medium-term planning. All the time, the network has sought to develop an overarching strategic approach for network activities and to understand the relationships among the various themes that have evolved over the past three years within the network in terms of the interests of policy-makers in the OECD countries.

Building on the issues and methodology discussed in this volume, this concluding chapter lays out a potential plan of action for the next phase in the development of education indicators. Since Network A does not, and should not, exist in isolation from

---

* Texte en français, page 220.

the other networks, from the technical group, and the Secretariat, or from the needs of Member countries, the intention of this chapter is to serve as input into a revised overall framework for the INES project. The content of this chapter reflects the thinking of the authors and the members of the Network; however, there have been other proposals which envision a narrower focus for the network's activities than is described here.

1. Brief History and Progress of Network A

The main objective of INES is to supply OECD countries with a framework within which they can co-operate to develop and refine a series of education indicators that can be used to evaluate education systems at the national level. Furthermore, the project aims to develop a system of internationally comparable education indicators that can be used to inform decisions and policy-making.

Network A was created to prepare student outcome indicators. In its initial years, and in keeping with the experimental nature of the INES project, Network A opportunistically examined subject-bound achievement data available from the International Assessment of Educational Progress (IAEP) in science and mathematics and the International Association for the Evaluation of Educational Achievement (IEA) in reading literacy. During this period the network also worked to develop a structure for indicator preparation and dealt with developing statistical and presentation standards.

As the chapters in this volume demonstrate, Network A has expanded beyond its original parameters and taken steps to implement a broader conceptualisation of student outcomes. The CCC and GOALS activities described in Chapters 4 to 7 and 8 to 10, reflect a desire by the network to provide additional measures of student outcomes and a context for interpreting the network's indicators. Although this evolution is seen by members to be positive, certain problems have surfaced:

- the original model for the overall project is no longer current;
- the relationships between indicators is not clear and should be investigated; and
- the balance between the domains has shifted and needs to be re-examined.

The INES indicator set which we are attempting to produce is rapidly reaching a size which is larger than ideal, in terms of cost, feasibility and utility.

2. Towards a Strategic Plan

A vital part of strategic planning is the concept of shared beliefs, vision, and mission. Until 1995, the network did not have a mission statement to guide its workplan. There have been several statements of what the network is responsible for, such as, "indicators of student achievement" or "the development and preparation of educational outcome indicators"; however, these definitions are not very precise, especially since the terms "educational outcomes" and "student achievement" are far from synonymous. Furthermore, some of the indicators being developed by the GOALS and CCC sub-groups are difficult to conceptualise as outcomes; and to complicate things further, indicators developed by other networks deal with what can arguably be regarded as "student outcomes" (*e.g.* graduation rates).

A formal mission statement will clarify the areas Network A is charged with examining. It will also convey to network members, and others, the underlying rationale for the network's working in a specific area of indicator development. Such a statement might be:

> "Network A exists to develop indicators of certain areas of knowledge, skills, and attitudes demonstrated by students. These indicators shall be relevant to policy development and shall allow valid comparison between education systems and over time."

To adopt this mission statement would imply several changes in Network A's activities. Student outcome indicators would be broader in scope than those developed during Phase III – and would include additional achievement topics and indicators which represent broad skills that are not bound to particular curricula, as well as student attitudes. In addition, information would be developed on education systems to provide a setting or context for the indicators and to allow more meaningful comparisons. Finally, indicators should be regularly measured over time. For example, an indicator that results in the statement that "Country A scores higher than Country B in subject X", only partly meets policy-makers' needs, especially since subject X is not chosen because of any specific policy imperative, but simply because an international data-gathering body has determined that it is next in the cycle. During this current period of significant educational reforms in most OECD countries, policy-makers also require information on the progress of their students in particular subjects in relation to stated goals or otherwise communicated expectations and in comparison with other countries. This requires that the network look beyond the bounds of currently planned international data collections and beyond existing data sources (see below, "Developing New Sources of Data"). Feasibility, however, should also form part of the mission statement. There must be moments where the results produced by the network are judged against what was intended.

Given the proposed re-design of Network A's activities, the following issues need to be looked at from a strategic viewpoint:

- Are the criteria for inclusion of indicators realistic, given financial and other limitations of data-gathering?
- Are the domains into which the indicators are grouped functional or merely labels of convenience?
- Are our data sources adequate, and appropriate for our data requirements – will they allow for regular and frequent reporting and do they cover a broad enough number of subjects and topics to describe the domain fully?
- Are the indicators that we produce the best fit for the Network A domains and the overall INES model, or are they mostly opportunistic, derived from whatever data are available?
- Do the results produced by the network satisfy expectations?

3.   Developing a Strategy for Regular Reporting of Certain Indicators

From its inception and through to the preparation of *Education at a Glance* (OECD, 1995), Network A has relied on the availability of data from the IEA and IAEP. This has resulted in the network preparing indicators in mathematics, science, and reading literacy. However, regardless of the other shortcomings of the indicators produced using IEA and IAEP data, it is significant that such sources of data do not ensure that progress over time can be measured.

Before going on to discuss issues of reporting strategy and data collection directly, it should be pointed out that agreement still needs to be sought on issues relating to the outcome domains that have been designated for Network A development; the domains are shown in Figure 12.1.

The outcome domains were developed more in response to the work the network had completed and planned rather than as a comprehensive overview of all areas of learning outcomes. If Network A succeeds in taking a broader view of all learning outcomes, the list of domains may need to be examined and revised accordingly. Similarly, if the network were to limit its activities to a more focused series of outcomes, the domains should reflect this. Developing a definitive list of domains may be an evolutionary process, but trying to clarify them now will allow us to define our goals better and will help to drive network activity, rather than allowing network activity to define our goals. At the very least, the domains should be critically examined for structural consistency

Figure/*Graphique* 12.1.   **Outcome domains**
Domaines où des résultats sont attendus

Source: Network A, INES, OECD.

since domain No. 1 is clearly superordinate to several of the others. They also need to be examined relative to the overall INES project, in order to reveal gaps or overlaps with other networks.

Having selected these domains, the network needs formally to adopt a system of classifying indicators under these domains. Such a system might be built around the following questions:

- Which student outcome domains do policy-makers think are important?
- Which indicators within these policy-relevant domains help policy-makers to understand student outcomes?
- How can the set of indicators be measured, in accordance with INES statistical standards?
- What are the sources of data?
- How frequently does the set of indicators need to be produced to allow a meaningful assessment of progress over time?
- What are the context, social norms, and education goals that eventually affect system implementation and student outcomes?

We should not be driven by the availability of data, rather we need to decide what information is needed, when and how often, and then to develop a strategy to obtain the data. In this regard, it would be essential to re-examine the criteria that we use to decide whether an indicator should be developed and included in the set of indicators. In addition, the network should set targets for how often it wants to include indicators in each domain.

The classification system should be reviewed by the policy review and advisory group. Currently, because work is just beginning in some areas, not all domains are covered. As work continues, there will be greater coverage of domains. In its expansion to other domains as well as refinements to current domains, the network needs to move away from an opportunistic search for new outcome indicators to one directed by trans-national policy interests. In order to do so, some market research might be done to understand who *Education at a Glance*'s audience is, how they use information, what information they want, and how that information should be presented. Assuming that market research confirms the general direction currently being pursued, the network should consider adopting the following three working goals:

- That indicators will be developed to lead to an adequate coverage of all outcome domains. (Ideally, the set of indicators would fully cover all outcome domains. This is not feasible; the network must limit the number and scope of the domains, or be prepared to initiate data-gathering to support the indicators developed by the INES project.)
- That once indicators in certain outcome domains appear in *Education at a Glance* or other OECD publications, those domains will be represented on a regular basis.
- That the network will undertake a bi-annual review of its development activities and the indicators produced for INES to ensure that they are consistent with the needs and aspirations of the Member countries.

Before beginning Phase IV of the INES project, the network should work through these issues and adopt a strategic plan. The implementation of that strategy can only be considered within the broader context of how the INES project is organised after 1996.

4. Developing New Sources of Data

It has been suggested throughout this chapter that one of the major challenges confronting Network A is the lack of appropriate data upon which to base indicators. That problem is not unique for Network A. In fact, it is a major issue of concern to the entire effort, led by the OECD, to create a stable set of international indicators of national education systems, but, because of the nature of the data to be gathered about student outcomes, it is especially difficult for this network.

To date, Network A has depended on existing sources of data concerning student achievement. The data utilised by the network were gathered for large-scale comparative studies undertaken by IEA and the IAEP, which resorts under the Educational Testing Service (ETS). While both agencies have produced useful information and insights, their studies are designed to be detailed, and are comprehensive beyond our needs. We must remember that the purpose of Network A is not to research education on an international basis, but to develop indicators. The type of data we require for even the most sophisticated indicator is still considerably narrower in scope than what is needed to answer the major research questions posed by studies such as TIMSS (IEA Third International Mathematics and Science Study). As a result, these studies are too expensive, too slow to report, do not cover enough domains, do not involve enough OECD countries (or all parts of the countries that do participate), and the OECD has little influence or control over the testing schedule.

In thinking about future data needs, Network A has to consider ways of producing high-quality and comparable student outcome data on a regular basis, in several domains, and at a reasonable cost. Improving efficiency and cost-effectiveness will necessitate a careful review of the priorities of the Member countries. Such a review might be undertaken under the auspices of the OECD. This organisation might also be invited to become more pro-active in large-scale data collection about student achievement. Exactly how this can be done remains to be considered, since it will require that priorities and budgets must be agreed upon by the countries involved, and clear directives should be established as to what is expected, and by what date. National governments are the bodies ultimately held accountable for the performance of the education system for which they are responsible, and thus they should have a significant role in clarifying data needs.

In order for internationally comparative indicators on student outcomes to become sustainable and integral in a set of international education indicators, the strategic plan must take into consideration the costs of the current fragmented system of collecting international student achievement data. While the broad involvement of nations in the IEA TIMSS, for example, attests to their interest in the study, the survey runs virtually independently of any country's national data collection system or, for that matter the OECD system on education statistics and indicators. Over time, the development of indicators could depend on a vertically integrated data system. Such a system would build on existing national assessments, which an increasing number of OECD countries are implementing, and encourage countries without national assessments to commit themsleves to an on-going data-collection system.

Another possible strategy is to re-direct the energies of the existing international research agencies to fulfil an agenda which reflects Network A's strategic objectives. The IEA/IAEP approach has the benefit of focusing on schooling (ISCED 1, 2 and 3), and the aggregations of the performance of individual students within that age range. Such surveys depend on long-term planning, which in turn makes for long periods between data becoming available. However, it should be possible nonetheless to negotiate a modified approach with research agencies if an agreed strategy required more frequent surveys. These might be based on a common format with guaranteed OECD participation through Network A.

Yet another alternative is for countries to re-deploy resources to support equivalent research under the auspices of the OECD itself. The idea that the OECD should become directly involved in data collection needs careful consideration. It would not be unreasonable, however, for the OECD, guided by Network A, to commission a suitable agency or agencies to organise regular comparative surveys. In this way the relevant expertise could be utilised under network control and with the minimum of additional in-house staff and financial costs. There would of course still be funding implications for Member countries, but if this option were pursued, there would be potential savings for national authorities (by discontinuing work with existing agencies) which could be used to fund the work commissioned by the OECD. One factor that must not be overlooked in considering these options is the wider community of non-OECD countries which take part in comparative surveys: adopting the latter approach might exclude such countries from international comparative work.

5. New Indicators

Despite the difficulty of finding data on the indicators which the network has identified, it is still useful to consider ideas for future indicators. These will arise naturally out of the process of identifying outcome domains, but new indicators may also be developed by examining different populations at different times and at different locations. For example, as an indicator of *labour force readiness,* the network could develop an indicator focused only on students intending to pursue a vocational course of study, or students whose schooling ends with compulsory education.

In similar vein, an examination of the results of the education system need not be restricted to student populations. Focusing on the knowledge and skills of entry-level workers would allow for a more direct assessment of the potential productivity of a country's labour force than would testing student populations. Another type of indicator might examine the retention of knowledge by means of a longitudinal study with the baseline being towards the end of a student's career and the follow-up five or ten years later, when the student is no longer at school or studying for examinations.

It is important, however, that the network should not "go fishing" for new indicators unless their relationship to the overall project and usefulness to policy-makers can be demonstrated. Network A must be confident that the indicators that are chosen are not merely interesting statistics, but are worth monitoring, and are critical to informing policy-makers about major educational issues relating to young people.

The process of inclusion of new indicators should include an examination of the following criteria as well as those that the network has already established for ensuring the quality of data. Indicators, in other words, must be:

- comparable over time and between jurisdictions, or against standards;
- acceptable to all stakeholders as meaningful measures of a stated value;
- responsive to changes in the underlying phenomena;
- substantively distinguishable from other indicators;
- modifiable through positive action; and
- supported by data that are, and will probably continue to be, accessible.

6. New Publications

The purpose of the INES project is, in part, to produce international education indicators and to make them accessible to policy-makers, the public, and the press. *Education at a Glance* is the primary forum for presenting network indicators. However, the first two editions (1992 and 1993) of the project's principal publication are too oriented towards technical audiences and, therefore, inhibit on-going use by policy-makers. At the same time, *Education at a glance* is "at a glance" and its style of presenting indicators with brief descriptions is recognised to be rather limited.

In addition, the network is undertaking work in the GOALS and CCC sub-groups, for example, which will yield much more information than is appropriate for *Education at a Glance;* therefore, additional supplements to *Education at a Glance* may be required. These supplementary reports could present information in a more in-depth and descriptive manner. Examples might be final reports of the various studies planned by the CCC and GOALS sub-groups. They would probably target a more specific audience than *Education at a Glance.* The inclusion of detail in such documents might free *Education at a Glance* to become more focused and less complex and thus more effective as a document to be read by senior government officers and politicians.

The network should, therefore, develop a more systematic publishing strategy which remains aligned with the overall INES project. The strategy should ensure that publications intended for policy-makers are more accessible, more policy-oriented, designed to increase the visibility of indicators, and provide more descriptive information across indicators in order to allow patterns and trends to be examined. In all likelihood, such a publishing strategy would result in a variety of reporting formats including a redesigned *Education at a Glance,* topical bulletins, key indicators, etc. The content and structure of the technical reports should be closely aligned with the needs of their intended audience.

7. Reviewing the Processes of Indicator Selection

Countries participate in the indicators project with a variety of objectives, including:

- to learn about education in other countries with whom they participate in a global economy;
- to focus interest and debate on domestic educational issues through international comparisons; and
- to target priorities on key issues.

Built into the strategic plan must be a mechanism to evaluate the degree to which Network A's indicators meet these objectives; that is, Network A needs to adopt performance indicators measuring its own responsiveness to the policy needs of Member countries. Performance measures should examine the use and usefulness of Network A's indicators and the degree to which they influence national policy through political debate, legislation, and practice. These measures require links to be forged between outcome indicators and indicators of educational process and curriculum. This logic is found in the work of the GOALS sub-group described in Chapters 8 and 11. Obviously, countries' willingness to devote financial and human resources to this activity is a useful performance indicator. However, this tells us very little about whether countries will continue to provide these resources in the future.

8. Conclusion

The network has experimented and evolved. Since the General Assembly meeting in 1991 in Lugano, Switzerland, Network A has produced student outcome indicators in mathematics, science, and reading literacy. In addition, significant headway has been made in the area of developing an indicator of cross-curricular competencies and a description of national goals. During this period, the structure of indicators and standards for data have been developed. If all of that is taken into account, the network has come a great distance in a relatively short time.

Some of the network's work has been opportunistic, building on readily available sources of data. Some, such as the structure of the indicators, was guided by pragmatism and the desire to contribute to *Education at a Glance*. Now, the network is beginning the difficult task of thinking strategically.

The activities discussed in this and earlier chapters will take time to achieve. They involve 1) the development of a consensus around what to do, 2) the acceptance of a data-collection strategy that depends on the commitment of governments, 3) the preparation of instrumentation, 4) data collection and analysis, 5) the development of new communication mechanisms, and finally, 6) feedback to reassess the validity of the strategic plan.

Two issues will shape the future of Network A:

- the need for a longer-term perspective and a greater commitment by participants and governments; and

- the need for the work of Network A to be embedded within a regularised system of data collection and reporting.

If these needs can be met, the network will be able to ensure that it measures progress in student outcomes – which is of central concern to policy-makers.

*

*   *

Vers une approche stratégique pour développer les indicateurs internationaux de réussite scolaire

Depuis 1992, le Réseau A a comparé la nécessité de produire rapidement des indicateurs de résultats scolaires à l'aide des données existantes et la nécessité de concevoir une stratégie de développement à long terme. La première partie de cet ouvrage, qui aborde certains des problèmes de méthodologie apparus pendant l'élaboration des indicateurs de résultats scolaires pour *Regards sur l'éducation* (OCDE, 1992 et 1993), représente l'approche à court terme adoptée jusqu'à présent. Les parties 2 et 3 renseignent sur les problèmes et procédés entourant l'élaboration d'indicateurs dans deux nouveaux domaines : celui des compétences transdisciplinaires (CCC) et celui des objectifs nationaux (GOALS), qui représentent une perspective à moyen terme. Pendant tout ce temps, le réseau a tenté de mettre au point une approche stratégique globale pour ses activités et de saisir les relations entre les divers thèmes qui se sont fait jour au cours des trois dernières années, dans l'optique des préoccupations des décideurs des pays de l'OCDE.

S'appuyant sur les questions et la méthodologie examinées dans le présent volume, le chapitre final trace un plan d'action susceptible d'être appliqué à la prochaine phase d'élaboration des indicateurs de l'enseignement. Comme le Réseau A n'est pas, et ne doit pas être isolé des autres réseaux, du groupe technique et du Secrétariat, ni détaché des besoins des pays Membres, le chapitre a pour objet de contribuer à l'élaboration d'un cadre global révisé pour le projet sur les indicateurs internationaux des systèmes d'enseignement (INES). Son contenu traduit la pensée des auteurs et des membres du réseau ; on notera que d'autres propositions ont toutefois été formulées prévoyant pour les activités du réseau un cadre plus restreint que celui décrit ici.

1. Bref historique et évolution du Réseau A

Le projet INES a pour principal objectif d'assurer aux pays de l'OCDE un cadre dans lequel ils peuvent mettre au point et améliorer, en collaboration, une série d'indicateurs de l'enseignement qui s'utilisent pour évaluer les systèmes éducatifs à l'échelon national. Le projet vise, de surcroît, à construire un ensemble d'indicateurs comparables au niveau international, susceptible d'être employé pour étayer les décisions et les politiques.

Le Réseau A a été créé avec pour mission d'élaborer les indicateurs de résultats des élèves. Au cours de ses premières années et conformément à la nature expérimentale du projet INES, il a opportunément examiné les données sur la réussite scolaire par matière, publiées par l'International Assessment of Educational Progress (IAEP) en sciences et en mathématiques et par l'International Association for the Evaluation of Educational Achievement (IEA) en lecture. Durant cette période, le réseau a aussi contribué à mettre au point une structure pour la préparation des indicateurs, ainsi que des critères statistiques et des normes de présentation.

Comme le démontrent les chapitres de cet ouvrage, le Réseau A a transcendé ses paramètres d'origine pour s'orienter vers une conception plus large des résultats scolaires. Les activités CCC et GOALS, décrites aux chapitres 4 à 7 et 8 à 10, indiquent qu'il souhaite fournir des mesures complémentaires de résultats des élèves et un contexte permettant d'interpréter les indicateurs qu'il met au point. Bien que les membres du réseau jugent cette évolution encourageante, certains problèmes se sont néanmoins fait jour :

- le modèle original du projet global n'a plus cours ;
- la relation entre les indicateurs n'est pas claire et devrait être étudiée ; et
- l'équilibre entre les domaines s'est rompu et doit être réexaminé.

L'ensemble d'indicateurs que nous tentons de produire dans le cadre du projet INES atteint rapidement une taille plus importante qu'il n'est souhaitable en termes de coût, de faisabilité et d'utilité.

2. Vers un plan stratégique

La planification stratégique comporte un élément essentiel : l'idée d'une vision, d'une mission et de convictions partagées. Jusqu'à 1995, le réseau n'avait pas d'énoncé de mission pour orienter son plan de travail. Plusieurs déclarations ont certes mentionné ce dont il est responsable, comme « les indicateurs de réussite scolaire » ou « l'élaboration et la préparation d'indicateurs de résultats de l'enseignement » ; mais ces définitions ne sont pas très précises, en particulier parce que les expressions « réussite scolaire » et « résultats de l'enseignement » sont loin d'être synonymes. Qui plus est, certains des indicateurs mis au point par les sous-groupes GOALS et CCC sont difficiles à conceptualiser en tant que résultats ; et pour compliquer encore les choses, quelques indicateurs élaborés par d'autres réseaux concernent ce qu'on peut considérer comme « les résultats des élèves » (par exemple, les taux d'obtention de diplômes).

Un énoncé de mission officiel permettrait de préciser les domaines que le Réseau A est chargé d'examiner et ferait connaître aux membres du réseau, et à d'autres, la raison sous-jacente pour laquelle le réseau travaille dans un secteur spécifique de développement des indicateurs. L'énoncé pourrait être formulé en ces termes :

> « Le Réseau A est chargé de mettre au point les indicateurs de certains domaines de connaissances, de compétences et de comportements des élèves. Ces indicateurs seront utiles à l'élaboration des politiques et permettront de procéder à des comparaisons valables entre les systèmes d'enseignement et au cours du temps. »

L'adoption de cet énoncé de mission impliquerait plusieurs changements dans les activités du Réseau A. Les indicateurs de résultats des élèves auraient une portée plus large que les indicateurs mis au point au cours de la phase III – ils engloberaient de nouveaux secteurs de réussite scolaire, des compétences générales non liées à des programmes d'études particuliers, ainsi que des comportements des élèves. En outre, des informations sur les systèmes d'enseignement seraient produites afin d'assurer un cadre ou un contexte aux indicateurs et de permettre des comparaisons plus significatives qu'auparavant. Enfin, les indicateurs devraient être évalués régulièrement. Par exemple, un indicateur qui donne lieu à l'énoncé suivant : « Le pays A obtient un meilleur résultat que le pays B dans la discipline X », ne répond qu'en partie aux besoins des décideurs, en particulier parce que la discipline X n'est pas choisie pour répondre à un impératif politique spécifique, mais simplement parce qu'un organisme international de collecte de données a décidé qu'elle était la suivante dans son cycle d'enquête. Comme la plupart des pays de l'OCDE procèdent actuellement à des réformes importantes dans le secteur de l'enseignement, les décideurs ont également besoin de renseignements sur les progrès qu'accomplissent leurs élèves dans certaines matières, en relation avec les objectifs énoncés ou les attentes et par rapport aux élèves d'autres pays. Il ne faut donc pas que le réseau se limite aux collectes de données prévues à l'échelon international et aux sources de données existantes (voir ci-dessous : « Nouvelles sources de données »). Cependant, la faisabilité devrait aussi faire partie de la mission du réseau. Les résultats issus du réseau doivent faire l'objet d'une évaluation par rapport aux objectifs fixés.

Compte tenu de la nouvelle conception des activités du Réseau A qui est proposé, il convient d'examiner les questions ci-après sous l'angle stratégique :

- Les critères d'inclusion des indicateurs sont-ils réalistes, vu les contraintes financières et autres touchant les collectes de données ?
- Les domaines qui regroupent les indicateurs sont-ils fonctionnels ou répondent-ils à des considérations purement pratiques ?
- Nos sources de données sont-elles satisfaisantes et conviennent-elles à nos besoins en matière d'informations – permettent-elle de diffuser les indicateurs de façon régulière et fréquente ; couvrent-elles un nombre suffisamment important de disciplines et de sujets pour permettre une description exhaustive de chaque domaine ?
- Les indicateurs que nous produisons correspondent-ils au mieux aux domaines attribués au Réseau A et au modèle global INES ou sont-ils essentiellement le

résultat des circonstances, en ce sens qu'ils dérivent des données disponibles, quelles qu'elles soient?

• Les résultats produits par le réseau répondent-ils aux attentes?

3. Mise au point d'une stratégie permettant la diffusion régulière de certains indicateurs

Depuis ses débuts et tout au long de la préparation de *Regards sur l'éducation* (OCDE, 1995), le Réseau A s'est fondé sur les données publiées par l'IEA et l'IAEP et a donc préparé des indicateurs en mathématiques, en sciences et en lecture. Or, sans même tenir compte des autres lacunes des indicateurs établis à partir de ces données, on peut remarquer que ces sources de données ne permettent pas de mesurer les progrès accomplis au fil du temps.

Mais avant d'entamer le débat sur les questions de stratégie de diffusion et de collecte de données, il faut d'abord s'entendre sur les problèmes relatifs aux domaines de résultats des élèves attribués au Réseau A; ces domaines sont présentés dans le graphique 12.1 page 214.

Les domaines ont été retenus en fonction des travaux accomplis ou prévus par le réseau, plutôt que pour constituer une vue d'ensemble de tous les domaines touchant aux résultats de l'enseignement. Si le Réseau A réussit à adopter une perspective plus large, il y aura peut-être lieu de vérifier la liste des domaines et de la revoir en conséquence. De même, si le réseau devait limiter ses activités à une série de résultats plus ciblée, il faudrait en tenir compte dans le choix des domaines. L'établissement d'une liste de domaines pourrait bien entendu constituer un processus évolutif, mais si les domaines étaient précisés dès à présent, le réseau pourrait mieux définir ses objectifs et orienter ses activités, au lieu de laisser ses activités définir ses objectifs. Les domaines devraient tout au moins être examinés d'un oeil critique pour s'assurer de la cohérence de leur structure, étant donné que le domaine n° 1 en domine manifestement plusieurs autres. Ils devraient aussi être examinés par rapport à l'ensemble du projet INES afin de mettre en lumière d'éventuels chevauchements avec d'autres réseaux ou de possibles lacunes.

Une fois les domaines choisis, le réseau devra officiellement adopter un système permettant de classer les indicateurs en fonction des domaines. Le système pourrait être organisé autour des questions suivantes :

• Quels sont les domaines de résultats des élèves que les décideurs jugent importants?

• Dans les domaines qui intéressent les décideurs, quels indicateurs les aident à comprendre les résultats des élèves?

• Comment l'ensemble d'indicateurs peut-il être mesuré, conformément aux normes du projet INES en matière de statistiques?

• Quelles sont les sources des données?

• A quel rythme l'ensemble des indicateurs doit-il être produit pour permettre une évaluation significative des progrès accomplis au fil du temps?

- Quels sont les normes sociales, le contexte et les objectifs éducatifs susceptibles d'influer sur la mise en œuvre du système et les résultats des élèves ?

Nous ne devrions pas nous laisser guider par la disponibilité des données ; nous devons au contraire décider de quelles informations nous avons besoin, à quel moment et selon quelle fréquence, puis concevoir une stratégie qui nous permette d'obtenir les données. A cet égard, il serait capital de revoir les critères que nous employons pour déterminer s'il y a lieu de mettre au point un indicateur et de l'inclure dans l'ensemble des indicateurs. En outre, le réseau devrait établir des objectifs concernant le rythme auquel il souhaite inclure des indicateurs dans chaque domaine.

Il serait bon que le Groupe de consultation et d'analyse politique examine le système de classement. En ce moment, comme les travaux ne font que commencer dans certains secteurs, tous les domaines ne sont pas couverts. A mesure que les travaux se poursuivront, un nombre croissant de domaines seront abordés. Lorsqu'il s'élargira à d'autres domaines et améliorera ceux qu'il traite actuellement, le réseau devra rechercher de nouveaux indicateurs de résultats non plus en tirant parti des circonstances, mais en se laissant guider par les intérêts politiques transnationaux. Dans ce contexte, il pourrait être utile de procéder à une étude de marché afin de connaître la composition du lectorat de *Regards sur l'éducation,* la façon dont il se sert de l'information, l'information qu'il souhaite obtenir et la manière de la présenter. A supposer que l'étude de marché confirme la voie générale dans laquelle il est actuellement engagé, le réseau devrait envisager l'adoption des trois objectifs de travail suivants :

- Les indicateurs seront établis de façon à couvrir correctement tous les domaines de résultats. (Dans l'absolu, l'ensemble d'indicateurs couvrirait entièrement tous les domaines. Mais cela n'est pas possible ; le réseau doit limiter le nombre et l'étendue des domaines ou être disposé à entreprendre une collecte de données pour étayer les indicateurs mis au point dans le cadre du projet INES.)
- Dès lors que les indicateurs relatifs à certains domaines paraissent dans *Regards sur l'éducation* ou dans d'autres publications de l'OCDE, ces domaines seront représentés régulièrement.
- Le réseau examinera deux fois par an ses activités de développement ainsi que les indicateurs produits pour le projet INES afin de vérifier s'ils répondent aux besoins et aux aspirations des pays Membres.

Avant de se lancer dans la phase IV du projet INES, le réseau devra régler ces questions et adopter un plan stratégique. La mise en œuvre de cette stratégie ne peut être envisagée que dans le contexte plus large de l'organisation du projet au-delà de 1996.

4. Nouvelles sources de données

Tout au long de ce chapitre, nous avons laissé entendre que l'une des principales difficultés auxquelles se heurte le Réseau A est le manque de données pertinentes sur lesquelles fonder les indicateurs. Le Réseau A n'est pas le seul à connaître ce problème. En fait, il s'agit d'un important sujet de préoccupation pour toute l'entreprise que mène l'OCDE en vue de la création d'un ensemble stable d'indicateurs internationaux des systèmes d'enseignement. Toutefois, vu la nature des données à rassembler sur les résultats des élèves, le problème est particulièrement ardu pour le Réseau A.

Jusqu'ici, ce réseau a dépendu des sources de données existantes concernant la réussite scolaire. Les données qu'il a utilisées ont été recueillies dans le cadre d'enquêtes comparatives à grande échelle menées par l'IEA et par l'IAEP – qui font appel à l'Educational Testing Service (ETS). Les deux organismes ont certes publié des renseignements et des indications utiles, mais leurs études sont très détaillées et dépassent nos besoins par leur ampleur. Nous ne pouvons perdre de vue que l'objectif du Réseau A n'est pas de faire de la recherche sur l'enseignement à une échelle internationale, mais de produire des indicateurs. Le type de données dont nous avons besoin pour élaborer même l'indicateur le plus complexe couvre un champ bien étroit au regard des informations nécessaires pour répondre aux grandes questions que posent des études comme la Third International Mathematics and Science Study (TIMSS) de l'IEA. En conséquence, ces études sont trop coûteuses, leurs délais de publication sont trop longs, elles couvrent insuffisamment de domaines, ne concernent pas assez de pays de l'OCDE (ou toutes les régions des pays participants), et l'OCDE n'a que peu d'influence ou de contrôle sur le calendrier des épreuves.

En réfléchissant à ses besoins futurs en matière de données, le Réseau A doit étudier les moyens de produire, à intervalles réguliers, dans plusieurs domaines et moyennant un coût raisonnable, des données sur les résultats scolaires qui soient comparables et de bonne qualité. Pour améliorer l'efficacité et la rentabilité, il devra examiner avec attention les priorités des pays Membres. Un tel examen pourrait être réalisé sous les auspices de l'OCDE. L'Organisation pourrait aussi prendre une part plus active dans le recueil de données à grande échelle sur les résultats scolaires. La façon dont cette stratégie pourra être mise en œuvre n'est pas encore décidée, car les priorités, ainsi que les budgets, doivent être adoptés d'un commun accord par les pays en cause, qui doivent aussi donner des directives précises en ce qui concerne leurs attentes et leurs calendriers. Ce sont les gouvernements nationaux qui, en dernière analyse, répondent de la performance des systèmes d'enseignement dont ils sont responsables, et il serait donc bon qu'ils aient un rôle important à jouer dans la définition des besoins en matière de données.

Pour que des indicateurs de résultats scolaires comparables à l'échelle internationale deviennent viables et puissent s'intégrer dans un ensemble d'indicateurs internationaux des systèmes d'enseignement, le plan stratégique doit tenir compte des coûts du système fragmenté actuel de collecte de données internationales sur la réussite scolaire. Si l'ampleur de la participation des pays à la TIMSS de l'IEA, par exemple, témoigne de leur intérêt pour l'étude, celle-ci ne dépend pratiquement d'aucun système national de collecte de données, ni d'ailleurs du système de statistiques et d'indicateurs de l'enseignement de l'OCDE. Au fil du temps, la mise au point d'indicateurs pourrait reposer sur un système de données intégré verticalement. Un tel système s'appuierait sur les évaluations nationales qu'un nombre croissant de pays de l'OCDE sont en train de mettre en place et inciterait les pays qui ne font pas d'évaluations à s'engager dans la mise en œuvre d'un système permanent de collecte de données.

Une autre stratégie possible consisterait à réorienter l'activité des organismes internationaux de recherche vers un programme qui tienne compte des objectifs stratégiques du Réseau A. L'approche de l'IEA et de l'IAEP offre l'avantage de se focaliser sur la scolarité aux niveaux CITE 1, 2 et 3 et sur le regroupement des performances des élèves appartenant à ces tranches d'âge. Le type d'études qu'effectuent ces organismes repose sur une planification à long terme, ce qui explique la longueur des délais de production des données. Mais il devrait être possible de négocier une nouvelle approche avec eux si une stratégie fixée d'un commun accord exigeait des enquêtes plus fréquentes. Celles-ci pourraient reposer sur un modèle de présentation commun, l'OCDE garantissant sa participation par l'entremise du Réseau A.

Une autre possibilité serait que les pays affectent des ressources au financement d'une recherche équivalente, qui serait menée sous les auspices de l'OCDE même. L'idée que l'Organisation prenne directement part à une collecte de données doit être examinée avec une grande attention. Mais il ne paraît pas déraisonnable que l'OCDE, guidée par le Réseau A, mandate un ou plusieurs organismes compétents pour organiser des enquêtes comparatives périodiques. Une expertise pertinente pourrait ainsi être utilisée sous la direction du réseau et avec un minimum de ressources humaines et financières internes complémentaires. Il est indéniable que cette solution aurait une incidence financière pour les pays Membres ; mais, si elle était adoptée, les autorités nationales pourraient probablement réaliser des économies (en interrompant les travaux menés avec les organismes en place), qu'elles pourraient utiliser pour financer les recherches commandées par l'OCDE. Un élément qu'il ne faut toutefois pas ignorer en examinant ces diverses options est la présence d'un groupe de pays non membres de l'OCDE qui prend part aux études comparatives : l'adoption de la dernière approche pourrait exclure ces pays des travaux comparatifs internationaux.

5. Nouveaux indicateurs

Bien qu'il soit difficile de trouver des données sur les indicateurs que le réseau a inventoriés, il est néanmoins utile d'envisager de nouveaux indicateurs. Ceux-ci pourraient certes découler de l'identification des domaines de résultats de l'enseignement, mais ils pourraient aussi dériver de l'examen de populations différentes, à des moments différents et dans des situations différentes. Ainsi, parmi les indicateurs de *préparation au marché du travail*, le réseau pourrait mettre au point un indicateur centré uniquement sur les élèves ayant l'intention de poursuivre une filière professionnelle ou sur ceux qui arrêtent leurs études au niveau de la scolarité obligatoire.

Dans le même ordre d'idées, l'examen des résultats du système d'enseignement ne doit pas nécessairement se limiter aux effectifs estudiantins. Si on se concentrait sur les connaissances et les compétences des travailleurs à leur entrée sur le marché du travail, on pourrait évaluer plus directement la productivité éventuelle de la population active d'un pays qu'en testant les populations scolaires. Un autre type d'indicateur pourrait analyser la fixation des connaissances au moyen d'une étude longitudinale dont le niveau de référence se situerait vers la fin de la carrière de l'élève ou de l'étudiant, et le suivi, cinq ou dix ans plus tard, lorsque l'élève ne serait plus dans un établissement d'enseigne-ment ni occupé à préparer ses examens.

Il importe toutefois que le réseau ne «déniche» aucun nouvel indicateur dont il ne puisse démontrer clairement le rapport avec l'ensemble du projet et l'utilité pour les décideurs. Le réseau doit être persuadé que les indicateurs choisis ne sont pas simplement d'intéressantes statistiques, mais méritent d'être suivis de près et sont essentiels pour renseigner les décideurs sur les grands problèmes touchant la jeunesse en matière d'enseignement.

Le processus d'inclusion de nouveaux indicateurs devrait comporter l'examen des critères ci-après, outre l'examen des critères déjà définis par le réseau pour vérifier la qualité des données. En d'autres termes, les indicateurs doivent être :

• comparables au fil du temps et entre les entités, ou par rapport à des normes ;
• considérés par tous les intervenants comme une mesure utile d'une valeur énoncée ;
• sensibles à l'évolution du phénomène sous-jacent ;
• fondamentalement distincts des autres indicateurs ;
• modifiables par une intervention positive ; et
• étayés par des données qui sont accessibles et continueront probablement de l'être.

6. Nouvelles publications

Le projet INES a, en partie, pour objectif de produire des indicateurs internationaux des systèmes d'enseignement et de les mettre à la disposition des décideurs, du grand public et de la presse. *Regards sur l'éducation* est le principal moyen de présentation des indicateurs élaborés par les réseaux. Toutefois, les deux premières éditions de la plus importante publication du projet (1992 et 1993) sont trop axées vers des publics spéciali-sés, ce qui empêche les décideurs de s'en servir couramment. De même, *Regards sur l'éducation* donne un «instantané» de la situation, et son style de présentation des indicateurs, qui consiste à donner de brèves descriptions, est notoirement assez limité.

En outre, par l'entremise des sous-groupes GOALS et CCC notamment, le réseau conduit des travaux qui dégageront une quantité d'informations bien trop importante pour *Regards sur l'éducation*. Il conviendrait donc peut-être de publier des suppléments à cet ouvrage. Ces rapports complémentaires pourraient présenter les informations de façon plus détaillée et plus descriptive ou servir, par exemple, de rapports finals aux diverses études prévues par les sous-groupes. Ils s'adresseraient sans doute à un public plus spécifique que *Regards sur l'éducation*. Déchargé dès lors de la publication des détails, ce dernier ouvrage deviendrait plus ciblé et moins complexe et serait donc un meilleur instrument de consultation pour les hauts fonctionnaires et les hommes politiques.

Par conséquent, le réseau aurait avantage à élaborer une stratégie de publications plus systématique qui demeure alignée sur le projet INES. Cette stratégie garantirait que les publications destinées aux décideurs soient plus accessibles et plus orientées vers l'action, contribuent à accroître la visibilité des indicateurs et offrent des informations plus concrètes permettant l'examen des tendances et des courants. Il est probable qu'une telle stratégie entraînerait la parution de toute une gamme de publications, comme des bulletins thématiques ou des recueils d'indicateurs clés, ou encore la refonte de *Regards sur l'éducation*. Le contenu et la structure des rapports techniques devraient se conformer étroitement aux besoins des publics visés.

7. Examen des processus de sélection des indicateurs

Les pays qui participent au projet sur les indicateurs poursuivent divers objectifs. Ils souhaitent notamment :
- se renseigner sur l'enseignement dispensé dans d'autres pays qui sont leurs partenaires dans une économie devenue mondiale ;
- polariser l'intérêt et le débat sur les problèmes pédagogiques intérieurs, par le biais de comparaisons entre pays ; et
- centrer les priorités sur les problèmes essentiels.

Le plan stratégique doit prévoir un mécanisme destiné à évaluer si les indicateurs du Réseau A répondent à ces objectifs ; autrement dit, le réseau aurait intérêt à adopter des mesures de performance susceptibles de juger de sa propre sensibilité aux besoins des pays Membres. Ces mesures auraient trait à l'utilisation et à l'utilité des indicateurs du réseau et évalueraient l'influence qu'ils exercent sur les politiques nationales par le biais de débats politiques, de législation et de procédures. Ces mesures de performance supposent que des liens s'établissent entre les indicateurs de résultats et les indicateurs de processus éducatifs et de programmes d'études. On retrouve cette même logique dans les travaux du sous-groupe GOALS décrits aux chapitres 8 à 11. Il est clair que la volonté des pays de consacrer des ressources humaines et financières à cette activité constitue un indicateur de performance utile. Mais il ne nous renseigne guère sur l'intention des pays de continuer à fournir ces ressources dans l'avenir.

8. Conclusion

Le réseau a fait des expériences et a évolué. Depuis l'Assemblée générale de 1991 tenue à Lugano, en Suisse, il a produit des indicateurs de résultats des élèves en mathématiques, en sciences et en lecture. De surcroît, il a considérablement avancé dans la mise au point d'un indicateur de compétences transdisciplinaires et dans la description des objectifs nationaux. Pendant cette période, il a aussi défini la structure des indicateurs et mis au point des normes concernant les données. Si l'on tient compte de tous ces éléments, le réseau a accompli de sensibles progrès en relativement peu de temps.

Quelques-uns de ces travaux, s'appuyant sur des sources de données préexistantes, se sont aidés des circonstances. D'autres, comme ceux portant sur la structure des indicateurs, ont obéi à des considérations pragmatiques et au désir de contribuer à

Regards sur l'éducation. A présent, le réseau entreprend une autre tâche difficile : l'adoption d'une optique stratégique.

Il faudra du temps pour mener à bien les activités évoquées dans le présent chapitre ainsi que dans les précédents. Elles concernent : 1) la constitution d'un consensus autour des activités, 2) l'acceptation d'une stratégie de collecte de données qui dépend de l'engagement des pouvoirs publics, 3) la mise au point d'appareils de mesure, 4) la collecte et l'analyse de données, 5) l'élaboration de nouveaux mécanismes de communication et, enfin, 6) un retour d'informations permettant de réévaluer la validité du plan stratégique.

Deux éléments façonneront l'avenir du Réseau A :

* le besoin d'une perspective à plus long terme et d'un engagement plus important de la part des participants et des pouvoirs publics ; et
* le besoin d'intégrer ses travaux dans un système régulier de collecte et de diffusion des données.

Si ces besoins peuvent être satisfaits, le réseau sera à même de mesurer convenablement l'évolution des résultats des élèves – ce qui est au centre des préoccupations des décideurs.

List of Abbreviations
Liste des abréviations

ACT	American College Test
CCC	Cross-Curricular Competencies
CERI	Centre for Educational Research and Innovation
COMPED	IEA Study of Computers in Education
ETS	Educational Testing Service
EVS	European Value Study
GOALS	Goals Orientation and Attainment in Learning Systems
IAEP	International Association for Educational Progress
IEA	International Association for the Evaluation of Educational Achievement
INES	International Indicators of Education Systems
ISCED	International Standard Classification of Education
NAEP	National Assessment of Educational Progress
NCES	National Center for Education Statistics, US Department of Education
SAT	Standard Attainment Tasks
SIMS	Second International Mathematics Study
SOCON	Social and Cultural Development in the Netherlands
TIMSS	Third International Mathematics and Science Study

ÉGALEMENT DISPONIBLES

Regards sur l'éducation - Les indicateurs de l'OCDE
FF 220 FFE 285 £35 US$ 54 DM 83

OECD Education Statistics, 1985-1992/Statistiques de l'enseignement de l'OCDE, 1985-1992 (bilingue)
FF 160 FFE 210 £25 US$ 40 DM 60

Measuring the Quality of Schools/Mesurer la qualité des établissements scolaires (bilingue)
FF 120 FFE 155 £20 US$ 29 DM 47

Education and Employment/Formation et emploi (bilingue)
FF 90   FFE 115 £14 US$ 22 DM 34

Public Expectations of the Final Stage of Compulsory Education/Le dernier cycle de l'enseignement obligatoire : quelle attente ? (bilingue)
FF 100 FFE 130 £16 US$ 25 DM 38

Les processus de décision dans 14 systèmes éducatifs de l'OCDE (à paraître prochainement)

MAIN SALES OUTLETS OF OECD PUBLICATIONS
PRINCIPAUX POINTS DE VENTE DES PUBLICATIONS DE L'OCDE

ARGENTINA – ARGENTINE
Carlos Hirsch S.R.L.
Galería Güemes, Florida 165, 4° Piso
1333 Buenos Aires   Tel. (1) 331.1787 y 331.2391
Telefax: (1) 331.1787

AUSTRALIA – AUSTRALIE
D.A. Information Services
648 Whitehorse Road, P.O.B 163
Mitcham, Victoria 3132   Tel. (03) 873.4411
Telefax: (03) 873.5679

AUSTRIA – AUTRICHE
Gerold & Co.
Graben 31
Wien I   Tel. (0222) 533.50.14

BELGIUM – BELGIQUE
Jean De Lannoy
Avenue du Roi 202
B-1060 Bruxelles   Tel. (02) 538.51.69/538.08.41
Telefax: (02) 538.08.41

CANADA
Renouf Publishing Company Ltd.
1294 Algoma Road
Ottawa, ON K1B 3W8   Tel. (613) 741.4333
Telefax: (613) 741.5439
Stores:
61 Sparks Street
Ottawa, ON K1P 5R1   Tel. (613) 238.8985
211 Yonge Street
Toronto, ON M5B 1M4   Tel. (416) 363.3171
Telefax: (416)363.59.63
Les Éditions La Liberté Inc.
3020 Chemin Sainte-Foy
Sainte-Foy, PQ G1X 3V6   Tel. (418) 658.3763
Telefax: (418) 658.3763

Federal Publications Inc.
165 University Avenue, Suite 701
Toronto, ON M5H 3B8   Tel. (416) 860.1611
Telefax: (416) 860.1608
Les Publications Fédérales
1185 Université
Montréal, QC H3B 3A7   Tel. (514) 954.1633
Telefax : (514) 954.1635

CHINA – CHINE
China National Publications Import
Export Corporation (CNPIEC)
16 Gongti E. Road, Chaoyang District
P.O. Box 88 or 50
Beijing 100704 PR   Tel. (01) 506.6688
Telefax: (01) 506.3101

**CZECH REPUBLIC – RÉPUBLIQUE
TCHÈQUE**
Artia Pegas Press Ltd.
Narodni Trida 25
POB 825
111 21 Praha 1   Tel. 26.65.68
Telefax: 26.20.81

DENMARK – DANEMARK
Munksgaard Book and Subscription Service
35, Nørre Søgade, P.O. Box 2148
DK-1016 København K   Tel. (33) 12.85.70
Telefax: (33) 12.93.87

EGYPT – ÉGYPTE
Middle East Observer
41 Sherif Street
Cairo   Tel. 392.6919
Telefax: 360-6804

FINLAND – FINLANDE
Akateeminen Kirjakauppa
Keskuskatu 1, P.O. Box 128
00100 Helsinki
Subscription Services/Agence d'abonnements :
P.O. Box 23
00371 Helsinki   Tel. (358 0) 12141
Telefax: (358 0) 121.4450

FRANCE
OECD/OCDE
Mail Orders/Commandes par correspondance:
2, rue André-Pascal
75775 Paris Cedex 16   Tel. (33-1) 45.24.82.00
Telefax: (33-1) 49.10.42.76
Telex: 640048 OCDE
Orders via Minitel, France only/
Commandes par Minitel, France exclusivement :
36 15 OCDE

OECD Bookshop/Librairie de l'OCDE :
33, rue Octave-Feuillet
75016 Paris   Tel. (33-1) 45.24.81.67
(33-1) 45.24.81.81

Documentation Française
29, quai Voltaire
75007 Paris   Tel. 40.15.70.00

Gibert Jeune (Droit-Économie)
6, place Saint-Michel
75006 Paris   Tel. 43.25.91.19

Librairie du Commerce International
10, avenue d'Iéna
75016 Paris   Tel. 40.73.34.60

Librairie Dunod
Université Paris-Dauphine
Place du Maréchal de Lattre de Tassigny
75016 Paris   Tel. (1) 44.05.40.13

Librairie Lavoisier
11, rue Lavoisier
75008 Paris   Tel. 42.65.39.95

Librairie L.G.D.J. - Montchrestien
20, rue Soufflot
75005 Paris   Tel. 46.33.89.85

Librairie des Sciences Politiques
30, rue Saint-Guillaume
75007 Paris   Tel. 45.48.36.02

P.U.F.
49, boulevard Saint-Michel
75005 Paris   Tel. 43.25.83.40

Librairie de l'Université
12a, rue Nazareth
13100 Aix-en-Provence   Tel. (16) 42.26.18.08

Documentation Française
165, rue Garibaldi
69003 Lyon   Tel. (16) 78.63.32.23

Librairie Decitre
29, place Bellecour
69002 Lyon   Tel. (16) 72.40.54.54

GERMANY – ALLEMAGNE
OECD Publications and Information Centre
August-Bebel-Allee 6
D-53175 Bonn   Tel. (0228) 959.120
Telefax: (0228) 959.12.17

GREECE – GRÈCE
Librairie Kauffmann
Mavrokordatou 9
106 78 Athens   Tel. (01) 32.55.321
Telefax: (01) 36.33.967

HONG-KONG
Swindon Book Co. Ltd.
13–15 Lock Road
Kowloon, Hong Kong   Tel. 2376.2062
Telefax: 2376.0685

HUNGARY – HONGRIE
Euro Info Service
Margitsziget, Európa Ház
1138 Budapest   Tel. (1) 111.62.16
Telefax : (1) 111.60.61

ICELAND – ISLANDE
Mál Mog Menning
Laugavegi 18, Pósthólf 392
121 Reykjavik   Tel. 162.35.23

INDIA – INDE
Oxford Book and Stationery Co.
Scindia House
New Delhi 110001   Tel.(11) 331.5896/5308
Telefax: (11) 332.5993
17 Park Street
Calcutta 700016   Tel. 240832

INDONESIA – INDONÉSIE
Pdii-Lipi
P.O. Box 4298
Jakarta 12042   Tel. (21) 573.34.67
Telefax: (21) 573.34.67

IRELAND – IRLANDE
Government Supplies Agency
Publications Section
4/5 Harcourt Road
Dublin 2   Tel. 661.31.11
Telefax: 478.06.45

ISRAEL
Praedicta
5 Shatner Street
P.O. Box 34030
Jerusalem 91430   Tel. (2) 52.84.90/1/2
Telefax: (2) 52.84.93
R.O.Y.
P.O. Box 13056
Tel Aviv 61130   Tél. (3) 49.61.08
Telefax (3) 544.60.39

ITALY – ITALIE
Libreria Commissionaria Sansoni
Via Duca di Calabria 1/1
50125 Firenze   Tel. (055) 64.54.15
Telefax: (055) 64.12.57
Via Bartolini 29
20155 Milano   Tel. (02) 36.50.83
Editrice e Libreria Herder
Piazza Montecitorio 120
00186 Roma   Tel. 679.46.28
Telefax: 678.47.51
Libreria Hoepli
Via Hoepli 5
20121 Milano   Tel. (02) 86.54.46
Telefax: (02) 805.28.86
Libreria Scientifica
Dott. Lucio de Biasio 'Aeiou'
Via Coronelli, 6
20146 Milano   Tel. (02) 48.95.45.52
Telefax: (02) 48.95.45.48

JAPAN – JAPON
OECD Publications and Information Centre
Landic Akasaka Building
2-3-4 Akasaka, Minato-ku
Tokyo 107   Tel. (81.3) 3586.2016
Telefax: (81.3) 3584.7929

KOREA – CORÉE
Kyobo Book Centre Co. Ltd.
P.O. Box 1658, Kwang Hwa Moon
Seoul   Tel. 730.78.91
Telefax: 735.00.30

MALAYSIA – MALAISIE
University of Malaya Bookshop
University of Malaya
P.O. Box 1127, Jalan Pantai Baru
59700 Kuala Lumpur
Malaysia   Tel. 756.5000/756.5425
Telefax: 756.3246

MEXICO – MEXIQUE
Revistas y Periodicos Internacionales S.A. de C.V.
Florencia 57 - 1004
Mexico, D.F. 06600   Tel. 207.81.00
Telefax : 208.39.79

NETHERLANDS – PAYS-BAS
SDU Uitgeverij Plantijnstraat
Externe Fondsen
Postbus 20014
2500 EA's-Gravenhage   Tel. (070) 37.89.880
Voor bestellingen: Telefax: (070) 34.75.778

**NEW ZEALAND
NOUVELLE-ZÉLANDE**
Legislation Services
P.O. Box 12418
Thorndon, Wellington   Tel. (04) 496.5652
          Telefax: (04) 496.5698

NORWAY – NORVÈGE
Narvesen Info Center – NIC
Bertrand Narvesens vei 2
P.O. Box 6125 Etterstad
0602 Oslo 6   Tel. (022) 57.33.00
          Telefax: (022) 68.19.01

PAKISTAN
Mirza Book Agency
65 Shahrah Quaid-E-Azam
Lahore 54000   Tel. (42) 353.601
          Telefax: (42) 231.730

PHILIPPINE – PHILIPPINES
International Book Center
5th Floor, Filipinas Life Bldg.
Ayala Avenue
Metro Manila   Tel. 81.96.76
          Telex 23312 RHP PH

PORTUGAL
Livraria Portugal
Rua do Carmo 70-74
Apart. 2681
1200 Lisboa   Tel.: (01) 347.49.82/5
          Telefax: (01) 347.02.64

SINGAPORE – SINGAPOUR
Gower Asia Pacific Pte Ltd.
Golden Wheel Building
41, Kallang Pudding Road, No. 04-03
Singapore 1334   Tel. 741.5166
          Telefax: 742.9356

SPAIN – ESPAGNE
Mundi-Prensa Libros S.A.
Castelló 37, Apartado 1223
Madrid 28001   Tel. (91) 431.33.99
          Telefax: (91) 575.39.98

Libreria Internacional AEDOS
Consejo de Ciento 391
08009 – Barcelona   Tel. (93) 488.30.09
          Telefax: (93) 487.76.59
Llibreria de la Generalitat
Palau Moja
Rambla dels Estudis, 118
08002 – Barcelona
          (Subscripcions) Tel. (93) 318.80.12
          (Publicacions) Tel. (93) 302.67.23
          Telefax: (93) 412.18.54

SRI LANKA
Centre for Policy Research
c/o Colombo Agencies Ltd.
No. 300-304, Galle Road
Colombo 3   Tel. (1) 574240, 573551-2
          Telefax: (1) 575394, 510711

SWEDEN – SUÈDE
Fritzes Information Center
Box 16356
Regeringsgatan 12
106 47 Stockholm   Tel. (08) 690.90.90
          Telefax: (08) 20.50.21

Subscription Agency/Agence d'abonnements :
Wennergren-Williams Info AB
P.O. Box 1305
171 25 Solna   Tel. (08) 705.97.50
          Téléfax : (08) 27.00.71

SWITZERLAND – SUISSE
Maditec S.A. (Books and Periodicals - Livres
et périodiques)
Chemin des Palettes 4
Case postale 266
1020 Renens VD 1   Tel. (021) 635.08.65
          Telefax: (021) 635.07.80

Librairie Payot S.A.
4, place Pépinet
CP 3212
1002 Lausanne   Tel. (021) 341.33.47
          Telefax: (021) 341.33.45

Librairie Unilivres
6, rue de Candolle
1205 Genève   Tel. (022) 320.26.23
          Telefax: (022) 329.73.18

Subscription Agency/Agence d'abonnements :
Dynapresse Marketing S.A.
38 avenue Vibert
1227 Carouge   Tel.: (022) 308.07.89
          Telefax : (022) 308.07.99

See also – Voir aussi :
OECD Publications and Information Centre
August-Bebel-Allee 6
D-53175 Bonn (Germany)   Tel. (0228) 959.120
          Telefax: (0228) 959.12.17

TAIWAN – FORMOSE
Good Faith Worldwide Int'l. Co. Ltd.
9th Floor, No. 118, Sec. 2
Chung Hsiao E. Road
Taipei   Tel. (02) 391.7396/391.7397
          Telefax: (02) 394.9176

THAILAND – THAÏLANDE
Suksit Siam Co. Ltd.
113, 115 Fuang Nakhon Rd.
Opp. Wat Rajbopith
Bangkok 10200   Tel. (662) 225.9531/2
          Telefax: (662) 222.5188

TURKEY – TURQUIE
Kültür Yayinlari Is-Türk Ltd. Sti.
Atatürk Bulvari No. 191/Kat 13
Kavaklidere/Ankara   Tel. 428.11.40 Ext. 2458
Dolmabahce Cad. No. 29
Besiktas/Istanbul   Tel. 260.71.88
          Telex: 43482B

UNITED KINGDOM – ROYAUME-UNI
HMSO
Gen. enquiries   Tel. (071) 873 0011
Postal orders only:
P.O. Box 276, London SW8 5DT
Personal Callers HMSO Bookshop
49 High Holborn, London WC1V 6HB
          Telefax: (071) 873 8200
Branches at: Belfast, Birmingham, Bristol, Edin-
burgh, Manchester

UNITED STATES – ÉTATS-UNIS
OECD Publications and Information Centre
2001 L Street N.W., Suite 700
Washington, D.C. 20036-4910 Tel. (202) 785.6323
          Telefax: (202) 785.0350

VENEZUELA
Libreria del Este
Avda F. Miranda 52, Aptdo. 60337
Edificio Galipán
Caracas 106   Tel. 951.1705/951.2307/951.1297
          Telegram: Libreste Caracas

Subscription to OECD periodicals may also be
placed through main subscription agencies.

Les abonnements aux publications périodiques de
l'OCDE peuvent être souscrits auprès des
principales agences d'abonnement.

Orders and inquiries from countries where Distribu-
tors have not yet been appointed should be sent to:
OECD Publications Service, 2 rue André-Pascal,
75775 Paris Cedex 16, France.

Les commandes provenant de pays où l'OCDE n'a
pas encore désigné de distributeur peuvent être
adressées à : OCDE, Service des Publications,
2, rue André-Pascal, 75775 Paris Cedex 16, France.

          1-1995

OECD PUBLICATIONS, 2 rue André-Pascal, 75775 PARIS CEDEX 16
PRINTED IN FRANCE
(91 95 06 3) ISBN 92-64-04358-6 - No. 47798 1995